PATERNO

PATERNO: BY THE BOOK

JOE PATERNO

with Bernard Asbell

Random House   New York

All rights reserved under International and Pan-American Copyright Conventions.
Published in the United States by Random House, Inc., New York, and simultaneously
in Canada by Random House of Canada Limited, Toronto.

Library of Congress Cataloging-in-Publication Data

Paterno, Joe.
    Paterno : by the book/ Joe Paterno with Bernard Asbell.
        p. cm.
    ISBN 0-394-56501-0
    1. Paterno, Joe.   2. Football—United States—Coaches—Biography.
3. Pennsylvania State University—Football—History.
I. Asbell, Bernard.   II. Title.
GV939.P37A3   1989
796.332'092—dc20
[B]   89-42788

Manufactured in the United States of America
24689753
First Edition

To my wife and friend, Sue.

I hope your goodness, talents, and
unselfish commitment to your family,
to people, and to Penn State glow as brightly
on every page of this book as your warmth
and concern have touched all who know you.

Because, you see, I love you.

And to the memory of my devoted mother,
Florence Cafiero Paterno,
who went to her rest after this book was
 completed.

Editor's Note: About the Authors

"You can't be a nice guy and do a job like this." Paterno said that early in the planning of this book. His remark might make a good opening sentence, I thought—but he and his writing partner, Bernard Asbell, decided otherwise.

Nice guy? The idea here is to say a few factual things about Joseph Paterno & Friend that they can't, or won't, say about themselves.

Joe Paterno is perhaps the most respected, beloved (in a few territories, reviled), and certainly most recognizable college football coach in America. Patrolling the sidelines in signature dark glasses during a game, he dares to wear his trousers rolled, with white athletic socks defining the difference between his football shoes and trouser bottoms. (It is a style my kids called "floods," as if the wearer were expecting one.) On the field, he is much of the time a model of concentration, control, and calm, except for those few fleeting moments when, screaming and flailing his arms, he feels it his civic duty to point out the deficiencies of the several discernibly handicapped persons in striped shirts who are supposed to be officiating. But, visible as he is, Paterno is in some ways too little known and not always understood. Here, he tells all. Well, if not all, most.

Paterno has paid his dues, has pungent opinions, and has earned the right to them. Though a youthful man, he began coaching football at the bridge of the Truman-Eisenhower years and this fall, 1989, he will have been at it for forty years. The football record is better known than the man—or at least is easier to quantify.* "Joe-pa," as students call him (his wife, Sue, a not-so-secret weapon, is "Sue-pa"), has directed the Nittany Lions to 212 victories, as of the end of 1988, second only among active coaches to Bo Schembechler of Michigan. His teams have made nineteen bowl appearances, with only Bear Bryant of Alabama appearing in more. Paterno's twenty-three-year winning percentage as head coach is .795, and he has coached six teams through undefeated seasons.†

More than fifty of his players have been first-team all-Americans and well over a hundred have gone on to play as pros in the National Football League.

But stats do not explain the special place the coach occupies in the consciousness, spirit, and affections of Penn State people—and beyond. (Paterno, like Notre Dame, has "subway alumni," people with no known connection to the university who approach him in airports, asking for his autograph. The women always say it is for their husbands or sons.) Each year, during Homecoming Weekend, there is an enthusiastic Paterno Look-alike Contest (Joe says: "I don't know why anyone would want to win"). Year-round, promoters sell by the thousands life-size, full-figure cutouts of his photograph, printed on suitably tough cardboard. People display these in their offices, bars, and front windows, at church socials or poker games, calling the easel-backed posters Stand-up Joes, or Joes-to-Go. Golf balls bearing his likeness are also a popular item

*Much of the data that follows is paraphrased, with a deep bow, from the program produced by the Penn State sports information department [[CHK]] for the "Blue-White" game, an intrasquad practice engagement in April that draws some 25,000 or so spectators, plus fifteen or twenty high school bands, to the university's Beaver Stadium.

†Coach Paterno is also a skilled and successful recruiter, and he tells some interesting stories about this without revealing his technique—which is to offer challenges to achievement, rather than inducements. An especially well-written and close-up look at Paterno on the road was done by novelist D. Keith Mano in *Sports Illustrated*, March 15, 1976.

(see one player's comment in a later chapter). Penn State's famous ice cream—almost as noteworthy as its football program (it spawned Ben & Jerry's renowned product)—has added to its select list of flavors Peachy Paterno, the College of Agriculture's version of the Nobel Prize.

But behind the scores, the merchandising, the cheerful name-calling, there is an even more astonishing fact: Joseph V. Paterno is an educator who happens to be a big-league football coach. Ask him about his statistics and instead of discussing wins and losses he's likely to tell you about his nineteen first-team academic all-Americans or his ten Hall of Fame scholar-athletes. To date, Professor Paterno has coached thirteen players who've won NCAA *post*graduate scholarships. He is also a leader in a major effort to raise millions to enhance Penn State's academic programs, one of his special enthusiasms being the university's libraries.

You're about to learn why the great Georgia Tech coach Bobby Dodd called Paterno "a class guy" and "an honest one." And why Joe Paterno has had a tiff with a U.S. president and the admiration of several others. Some good players have complained not only of what Paterno demands but of how he demands it. As one said, "He's always in your face." But when the all-American, all-pro linebacker Jack Ham was to be inducted into the Hall of Fame in 1988, "It took me about five seconds to decide on Paterno to present me." Wasn't Joe in Ham's face, too? "When you're an eighteen- or nineteen-year-old kid going to college, you can go in a lot of different directions. Joe got me going the right way. He didn't make football players larger than life . . . he made me realize that football was not the most important thing in my life . . . He made sure . . . it was your education, your family, and then football."

Dr. Dave Joyner, an all-American and now an orthopedic surgeon at Penn State's Hershey (Pa.) Medical Center, said: "He's a human being and he makes mistakes . . . he expects a lot out of you . . . His primary interest is in his football players as members of society ... People ask me, 'Is he for real?' And I say, 'Yes ...' I think Joe believes everything he says ... and tries to make it come true."

Thus, he may not claim to be or even care to be "nice." But when Bob White, defensive co-captain of the Lions 1986 team, said, "He's not the type who jokes with you but the type who helps you, forces you, to develop," he added the coup de grâce: "Joe Paterno is a good guy."

When I nominated another good guy to help Joe produce his book, Bernard Asbell responded by saying, "But I don't know football." To which I gave the obvious answer "Don't worry. He does."

The book was not to be "about" football. Sure, football would be at its center, just as Penn State is at the center of Pennsylvania. But given that Paterno himself is not just about football, the book was to go beyond the retailing and retelling of games.

Asbell set aside a book-in-progress, and met Joe. He experienced the usual instant epiphany, or conversion after touchdown, and went to it.

Previously, Asbell had worked with or written about Senator Edmund Muskie (*The Senate Nobody Knows,* a best-seller in Washington—where they thought they knew—is now used in colleges); Franklin Delano Roosevelt; Eleanor Roosevelt; their daughter Anna Roosevelt; as well as with scientists and educators and celebrities of several sorts. His first book, *When F.D.R. Died,* was a national best-seller and he was known to mainstream magazine editors as a writer who could be depended on to go beyond what was asked. If Paterno ran a writing team, Bernie would be a starter.

When Penn State recruited Asbell for a teaching post, he fell in love with the special place that is referred to wryly as Happy Valley. There, the central campus of the university system is located in a bowl (fittingly) of the Nittany Mountains, a setting often described as lovely and also equally inaccessible from all points.

Unlike some autobiographical collaborators, Asbell emphasizes finding the author's voice as well as points of view. Here, he has not prettied up Joe's words or imposed a fussy feeling for grammar, nor has he been merely phonographic and too-true-to-tape. He has preferred instead to catch Joe in the vernacular, on the run, as well as capturing the essence of the thoughtful, probing hours of conversation they have shared on campus, in the stadiums, locker rooms, airplanes, buses, and at Joe's hideaway on the Jersey shore.

The results of this team you are about to judge for yourself.

—SAM VAUGHAN
Senior Vice President and Editor
Random House
(and, declaring an interest, Penn State, '51)

Acknowledgments

The authors are especially grateful for the counsel of Mervin Hyman, formerly of *Sports Illustrated,* whose deep knowledge of the world of college football, present and past, and of the career of Joe Paterno, helped light the way through this book.

They are indebted also to Sue Paterno, not only for her time and enthusiasm, but also her boundless memory. One of the authors, the one not married to her, was constantly surprised by the rich and unerring detail of her recollections.

Also, they have been supported, backstopped, and frequently saved from fumbling by Joe Paterno's longtime and loyal administrative aide, Cheryl Norman, and her right-hand assistant, Cynthia Ault, as well as the secretarial staff, Mel Capobianco, Marcy Collitt, Michaelene Franzetta, and Patti Shawley.

The happy partnership of the authors was foreseen and matchmade by Samuel S. Vaughan, who edited the book for Random House, and whom both have known, admired, and trusted for many years. To say he made the book better is not enough. He made it exist.

Bernard Asbell is indebted to Joe Paterno's entire coaching and administrative staff for uncountable instances of assistance and good cheer. He risks singling out Jim Tarman, athletic director, and L. Budd Thalman, associate director for communications; Frank Rocco, assistant athletic director, and Tom

Venturino, his right-hand man, for arranging seats on team buses and planes as well as other precious amenities for a nonathlete; Jerry Sandusky and Fran Ganter, defensive and offensive coordinators, as well as assistant coaches Tom Bradley, Jim Caldwell, Craig Cirbus, Ron Dickerson, Chet Fuhrman, Bob Phillips, Joe Sarra, and Jim Williams for making an interloper feel like an honorary coach; John Bove, administrative assistant, for leading the outsider through some of the secret mazes of recruiting football players; and Jim Caltagirone of the Penn State sports-information staff, for valuable help in fact-checking.

The coauthor is also grateful to the Reverend Thomas Bermingham, S.J., and to George Paterno for generous gifts of time in recalling Joe Paterno's early life.

Counsel and support in a variety of ways were given by Professors John Buck, Christopher Clausen, John Moore, and James Rambeau of the Penn State English department.

Research papers by Dennis Booher and Don Sheffield provided useful information, as did the book *Road to Number One*, by the late Ridge Riley.

And when at times the game stalled and this player stumbled wearily, dear Jean Brenchley always knew when and how to keep pointing to the goal posts.

The prize for endurance, devotion, and caring goes to Nicki Caldwell, who transcribed dozens of interviews, helped assemble notes, and seemed always to remember the whereabouts of a detail when the coauthor was drowning in floods of details.

Contents

PATERNO

1· The Call of a Patriot

I remember the night I was forced to decide who I am.

All night I lay awake wrestling with my past, trying to make sense of my future. Why am I in this place doing this thing I do? Me, Angelo Paterno's first son: tutored by Jesuits in Latin and Homer and Virgil, four Ivy League years burying my nose in English literature, all on a clear, straight road to making myself into a lawyer, a judge, to fulfill my parents. How did I get into, of all things, *coaching football?* And what keeps holding me to it?

Naturally, I remember—almost word for word—the unexpected conversation that hammered those questions into my head. It was a few nights earlier during those closing days of 1972. There I was, sitting around in my bedroom slippers, a telephone in my hand, knowing I had to dope out the meaning of this call, the meaning of those winds up there that shift around and play with a man's destiny. What were they trying to tell me? Who sent this guy to offer me a deal that would upset my whole life and make me rich?

He said, "I want to meet with you to talk about coaching my team."

I said, "You know, I've had other offers from pro teams, and I could never work up much interest—"

"Coach, I'm ready to make you an arrangement that would insure your family's well-being. You'd never have to worry about them again."

"What do you mean?"

"Owning a piece of the Boston Patriots."

I took a breath. "Well, that's the only thing that might get me interested, Mr. Sullivan. So we don't waste our time, there are two things I'd need to get us talking. Part owner is one. The other is how much control I'd have over the club. And I wouldn't want to waste your time if you thought—"

"You'd have control over the whole operation."

"The whole thing?"

"Coach and general manager."

That sounded like he might mean the whole thing. I told Bill Sullivan I'd meet and talk with him, but that I couldn't make any decision right away. My kids had only one scheduled game left to play in the 1972 season, against Pitt—the University of Pittsburgh—the traditional rival of Penn State long before I came. (The previous Saturday we had pounded Boston College, 45–26, which, while saddening most of Boston, probably impressed Sullivan. He understood about poundings. The Patriots he owned were getting them regularly from most of the National Football League.) Furthermore, we had just been picked to go to the Sugar Bowl for a big New Year's game with Oklahoma.

Soon after we beat Pitt, I flew to New York and sat down with Sullivan in a room at the Plaza. He started out the same way as before:

"Joe, I want to put you in a position where you'll never have to want."

First he hit me with a four-year salary-and-extras package that was quite a conversation opener: a paid-up deed to a $200,000 home, a two-car garage—with two cars in it, a salary of $200,000 the first year, rising each year in 25K jumps to $275,000 the fourth year. The prize bag came to about $1.4 million.

At Penn State, after starting as assistant coach in 1950 at $3,600 a year, and serving for sixteen seasons with normal increases, then becoming head coach in 1966 at $20,000, my pay after seven years of successful seasons had risen to a grand $35,000. The money had always satisfied me.

Next, we talked about stock in the club. As I recall, Sullivan mentioned 3 percent, and soon we were talking about 5. (The Boston Patriots franchise is worth about $160,000,000 today, although only a fraction of that in December 1972.) I had never possessed a share of stock in anything. Back in State College, Pennsylvania, we did own a modest, mortgaged house, one car, and five young kids, the youngest an infant. My wife, Sue, didn't care about lots of money any more than I did. Yet everything about the deal Sullivan was offering, frankly, made me dizzy.

I looked at the salary part, then the stock part, and said to myself, "Holy smoke."

Only once before had I ever gotten serious about a feeler from a pro team, the Pittsburgh Steelers, after we won the New Year's Day, 1969, Orange Bowl. But Sue's lack of enthusiasm for leaving our town of State College helped me follow my instinct, and I turned it down.

Another contact, through an intermediary, went halfway to seriousness—in fact, exactly halfway, which makes it worth telling. Wellington Mara of the New York Giants didn't get scared away, so far as I know, when I said I wanted something beyond a straight salary for coaching. I sent word that I'd be satisfied with only one quarter of 1 percent of the Giants' stock, but a very special quarter of 1 percent. Wellington Mara owned exactly 50 percent of the Giants. When his brother died, the other 50 percent had gone to Wellington's nephew. Of the tiny share I asked for, I said I wanted one half to come out of Wellington's stock, the other half to come out of the nephew's. I knew I could get along with Wellington, but I didn't know the nephew. What if Wellington and I agreed on, say, some important player trade, but the nephew said no? He could veto anything. So, if I owned that sliver of stock out of each of their shares, I'd have the controlling vote. Wellington Mara might have gone along with that. But, the way I heard it, the nephew—or maybe the nephew's lawyer—wouldn't.

Another approach from the pros was a subsequent offer from the Patriots—and with another Sullivan, Pat, Bill's son. Pat, too, said, "We'll let you have complete control."

"Okay," I said, testing, "I want to trade a guy right now. Can I do that?"

"Well, naturally," Pat said, looking nervous, "we'd expect you to consult with Bucko." Bucko Kilroy, sitting beside him, getting a little red in the face, was the team's general manager.

"Bucko, if you and I don't agree, do we make the trade or don't we?"

"You know, Joe, that I've been in the league a long time, and naturally I hope you—"

"All I'm asking you, Bucko, Do I have control when I want to make that trade?"

"You and I can always work out—"

"Okay, I don't want to kick a dead horse. Let's go to something else. I want to draft a certain guy. Do I have control to do that?"

They both started telling me about Dick Steinberg, their personnel man, and what a great personnel guy he was. Which I knew.

"But who has the say in the draft?"

"Well, we'd hope you would—you know—"

So I couldn't make a breakthrough on the biggest problem of coaches in professional football—the traditional roles of two or three key front-office people and how they jealously protect their turf. The general manager, who's often a former coach, is not about to give up his say on player trades and free agents. The personnel guy, in charge of following college prospects, has his own staff that he won't give up without a nasty fight. Usually, he reports to the general manager, sometimes directly to the owner.

So, say, I'm the coach and some tackle on my team is loafing. I try to give the player a stern message by not playing him. That doesn't spur him to fight for his job, so I tell him straight out: "If you don't get off your butt, I'm going to trade you." But suppose the general manager isn't too happy about proving he can bring off a hotshot trade for this guy. Or he may have spent heavily to get this lazy guy in the first place. Maybe he doesn't like to admit a bad deal. So as coach, without control of the coming and going of players, I'm stuck with him.

That's part of why those earlier conversations hadn't tempted me away from college football. But now, Bill Sullivan's offer looked like the real thing.

"Think about it," he said, "and I'll call you next week."

"No, I don't want to think about it now or next week. Let's put it out of our minds till after the Sugar Bowl. Then we'll talk."

He looked at me as though I were kidding, then said, "Right."

Landing with my team in New Orleans on December 26 made me wonder about Sullivan. Right away, sportswriters started digging at me about rumors I was about to quit Penn State to go pro with the Patriots. They even asked who'd succeed me, one of my assistant coaches or someone from elsewhere. Those rumors, which certainly hadn't started with me, were the last things I wanted my players to fret about. Some of my most promising kids, favorites as both players and people—John Cappelletti (on his way to a Heisman Trophy the following year), Mark Markowich, Eddie O'Neil, others on that good team—had another year to play at Penn State. I couldn't send them into a major bowl game on national television with feelings of uncertainty about their coach and his future—about *their* future. For some kids, that's like worrying about their father walking out on the family. In fact, this terrific bunch I had was starting to think that next year we could capture the national college championship. Did they need rumors now, of all times, that their coach might abandon them?

During the week of the game, the Sugar Bowl committee threw a dinner at Antoine's for the coaching staffs of both teams and the media. I'll never know what possessed him to show up in New Orleans or how he wangled an invitation to this private dinner, but suddenly, there he was, Bill Sullivan himself, with his lovely wife on his arm. And, of course, he threw me a big wave and a significant smile that made me want to shrink, as though I'd got stuck accidentally catching the roses at a wedding.

Back in Pennsylvania after the Sugar Bowl, Sue asked, as neutral-sounding as could be, "Well, what do you think?"

I said, "I've got to give myself a couple of days."

The rumors were now the talk of the street in State College. Mimi Barash (now Coppersmith), a magazine publisher and one of our town's civic activists, distributed bumper stickers, buttons, printed postcards, and whatnot, with a slogan, "Don't Go, Joe." I couldn't help but feel good about the hundreds of cards and the flashing lapels, but I couldn't let that make up my mind for me.

I knew there was no way I could turn down Sullivan's deal. It gave me everything I'd ever dreamed of: the summer house on Cape Cod that every rich Yankee kid I'd met at Brown assumed was coming to him, the same as inheriting his dad's club membership. It meant bringing up my kids around Boston, a lively place that had always appealed to me. Pro football would mean more time to spend with Sue and the kids. No more week after week on the road, recruiting high school players from the end of the playing season till spring. Fans and alumni don't understand the wear and tear and drudgery of that part of college coaching.

I liked the bright prospects of the Patriots. Two years earlier they had signed, as their number one draft pick, Jim Plunkett, the Stanford quarterback and Heisman Trophy winner. I'd got to know him as a member of the college all-star team I coached that year in Hawaii's Hula Bowl. Jim's combination of physical talent, personal character, and quick mind made him my kind of player.

But most of all, I was drawn to the deal by that once-in-a-lifetime chance to be top man.

After a couple of days, I said to Sue, "I have to take the job."

Sue just said, "Joe, whatever you want to do is fine with me. If you want to go, we'll go."

I could tell she wasn't crazy about it.

After dinner—this was on a Thursday night—I called Sullivan in Boston and told him we had a deal. We agreed to meet at nine the next morning, again at the Plaza. I called a friend who operated a private charter service and arranged for the 250-mile flight. Then Sue called Jim and Louise Tarman to come over to celebrate. Jim, a close friend and now director of Penn State athletics, was then sports information director. I had asked him to come with me to Boston. We poured champagne and toasted and talked about our good new life.

We talked about lots more too. Sue told how she'd miss our family doctor, John Light, who had delivered four of our children. Sue had been at Penn State since coming as a college freshman and had trouble trying to think of any other place as home. She had attended a pro game only once in her life: the Steelers. She said that all that she could remember was a lot of beer drinkers and loudmouth rowdies. "I don't know if I want to be in that kind of crowd," she laughed, and Jim and Louise and I laughed with her. Our son David, then six, had heard us talking, got out of bed, and began crying in Sue's lap. He didn't want to leave Ron, his friend since he was three.

"We'll fly home some weekends," Jim said bravely.

"Sure," I said.

A job's a job. When opportunity calls, you go where it takes you.

Then Jim, sipping at his second champagne, began remembering the good times we'd all had at Penn State.

Sue wondered about the coaching staff. Would my successor

keep them? At least a couple of the most seasoned—Jim O'Hora and Frank Patrick—were close to eligibility for retirement. Could they get jobs elsewhere if my successor brought in his own people?

This was turning out to be the most cheerless celebration party I'd ever been at. Sue says she can't remember anybody saying a jubilant, or even a positive, thing all evening. Still, it was filled with curiosity and excitement about getting on with our new life.

At bedtime I said to Sue, "Okay, kid. Tonight you get to sleep with a millionaire."

At two in the morning, Sue was sitting in her rocking chair nursing Scotty, our justborn. I'm sure she thought I was asleep. Sue had never said she didn't want to go to Boston. But now, tears were slipping down her face. I could almost hear them. I know the way she breathes.

I lay there thinking strange and irrelevant things—remembering a time one spring when I was walking across our beautiful campus and some student waved to me and said, "Where you headed, Coach?" And I told him. I remember that because it sounded funny: I was headed clear across campus to check on the blossoming of two azalea bushes. I'd always loved those particular bushes as though they were my own. I thought of mornings I'd walk my eight-year-old daughter, Mary Kay, to the corner and wait for the school bus.

When is it right for a guy to say good-by to a place he loves, the place he found his wife, where his kids lived all of their days? And my other kids—those young, tough, thick-necked, fragile-hearted football players—the ones who grow and ripen before your eyes before they go off to cut their own pathways in the world? Out of the hodgepodge picture of them all, I saw especially John Cappelletti, the shining star of that year whose heart was broken when he was too sick to play at the Sugar Bowl and who took the 14–0 defeat all on himself.

Would those players see me as quitting after a defeat?

But if I didn't go, would people think I was afraid to coach pro football? Would they say Paterno's scared because pro football is tougher than college?

That's a bunch of baloney. Despite what a lot of fans assume, life is easier for a coach in the pros. The play is tougher, sure, but the coaching's easier. The pro coach has his guys all day for meetings and practice. College kids have to go to class and follow NCAA restrictions on the number of days for practice. For coaches like me, college is especially tough because we insist that the kids *really* go to school, shoot to excel in classes. Some of us coaches insist that the most important thing that happens in a college player's career is not receiving a fifty-yard pass, but a diploma. Yet sometimes we play against coaches and teams who reverse those priorities. Pro football coaches don't have those problems.

Hey, what the hell was going on in my head? Why did I keep batting this back and forth as though I couldn't make up my mind? I'd *made* up my mind. Why was this thing tossing and turning around, keeping me awake, nagging me, chattering in my brain. It was time to get logical about this.

No, not logical. If something was my destiny, no logic in the world was going to get me out of it.

Was going to Boston my destiny?

Was staying at Penn State my destiny?

What to do? Go or stay?

Destiny is a trick bag. How's a guy to know? God gives each of us a destiny, then confuses us with the power of free will. We're still stuck with having to decide every step of the way.

Sometimes what you're destined to do and what you *want* to do are one and the same. Then it's easy. But sometimes you really want to choose *this*—you want it so much it looks like it *must* be right—yet you really have to choose *that* because you *know* that's your destiny. And when you choose wrong, as Aeneas himself found out, life comes down on you with some terrible whacks.

What was pulling me to Boston? What made me tell Sullivan I'd come? What was it that wasn't letting me go to sleep?

Boston was a great city. It was a new challenge. It was—

Come on, *face* it. I knew damn well what it was. The *money.* The house on Cape Cod. Hobnobbing with the hottest shots in a big-time town, in high-tone bars, being their hero. Not having to worry, for once, about the example I have to set in a small college town, being watched by kids. *It was the only chance at a million dollars I'd ever have.*

But already I had enough money for anything my family needed in this world. Sue loved it here. When I turned down the Steelers, her face looked as if I'd given her the gift of life. And look what I was about to give up for money: Suddenly I saw, like a circle around me, the life I was selling out for it. I saw the students, the granite statue of the Nittany Lion, the Blue Band, the eager, sweaty tryouts for the squad. I saw squads of the past, gone and graduated, grown men who write to me, who call on the phone, who come back and tell me what it was for them. I saw a long stream of those kids playing, studying, growing. And I saw the pro players, the Patriots, the Steelers, the Giants. Good teams, good guys, some of my kids there.

But I saw them playing only to *win.* No other reason to play. Even more than pro players are compelled to win, coaches are compelled to win.

It was like I suddenly made a direct connection. I knew what I had to do. I felt myself riding on that soaring, free-floating lift of knowing that my destiny and what I *wanted* to do were one and the same.

At five-thirty in the morning, Sue woke up to take care of Scotty. I was sitting by our bedside phone.

She said, "Why aren't you dressing? You have to get to the airport."

I said, "You went to bed with a millionaire, but you woke up with me. I'm not going."

The first words that went through Sue's head, she later told me, were "Oh, thank God."

I called my charter pilot and canceled, then agonized over how to tell Sullivan. He, too, was about to leave for New York and I had to head him off.

"Bill," I heard myself telling him, "I'm not coming. I don't know how to tell you this, but it's not right for me."

He said, "I'm terribly disappointed."

"I just wanted to get to you before you left."

"Can we talk about it?"

"We've talked. You've been more than fair and generous."

"Take another day or two to think about it."

"No, it wouldn't be fair—to you or anybody. That's it."

Early as it was, I then called Bob Patterson, a vice president of the university.

The sudden switch of decision had at least two unexpected happy results. Later in the morning, Patterson called back and "ordered" me to fly with him immediately to Pittsburgh to see a lawyer. Penn State didn't want any more close calls. That day, we drafted the first job contract I'd ever had.

The other result was happy for somebody else. Bill Sullivan called later in the morning to ask what I thought of Chuck Fairbanks as a coach. What could I say about the guy who'd just beaten me in the Sugar Bowl? I said I thought Fairbanks was a fine coach. Next thing, Fairbanks called and wanted to know what Sullivan had offered me. "Chuck," I had to say, "I don't think that's kosher." He pressed, playing on the fraternal relationship of coaches. But Sullivan had been too fair with me. I had to tell Chuck I couldn't discuss it. Chuck became the next coach of the Boston Patriots, and I took pleasure in having created the job opportunity.

That Friday morning, newspapers in both Boston and State College headlined that I was going to the Patriots. On the previous night, Sullivan apparently had put out the word that my move was all set, which it was. In fact, the morning papers even reported follow-ups and aftermaths, like quoting one of the investors in the Patriots who was mad as hell because he felt I could have been bought for a whole lot less than Sullivan had agreed to pay me. Sue and I enjoyed that.

Jim Tarman pulled together a press conference for me at ten o'clock Saturday morning, where I waved my new Penn State contract and put an end to the story.

I soon learned who my most enthusiastic supporter probably was: a minister from Reading, Pennsylvania, the Reverend Elton P. Richards, Jr., who was not a Penn State graduate but could teach a number of our highly charged alumni a lesson or two in enthusiasm. A year earlier, before the Cotton Bowl game against Texas, the announcement board outside his church told the world, GOD IS IMPARTIAL. BUT SOME MINISTERS ARE NOT. GO PENN STATE! And to herald the Sugar Bowl he posted: NOW IS THE TIME FOR ALL CHRISTIANS TO ROOT FOR THE LIONS. GO PENN STATE! Mr. Richards organized a statewide "Joe Paterno Day" in Camp Hill, a suburb of Harrisburg. He somehow rounded up my old high school coach and some teammates and brought them to Camp Hill, as well as teammates and fraternity brothers from Brown, a slew of ex-Nittany Lions, state officials, even our new Penn State president, the warm and affable John W. Oswald, and enough fans for the world's largest tailgate party. Finally, Mr. Richards and the crowd bowled me over with a gift: a trip for Sue and me to Italy! I'd never been there.

From the moment of revelation that had come just before making my early morning phone call, I now knew clearly, exactly, and forever, just what college football means to me—and what professional football never could.

2· What College Football Means to Me (and What Pro Ball Doesn't)

PRO football is about winning. Only winning.

Winning, and the big money that's paid for winning, seizes the concentration, the lives, of players and coaches alike.

Just winning is a silly reason to be serious about a game. Also, dangerous. For a kid still in school, devotion to winning football games at nearly any cost may cripple his mind for life. Institutions of higher learning don't have the moral right to exploit and mislead inexperienced kids that way. Neither do the fans who worship the glories of their college football teams.

Later, I'll spill a barrel of thoughts I have on the subject of winning and losing. Those ideas are central to my life and to the way I teach my squads to approach football. But for now I ask you to stop and consider where a young man's mind and emotions are when he enters college. Getting his high school diploma often signifies his graduating out of eighteen years of a high-fenced, blind-sided little world. He's probably lived all his life in the same tight little country town, or the same one-class, one-race, designer-label suburb, or the same cramped, dark-hall tenements of the same inner-city ghetto. He's lived fairly locked in a circle of his parents and uncles and aunts and their values, which are probably not too different from the values of the parents and uncles and aunts of his friends.

That's how it was for me. On the streets of Flatbush, everybody was a Dodger fan. Everybody had the same dialect. Everybody thought the same. Then I caught the brass ring of a college scholarship—for playing football. What a break! What a wide world—*worlds!*—suddenly opened for me, worlds of art, history, literature, music, politics, all-night arguments about the way society is, the way it ought to be, how to change it. Surrounded by that intellectual feast, was I going to limit my life just to playing a *game?*

Because I loved it, football became my main extracurricular activity, as debating, the band, or the theater club was for others. I gave it my best. It gave me a lot back. But it wasn't my *life.*

At Brown, we football players weren't ordered to lock ourselves away in a deluxe, carpeted athletic dorm like the one Coach Bear Bryant soon built at the University of Alabama. Maybe Bryant believed in protecting his Red Tide from the mental distractions of a university. He sheltered his squad of stars from the student who didn't play serious football. Thank God I wasn't "protected" that way at Brown, and today I wouldn't for one minute consider segregating my players that way at Penn State.

I want them to discover themselves—by discovering all the kinds of people they can meet among the thirty-seven thousand students on our campus. It's easy for fans to forget that a six-foot, two-hundred-pound bruiser who plays college football, like every other college kid, is hungry for full adulthood. The hero whose picture you see most often may also have the least emotional experience, is probably uncertain about who he is and who he's supposed to be. Inside, he's tender and fragile. Discovering himself is his main job. Often these kids focus too sharply, too much of the year, on their bodies, on athletics. Sometimes I see a kid spending too much time building his muscles in the off season, and he says, "There's not much else to do." I tell him I suppose there was nothing much to do around the Lake Country of England two hundred years ago, and that's why those bored Romantic poets started writing their poems. "Get involved," I hound my players. "Don't let the world pass you by. Go after life. Attack it. Ten years from now I want you to look back on college as a wonderful time of expanding yourself—not just four years of playing football." All the more so if a kid's here on a football scholarship. I tell him, *Use* it—for more than just football. It's a ticket to the world.

The purpose of college football is to serve education, not the other way around.

Often I get asked to name the best team I ever had. Knute Rockne was asked that long ago. He said: "I'll find out what my best team is when I find out how many doctors and lawyers and good husbands and good citizens have come off of each and every one of my teams." That's my feeling exactly. When I can look back and see what my squads have contributed to society, I'll have no trouble naming my best team.

Yet if I said that out loud today in a gathering of coaches, some would want to laugh me out of the room.

I love winning football games as much as any coach. My players love winning. Without that, Penn State teams couldn't have come out winners season after season or win national championships. But we also draw on an underlying layer of strength and power that gives us an advantage: While committing everything we've got to playing our best game, we know there's something that counts for more than winning.

I'm not dragging out the old hymn about football being a builder of character. Football doesn't automatically build character. It especially doesn't if you teach your guys to be a bunch of bullies. Where's the character building for a recruit who knows the NCAA rules that honest schools live by, yet who is offered—and accepts—a car or cash to sweeten his athletic scholarship? Where's the character building when he also learns his academic record will be "taken care of" no matter how many classes he skips? Or when a team is encouraged to climb off a plane for a national championship bowl game wear-

ing combat fatigues? Why not hang bayonets and hand gre-
nades on their belts, too, and lead them in the infantry cry "Kill
or be killed"?

Nor does the larger atmosphere around football necessarily
help build character. People who buy tickets to football games,
on the whole, aren't thinking about character. They want the
satisfaction of seeing the team of their choice beat the opposing team. Many just want to make heroes of the guys who
passed the ball or caught the ball or ran the ball to score the
winning touchdown. That may build egos, but not necessarily
character.

Yet despite all that, I watch almost all of our players grow
in the game, grow in their personal discipline, grow in their
educational development, grow as human beings. After a season, maybe ten kids emerge visibly different—better people.
Maybe more. Of all the statistics that magazine writers hang
around my neck, the one that means most is that 85 percent
of all the players I've coached have earned college degrees.
That list of players includes ten winners of national postgradu-
ate scholarships and six named as scholar-athletes by the National Football Foundation Hall of Fame. That is a big, deep,
lasting reward. It counts for more than winning and losing—
and I don't care how corny some people say that sounds. I don't
see how I'd get that payoff in pro football, where winning the
game is all that's asked of a coach.

Sure, many pro football players, too, are young and their
minds, too, need nurturing and guidance. But that's not what
a pro coach is hired for. Many pro coaches have told me they're
repeatedly surprised at how naïve some of their guys are, even
after finishing college. Then they add, "But that's all right.
There's always an agent or a lawyer to protect them." Those
coaches get so wrapped up in their professional football world,
they start to see a player's mind only in terms of how he uses
it in his business—the football business.

Let me tell you what one pro player got out of football—

college football. A few years ago, a high school English teacher named Libby McKinney wrote to us from Pineville, West Virginia. She told us about a kid in her class who was raised by his grandfather. He was the only black student in the school. You can imagine the isolation and the consequent pounding on his self-esteem that that kind of distinction forces on a youngster in a border-state small town. The teacher was excited by his natural brightness. She urged us to look at him and said she hoped his football talents would earn him a ticket to Penn State, where, she said, she knew athletics would not be permitted to overshadow his education. Her values were in the right place. That teacher's protégé, Curt Warner, became the tailback who led Penn State to its first undisputed national football championship in 1982. The Seattle Seahawks chose him in the first round of the draft, and today he's perhaps the best running back in the National Football League. But at least as important to me was that Curt graduated as an outstanding student in communications. After his pro football years are ended, he'll have no trouble creating another kind of productive career.

The example of Bobby White is different, but no less impressive. Bobby, too, was born into disadvantage—in Florida. He had a lousy school record, and no wonder. When the orange-crop was ready, he had to drop his studies, miss his classes, and pick oranges. Well, a schoolteaching couple from Freeport, Pennsylvania, who vacationed in Florida, came to know Bobby and got caught by an infectious light in him. They persuaded him to come to Pennsylvania—not just to visit, but to live with them, like a member of the family, while he finished high school. He blossomed out as a great school athlete. All sorts of colleges made offers to him, but he'd set his heart on playing football at Penn State. I didn't see how we could take him. Impossible as this may sound for a Pennsylvania high school, here was a kid who had never read a whole book! How could he remotely hope to do our level of college work? Bobby and my assistant coaches urged me: Give him a

chance to succeed—or fail. I offered him a deal: "We'll take
you into Penn State, but you've got to consent to extra tutoring
in English. By my wife, Sue." (We do have a special system
of academic favoritism at Penn State. With academic-problem
kids, we won't fix a grade. We *never* tap a professor for a little
"special understanding." But we do have a secret weapon for
a special few: personal tutoring by Sue.) Sue started him on
Huckleberry Finn. During his first year, he hung on just by his
fingernails. Four years later, he graduated as an outstanding
major in hotel administration and food service. Bobby's genuine charm and enthusiasm just naturally lifted him to become
the spirit of the 1986 national championship team. When that
triumphant team returned home to an ecstatic, late-night rally
outside our Rec Hall, Bobby was the natural choice as master
of ceremonies.

In the draft, the San Francisco 49ers took him, then cut
him. After a while, the Cleveland Browns signed him. If he
didn't make it there, he confidently told me, he planned to get
going in a career for which he had well prepared himself, as a
hotel manager, perhaps an owner. Well, in August of 1988, he
fell short of making it in pro football. But I know—and he
knows—that nobody has to worry about Bobby.

There are a few I would seriously worry about, if only they'd
worry a little about themselves. In the class that graduated in
the spring after the 1987 season, we had more than our usual
small share of guys who had taken coaching from us, but
wouldn't give back the one main thing we asked in return—
academic effort. A few cared only about getting into the pros.
These guys make a halfhearted show at schoolwork, just
enough to make us keep working with them. They use us as a
sports camp, a farm club, where they train for the pros, exploiting us just as blatantly as some schools exploit their players.

That brings down the whole team. I get thoroughly p.o.'d
and don't feel good about coaching guys like that. In the
middle of the night, I spend my lying-awake energy being mad

at them instead of thinking up ways to improve guys who are trying to improve themselves. I get so riled up I've decided I won't let guys like that use our facilities to keep in shape during their final spring semester while they wait around for the draft. Those facilities are the only persuader I have to keep a senior studying until he graduates.

But more than that, we have to make—and enforce—rules that enable us to get word to kids down through the high schools and through the elementary schools: If you have an ambition to be a college athlete but you don't want to study, you're not going to get to college. You're not going to be able to see yourself on television. You're not going to get to wave into the camera at your friends and say, "Hi, Mom!" We have to use that carrot to get these kids to study—and to convince teachers that they owe these kids special personal attention. Everywhere I go recruiting, I find some teachers who assume that because a kid can bounce a basketball or catch a football and he can run with it, and because that kid isn't interested in study, and because he comes from a family that doesn't own a book, and maybe he's black, that that kid is *ipso facto* dumb. In my experience, though, sometimes he's quick and smart as hell, but all the lessons of his life have twisted his priorities out of whack.

When I talk about this view of football and education to other coaches, some go away whispering that I'm sanctimonious, trying to build some kind of image. The few who see it as I do usually don't want to risk the embarrassment of saying these thoughts out loud. So when coaches gather, we rarely talk this way. We play it safer: We talk about football.

There are exceptions, and one is Tom Osborne, the Nebraska coach. He, too, warns his kids not to worship at the altar of football—yet he comes up year after year with powerful teams. Tom lectures his players with a set of deglamorizing statistics: In the average year, about eight Nebraska players are picked in the pro football draft. Of those eight, about four stay a while, and only two play for what might be called a full "career" (eight or ten years if a guy is lucky). The average pro football career lasts three and a half years. Fully 50 percent of pro players are broke when their playing days are over. Eighty to 85 percent of pro players wind up divorced. The average life expectancy of a pro football player is fifty-four years.

Yet player after player in college who "majors" in football gets blinded by the imagined big money and glamour of going pro. Far worse, many colleges and coaches, blinded by *their* zeal for winning, exploit these kids by doing little or nothing to dispel the cruel illusions.

"What they should do," says Ron Bracken, a savvy sportswriter in my hometown newspaper, *The Centre Daily Times,* is post those deglamorizing figures "in every high school and college locker room in the country. Better yet, they should be in large type at the top of every letter of intent, not unlike the surgeon general's warning on a pack of cigarettes." Ron's got it exactly right.

Some people still wonder how Penn State manages to recruit first-rate high school players when the kids know we'll load them with the full demand of college courses and passing grades. I believe the really ambitious player is flattered when we go after him. He knows we're interested in his *life* and what we can help him make of it, not just what we can get out of him as a football animal. The players who have been most important to the success of Penn State teams have just naturally kept their priorities straight: football a high second, but academics an undisputed first.

In 1986, John Shaffer, our steady-as-she-goes quarterback, led us to a national championship. What also makes me proud of John is that he stayed at Penn State to earn his M.B.A. and went on to an internship with Merrill Lynch. John is just a natural winner who will be successful in whatever he does.

Brian Siverling of that same team maintained a grade-point average of 3.6 (about A-minus) in engineering throughout a

Penn State football career. There's John Greene, who stayed on for graduate school in finance, and another alumnus I'm especially proud of, Lance Hamilton, of a family of Penn State football-playing Hamiltons, who went on to Yale Law School. His brother, Darren, soon followed—into Penn State's graduate school of education, where, as a doctoral candidate, he is doing research on black athletes and the difference education makes for them. Those guys, and many others like them, not only played well, they never lost sight of the reason to go to college.

I sometimes have to struggle not to lose sight of it either. When I feel that focus start to blur, I pull back into myself and run a replay of some of my early days. Our driving motivations and deepest beliefs get shaped early, and we don't have a lot to do with shaping them. The biggest shaper of our lives—call it accident or call it destiny—is who our parents were and how our patterns of reacting to them shaped us as children.

Maybe the best way to understand why I'd rather coach college students like Curt Warner, John Shaffer, Bobby White, Brian Siverling, John Greene, or Lance Hamilton than own a piece of the Boston Patriots is to come with me to the streets of Flatbush, to meet my family, visit my school, and follow some of the roads that opened to me during those early days.

3· A Family Tree Grows in Brooklyn

FOUR days before Christmas 1926, on Eighteenth Street in Flatbush, the first child of Florence de la Salle Paterno and Angelo Lafayette Paterno arrived. My mother expressed her love and respect for my father in the most sincere way a good Italian mother could. She urged that I be called Angelo Lafayette, Jr. That led to a difference of opinion, one of the few arguments that my gentle dad ever won over my mother's powerful will. So I became Joseph Vincent.

Barely twenty-one months later, my brother George checked in. Then another Paterno boy, Franklin, but he died at the age of fifteen months. When I was eleven, George and I were given a wondrous surprise, a baby sister, named Florence.

Even though both my parents were born and grew up in Brooklyn, our home was quite Italian in atmosphere. That means we spoke with flying hands as well as competing voices, especially when my mother's six sisters and three brothers all piled in to visit at the same time to eat and outshout one another. When Mom's parents came, the vocabulary respectfully shifted to Italian. My mother didn't encourage us kids to learn Italian, however, because our neighborhood was mostly Irish, German, and Jewish. She was fervent that outsiders not think of us as a family of wops. Mothers of the other kids from the other groups, each with its own cruel name—mick and Kraut and Jew-boy—had the same fears for their kids. That was New York in those days.

Yet ethnic identity was important, almost like your name. Where we lived, when a kid asked, "What are you?" he didn't mean are you a second baseman or a baritone. He meant, "Are you Irish or German or Italian or Jewish or what?" Religion— just having one, and believing your religion was the truth—was important, too, even if yours wasn't the same as the other guy's. When a Jewish kid had to abandon the stickball game to get to *shul* on time on the High Holy Days, the rest of us understood. And on those days I felt chosen when that kid's family asked me in to light their stove because they weren't supposed to strike matches. I was the *shabat goy*. Of course, everybody knew your family was important to you, and you assumed the other kid's family was important to him.

Although my father grew up as an Italian, his family actually was from Albania. Generations before he was born, his ancestors moved to the Italian province of Calabria, right at the toe of the Italian boot, where it's about to kick the football of Sicily, and where today there is still an enclave that speaks in Albanian. (After World War II, the Soviets swallowed up quiet, hardheaded Albania. But the Albanians, like their neighboring Yugoslavs, refused to go down easy. The confounded Russians finally had to let the Albanians go their own way. That's the way we are.) Sometimes my mother got exasperated at my father. Losing her sense of the map east of the Adriatic, she'd yell, "I *knew* I never should have married a Greek!"

My father's quiet way made people lean in, listen harder. That's a good starting point for persuading people, and my father liked to persuade on two subjects: the greatness of President Franklin D. Roosevelt and the intricacies of the game of football. He played on Sundays with a semipro team that visited around the metropolitan area of New York from their base in Bay Ridge, just one neighborhood away from Flatbush. They must have been pretty good. Even in the Great Depression, people paid to see them.

Every chance he got, my father tuned in the Saturday after-

noon live broadcasts of the Metropolitan Opera to make sure
we kids got indoctrinated in the single best thing in life. We
did. Fifty years later, I still don't like having to play most of
our football games at the very hour the Met is on the air.

My father was wry and straight-faced, and half the time
George and I didn't know when he was kidding. He'd tell us
he once kicked a lead football sixty yards. In awe, I'd announce
the feat to my friends. They'd take the tales home and next
day bring back whoppers about what *their* old man had done,
like swimming the length of the Hudson River underwater,
which, of course, a smart kid like me was not about to believe
for one minute. When one of us got banged up in a street
game, my father would inspect the injury and announce,
"Nothing but a little scrape. You should have seen me when
the other team broke my arm. I threw three touchdown passes
with it, and we beat 'em."

My father taught me to look after George and taught
George to show his older brother respect. He taught us well.
George and I always played football together as little kids in
the streets, as well as through high school, and through four
years at Brown. People called us the Katzenjammer Kids, after
a comic strip about two scrappy brothers. (Just before I became
head coach at Penn State, he became head football coach, then
served for a while as athletic director, at the U.S. Merchant
Marine Academy on Long Island. Today, in addition to his
current faculty duties, he's the color announcer for Penn State
football radio and television broadcasts.)

Scrappy brothers? Us? We were a couple of mild, mutually
respectful lambs, and George still shows his busted and scarred
nose to prove it. That's where I zonked him with the serious
end of a rake. But, of course, he'd started it by first kicking me
in the shins. Another time, just at the moment I had done
something he considered unlovable, George grabbed a length
of chain lying in the street at Avenue U and 25th Street. He
swung that chain and had the bad luck to hit me with it. I

picked it up and heaved it back. It might have been one of my better passes, except George ducked just in time. The chain crashed through the huge plate-glass window of Thom McAn's shoe store. Suddenly seized with brotherly love, George and I ran like hell.

At home, George scrambled under the bed, but not me. When my father asked what happened, I told him. I had learned that one thing he wouldn't tolerate was not telling the truth. He summoned the corner cop (a friend of his), who trooped into the house and scared the hell out of us—with George still under the bed. You can bet we didn't soon forget the high price of a new store window that my father had to put out. He drummed into us that if you're forthright about a mistake, the problem would solve itself. You don't sneak around it or compound it by lying. Looking back, I wonder why George didn't sometimes get furious at me for telling the awful truth. But he never did. He simply accepted "facing up" as *my* role.

I guess I was shaped, too, by the way my father sloughed off injuries. One day, when a bunch of us were playing touch football in the street, I dodged a parked car and smashed head-on into a tree. Three teeth stabbed through my lower lip. I tried sucking down the blood, hoping the others wouldn't see. Our team was behind, so I felt I had to keep playing. But George forced me to go home. I still have that scar.

For an easygoing guy, my father didn't find the going easy. In 1916, when the United States was about to enter the Great War, like many patriotic and adventurous kids he dropped out of high school to enlist. The army sent him first to Mexico with General Pershing to fight Pancho Villa, then to Europe for some of the worst infantry battles. After the Armistice he worked by day and finished high school by night, then spent years more of his evenings going to college and St. John's Law School. People liked him, and a friend helped get him a clerical job in the Appellate Division of the New York State Supreme

Court. After a while, he worked his way up to becoming a court clerk, a judge's administrative right arm. All during the Great Depression, he was one of the lucky ones who had a good, steady job, although it didn't pay much.

Nothing was more important to my parents than family. My father would barely manage the means to send us to summer camp for a couple of weeks, and my mother would say, "We can't send Joe and George without sending Nicky." The parents of Nicky, or some other cousin, couldn't afford camp that year. So my dad found a way to foot that bill, too.

In 1941, the year of Pearl Harbor, when he was forty-four, my father passed the New York State bar exam. While he remained on a civil service salary as court clerk, he took in bits and pieces of private law work, sometimes for modest fees, often for free just to help someone in need. Anyone in our vast extended family who got in a jam knew to call Uncle Pat (for Paterno), even at two in the morning.

My father's life drilled two important attitudes into me. When, as a little kid, you keep hearing of how your father finished high school at night, and then you see him come home late every night from college classes, and then at the age of fifteen you see all your uncles and aunts and cousins and neighbors celebrate because your father passed the bar exam, you get the feeling that education is really important. That was Attitude One. The second was what you play games for. Every night when we came in from playing, he'd always want to hear about the game. I don't remember him ever asking, "Did you win?" His question always was, "Did you have fun?"

When George or I brought him a question from our homework, or about current events, or about some argument we'd had with a kid, my father would question and challenge us to *think*, think *harder*. He'd remind us that one of my aunts taught languages on Long Island and that she was someone to be proud of, that my Uncle Freddy, even though he never graduated from high school, was an editor of the Brooklyn

Eagle, a large and important newspaper at that time. His constant challenges to *think,* think *harder,* made me mentally aggressive exactly the way games in the street pushed me to become physically aggressive. In both ways, I always had the feeling that I had to compete, had to stretch; that what I'm able to do at present is not quite enough, that there's more, always a little more.

In 1955, when I was twenty-eight and a green assistant football coach, and he was fifty-eight, my father collapsed and died of a heart attack. The life I have led since that year might have given him a lot of pleasure and gratification. I guess my deepest regret is that he didn't get to see some of it.

While my father's caring for the people around him helped shape me, I came to have more drive, more intensity, than he had. I attribute that to my mother.

Mom's people came from Naples, which means you always know what she has on her mind because she tells you flat-out, even today in her nineties. While my father was alive, she freely gave him what-for. He'd just let it bounce off, then do what he originally intended to do. But she was stern and firm with us, having clear images of what she expected each of us to do and be, how she expected us to grow up.

Mom never took a back seat to any one, any place, any time. If she couldn't be at the head of the pack, she wouldn't go. So, as the first son, in anything I did I had to be at the top. If we had a classroom spelling bee, I was expected to win it. I had to be able to do multiplication tables faster than anyone else. At St. Edmond's, the parochial grammar school we went to, when a nun asked a question, my hand always shot up first. Why? Because of the image in the back of my head of my mother expecting me to defend my honor, our family honor.

I guess I got my sense of rigid discipline from her, too. One day at school, I got into a little chalk-throwing contest while Sister's back was turned. The nun gave me a smart swat across the knuckles with her ruler. When I got home, my mom asked, "What's the matter with your hand?"

"Aw, it got scraped."

"Were you in a fight?"

"No."

"How'd your hand get red like that?"

"Sister hit me."

"Sister *hit* you?"

"Yeah, but I didn't do any—"

Mom gave me a shot right across the head. "That's for giving Sister problems."

My mother fretted constantly about how we kids would appear to the neighbors. Every morning, she was up at five-thirty, fixing our clothes so we'd go to school looking like a million bucks. We didn't have a washing machine, so she'd wash our shirts and sheets on a scrubbing board, then iron them. I nearly had to put on a tie to take out the garbage. She always imagined some kind of striving we had to do to fit socially into a predominantly Irish and German grammar school and later into a classy Catholic high school, Brooklyn Prep, that was economically a bit over our heads. Because of her undertone of fear that we might not be good enough, I have trouble to this day getting on familiar terms with accomplished friends, some inner voice prodding me to address them as Doctor or Mister or Father.

My mother's family story, like my father's, is cut from the saga of millions of Americans whose parents and grandparents crossed the Atlantic in the steerage class of crowded, smelly ships, out of sheer faith in the promise and mystery that called them to America. Her father had managed his way here before the turn of the century. He was only sixteen. From scrimping out of an immigrant's wages of less than a dollar a day, he put together enough to go back to Italy in his thirties. There he found the wife who was to become my maternal grandmother. She was fifteen. Her life in America brought her a huge brood of seventeen—or was it eighteen?—children, of whom ten survived. Even with all those mouths to feed, my grandfather managed to buy a horse-drawn wagon, a valuable capitalist property. He knew a man—they'd become Americans together over the years—who bought and sold peanuts and cashews, wholesale. My grandfather delivered for him, mostly to Garden City, Long Island, a big distribution center. As his friend's business grew, my grandfather bought a truck, then another. His business grew, too, and he and his young wife fed, clothed, and schooled their ten kids, making a good family life in a tenement on Troy Avenue, right off Atlantic Avenue, in the Bedford-Stuyvesant neighborhood of Brooklyn.

To this day, my mother will have you know that she was the first Italian to be hired by New York's telephone company. I don't know if that's precisely so, but the fact is she got through high school and got that good operator's job. Her oldest brother, Tony Cafiero, sent his oldest son, Gene, to Dartmouth. Gene eventually became president of the Chrysler Corporation (to be replaced one day by another *paisano*, Lee Iacocca).

Often, all our relatives with all their kids gathered in one place, say, at my Uncle John's house in Coney Island. Uncle John had once been a policeman. He stood as upright as the Empire State Building and expected us to do the same. After Sunday dinner, he'd pair us up, more or less according to age and size, and we had to go at each other in boxing matches. At six years old, I was defending myself boxing. Uncle John "taught" us all to swim. He'd lead us all out to the end of an ocean pier and throw us in, one by one. The choice was swim or die. While I learned I could swim, I never again had an urge to go leaping into the ocean.

Uncle John had a plumbing business, and he gave some of my cousins summer work at good money, two dollars for up to a fourteen-hour day, usually for the dirty jobs. I tried it for one day and never asked for more.

Sometimes the whole clan gathered at a relative's farmhouse at Syosset, Long Island. All of us young cousins—maybe as many as forty or fifty of us—would share the "kids' rooms," sleeping maybe four or five to a bed. One of my early memories was toward the end of Prohibition. Each year my uncles fermented their own illicit beer and wine to consume during a future year's card games at Syosset. They'd send one of the older kids down to the basement for a jug of wine, and the rule was that the kid had to whistle all the way down the stairs and back to prove he wasn't sipping any. If he stopped whistling, he got a crack across the head.

Those were fun times. Today, people move around a lot and they frantically reach out to make new friends. In those days, our family *were* our friends.

From the time George and I started playing serious football in high school, my mother said novenas for us every hour on the hour, from 9 A.M. to 6 P.M., every day of the season. After we both became coaches, her prayers became, if anything, more earnest. I guess I got feelings of support from that, except for her 9 A.M. prayer. She always addressed that one to Saint Jude, the patron of lost causes. But her favorite prayer went to the Infant Jesus of Prague, whom she called her "little guy." During the week before a tough game, she'd tell me not to worry about my team because the "little guy" would look after us.

My mother had us move from house to house a lot, to be near one of her six sisters, then another, and another, but all the moves were in the same general section of Brooklyn. One was a house we rented on Twenty-third Street between Avenues S and T, near St. Edmond's. It was a nice street, lots of playing room, lots of kids to play with, and we played all day in summer, all afternoon the rest of the year. Playing daily at sports was our work: not only touch football, but also punchball and stickball, using a high-bounce ball made by A. G. Spalding Company, which any street kid knew was called a Spal*deeeen.*

At stickball, when the wind was right, I could hit two-and-a-half sewers. (Anybody who needs that explained never lived in New York.)

One really important guy on the block, an adult, was named Jack Smith. What made him important was not his family, or his religion, or his ethnic group, none of which I knew anything about. He was a famous *sports* writer—and for the greatest, most important information medium of any kind anywhere in the entire world, the New York *Daily News*. On almost any day of the week, you could see his *name* there, at the top of articles he actually wrote. But that wasn't half of why we valued him as a neighbor. One of his good friends—he knew him *personally*—was Tommy Henrich of the New York Yankees, who every afternoon played the outfield beside Joe DiMaggio and George Selkirk. More than once, Jack Smith came walking from the subway station just a couple of hours after a game, bringing Tommy Henrich himself home for dinner. We might have heard his name on the radio that very day, hauling down a spectacular catch, or parking one in the upper deck, and here he was on Twenty-third Street! Jack Smith would introduce him to each one of us by our names, and then Tommy Henrich would throw us a few passes. I couldn't imagine any greater thrill, except his being a Brooklyn Dodger instead of a Bronx Bomber. I'd go to bed with goose bumps from the excitement.

When I was finishing at St. Edmond's, we had moved to Twenty-sixth and Avenue R, just one block from James Madison High School, a very good public school. At the bus stop on our corner, James Madison kids unloaded every morning by the hundreds. I guess I expected to become one of them, but my dad said, "No, I want you to go to a Catholic school." That meant he'd have to pay tuition of twenty bucks a month. At today's dollar, that might correspond to two hundred bucks a month or more. He had to take an extra job to pay for it. Never once did I hear my parents say, "We can't afford to send you."

My father enrolled me at Brooklyn Preparatory School, run

by Jesuits. (Brooklyn Prep is closed now. The buildings, which included a church and rectory, were later sold to the City of New York, and they are now Medgar Evers Community College.) A year and a half later, George was to go to St. Augustine's, a diocesan high school that was very good and where he'd have a cost-free scholarship. By the time George was ready to go, I had begun playing football at Brooklyn Prep. St. Augustine's didn't have football. George pleaded that if he could go to Brooklyn Prep, too, he'd play his heart out at football and win a college athletic scholarship. My father went to see the headmaster, Father John Hooper, and struck a deal for us both to go to Brooklyn Prep at a cut rate. So now he had to put up thirty bucks a month. After my dad died and I had to get all his financial records in order, for the first time I got a full view of what my parents went without to give us what we had. He died with empty pockets.

4· Virgil

WHEN I showed up at Brooklyn Prep in February 1941, itching to impress my new school with the athletic gifts I'd brought, I was a skinny kid of 125 pounds. The closest I got to the football varsity that year was attending every game as a spectator. In my sophomore year, I saw a little action as a kickoff receiver, because I was fast.

Finally, as a junior, I got my break from our new coach, Zev Graham. He was named after a horse and had been an all-American quarterback at Fordham University in the Bronx, which, at that time, fielded great football teams. I wanted to try out for center, but my light weight forced me to settle for offensive guard, staying in on defense as a linebacker. Today's two-platoon system hadn't come in yet, so most of us played nearly every minute of every game.

George, who was a year behind me, and I weren't the Katzenjammer Kids anymore. The papers called us "the Gold Dust twins." In my junior year, we won all of two games.

Meanwhile, I had also been playing basketball, and I felt myself more naturally suited to that than to football. By my senior year, I was starting guard on the basketball varsity, opposing players like Jack Kaiser, who later starred at St. John's University, where he is now athletic director; George Kaftan, who went on to lead Holy Cross to its 1947 national championship, and the great pro-to-be, Bob Cousy. Also I played against a star of St. John's Prep, John Bach, who later became my colleague as Penn State's head basketball coach.

During that senior year, Graham made me a starting full-back and flattered me pink by letting me call the plays without a huddle. I think he considered me fast in the head as well as on my feet. Later that season, he moved me to quarterback, but not because I had earned any medals as a thrower. In those days, the quarterback didn't necessarily throw the passes, and we didn't throw very often anyhow. Still, I was afraid I might lose the job because my arm wasn't good enough. I couldn't stand not being good enough, so at home after practice I'd throw a football against a padded wall in our cellar for hour after hour after hour. My mother thought some raging demon had possessed her oldest boy.

More than once I overheard my mother cautioning George, who she suspected was a stronger athlete, to hold himself back in games. Being a good Italian mother, she reminded him that, after all, I was the older brother and he had to be careful not to make me look bad. I'm sure George overlooked the advice. But I did have those doubts about how good a natural athlete I was, especially with George's gifts to compare mine against. More important was that I *feared* I didn't have the physical abilities I wished I had. Today, I think I owe a lot to those fears. Where I felt I had strong talent, as in running and agile footwork, I figured that was the way it was supposed to be. But where I had the slightest doubt I was tops, as in throwing, the fear of deficiency made me push myself to the limit. If you let them, the fear of weaknesses and adversities can whip you down. But they can also whip you up. And between those two choices, I already instinctively sensed, every person has the power to choose.

In my senior year, we were the best Catholic-school team in New York. We lost only one game, to St. Cecilia's High from Englewood, New Jersey, which had a sharp, intense young coach named Vince Lombardi. I had hurt my arm the previous week, and all through the St. Cecilia's game I had to conceal my pain—not from the other team, but from my own coach. I was afraid he'd pull me out.

*   *   *

Don't get the wrong idea. Football was not the most important thing for me at Brooklyn Prep. Student politics and government fascinated me, too. Every year my classmates elected me a class officer, finally class president, and then they picked me for vice president of the student council. But that wasn't the main part, either. What school was really about, and I never had a moment's confusion about this, was getting an education.

Every one of us at Brooklyn Prep had to take four solid years of mathematics, four years of Latin, and two years of a modern language. Also we needed to study science or Greek. I took the Greek, but the coming of World War II soon forced science on us all. Our teachers, those who weren't Jesuit priests, were scholastics, young men on their way to becoming Jesuit priests. All of them burned with idealism, and that made them marvelous teachers.

If destiny guided me anywhere, anytime, during my four years at Brooklyn Prep, it was through the door of my Latin class on the first day of my third year. The teacher up front, a black-robed scholastic with a bony-cheeked, long, ascetic face atop the wiry body of a welterweight, looked us over through cool, glassy blue eyes. A stranger to us all and probably hiding a quiver or two, he was an absolute rookie, facing the first meeting of the first class he had ever taught. Thomas Bermingham—Mr. Bermingham, as we addressed this future priest—moved the length of the blackboard, the width of the room, slowly, serenely. He was twenty-five. I was going on seventeen.

For him, this was not only a first class, but the first day of a long period within the thirteen-year trek to becoming a Jesuit. It's called the "regency period." For three years, with fellow seminarians, he had shut himself away, almost in confinement, with books, writings, and meditations all on a single subject, philosophy. Ahead of him lay four more years, equally locked away, all devoted to theology. But between those two periods, the seminarian is given a three-year time of change. He gets to return to the world of people, reminding himself of the lives of others, taking responsibility and serving them as a teacher—or regent. Here he was in our classroom, suddenly sprung.

This new teacher knew exactly where he wanted to bring us, he told me years later, but first he had to find out where each of us was starting from. Before even asking our names, Father Bermingham (that's what I'm going to call him from here on because that's how I address my lifelong friend today) passed out pieces of paper and said, in a surprisingly deep voice for a little guy: "I'm going to start by giving you a quiz. Don't be upset. It's the one exam you'll get that will be graded not for correct answers or anything like that, but for being honest. How will I know if you're being honest? You've got to convince me.

"I want you to draw up two lists of books you have read. On the left side of your sheet, I want you to list books you've read that you have really disliked. On the right side, anything you've read that you liked very much. If you try to start thinking about what will impress me, it will just throw you off and I'll know it. I just want the truth, and I'll know that, too. Remember, I'm grading only for honesty. That's the only thing you can impress me with."

That was the most puzzling darn test I'd ever heard of. After class, I got hold of one of my buddies, Frankie Snyder, a smart kid whose father ran a bar and grill around the corner from school, and we compared experiences. What Frankie said he'd done struck me as pretty daring and maybe a little crazy. The school had issued us a basic English literature textbook called *Prose and Poetry* that we used year after year. In a way, I liked the book because some stuff in it was pretty exciting, even though a lot of it put me to sleep. But Frankie hated the book, hated it cover to cover, page by page. So he put down on his left-side list *Prose and Poetry*—admitting right out loud that he hated a regular schoolbook. Worse still, under books that he *liked* he had the nerve to write *The G-String Murders* by

Gypsy Rose Lee, a best-selling mystery of the time by the world's most famous stripper.

I don't remember what I put down for books I hated, but I remember nervously admitting what I liked—stories by Ernest Hemingway and John Steinbeck—and wondering whether they were okay to confess.

My grade seemed to confirm that they really *were* bad: I got an A for my honesty. But Frankie Snyder did better—an A+.

A couple of days later, Father Bermingham asked me to see him after school. He got me talking about what interested me outside of classes. I told him about my football, basketball, and baseball and that I was starting to think I'd have to drop baseball to focus properly on the other two. He got me to tell him about my elections to class offices, and we talked about clubs I belonged to and liked: the Book Discussion Club, as well as the Sodality Club, a religious discussion group that also gave us an opportunity to work in the neighborhood among the poor or whoever else we could serve.

"That's a lot of activity," he said. "I'm not sure you'd have time for something else I had in mind."

He paused.

I waited.

"I had the thought that you and I might do up a list of further readings that we might go into together, but—"

Alarm flamed through my chest. I was scared that he was going to think me too busy and not give me the chance. I must have shown it.

"Would you be interested in my guiding you further along these lines?"

I couldn't blurt out "Yes" fast enough.

Starting from his first day as a teacher, Father Bermingham always kept an eye out for kids who had begun what he calls the most important task in education: their self-education. He meant kids who showed signs of taking responsibility for their own expansion instead of waiting for teachers to do it for them.

Even the most talented teacher can try what he or she thinks is "teaching," but it won't really take unless the student takes charge of the more important job: learning.

He was not alone in looking for students ready to be coached either one-on-one or in small groups. Jesuits believe in doing that. The headmaster himself, Father Hooper, had already picked out four or five of us and we met with him now and then to talk about his special interest, leadership, the importance of it and how to develop it in ourselves. One of the kids in school at that time was William Peter Blatty, who later wrote *The Exorcist* and other successful novels. (Father Bermingham appeared in a minor role in the film of *The Exorcist* and was technical adviser for the religious practices used in it.)

I was impressionable, eager, proud of my mind, probably overly so, simmering with intellectual curiosity. Two or three afternoons a week, Father Bermingham and I sat, usually in his classroom at two student desks, or in the scholastics' quarters next door, almost like equals. We'd spend forty, forty-five minutes talking about something he'd told me to read, and then I went to the gym for basketball practice. Members of the basketball team had to shoot a certain number of fouls every day before the practice hour. So I had to ask Coach Graham (he coached basketball and baseball as well as football) for permission to shoot my fouls in the morning, before school, so I could meet for those sessions with Father Bermingham. Maybe that contributed to the habit I observe to this day of getting up at five-thirty in the morning and doing close to a half day's work before breakfast.

At the beginning of my senior year, this austere big brother of a priest-to-be led me to Virgil. Father Bermingham told me that Virgil was the greatest of the Roman poets, that he lived just three or four decades before Christ, and that he is known mostly for his epic poem, *The Aeneid.* Father Bermingham asked if I'd like to read it with him.

"Sure," I said.

"What I had in mind," he said, "was reading it together in the original Latin."

"In Latin? A poem as long as a book?"

"Yes."

The book was on his desk, more than four hundred pages thick. As a schoolkid, I always had the attitude about any challenge, "Hey, if it's difficult, let's do it." That made it more fun.

"But if it's in Latin," I asked uncertainly, "will we be able to cover all that?"

"What's important," he said, "is not how much we cover. I don't like that word, 'cover.' It's not how much we do, but the excellence of what we do."

Excellence. The way he pronounced that word made it shine with a golden light.

I'll never forget the majestic ring of the opening lines and of how we approximated them in modern English:

> *Arma virumque cano, Troiae qui primus ab oris . . .*
> *Of arms and the man I sing.*

It made me hear cymbals and trumpets, and I envisioned a procession of gallant gladiators. At their head, on a huge horse, rode the most gallant of all, a king or a prince or some kind of general. It rang in my ears:

> *Of arms and the man I sing.*

And then:

> *From the seacoast of Troy in the early days*
> *He came to Italy by destiny . . .*

I still feel the spell of that young robed cleric's eyes searing into me, reminding me that I was special and that this was important. He never talked down. Instead of telling me thoughts, he'd pull them out of me. He'd ask, "Why do you think he used that word?" I'd think about that, and developed feelings not only for the precision of words, but also for the subtle shadings of Latin.

So Virgil, and his hero Aeneas, the founder of Rome, entered my life. More than entered it. The adventures of Aeneas seeped into far corners of my mind, into my feelings about what is true and honorable and important. They helped shape everything I have since become. I don't think anybody can get a handle on what makes me tick as a person, and certainly can't get at the roots of how I coach football, without understanding what I learned from the deep relationship I formed with Virgil during those afternoons and later in my life.

The story of Aeneas tells how the city of Rome was founded. By birth Aeneas is a Trojan, the son of the goddess of love, Venus. As Troy is ransacked and conquered through trickery by the Greeks, Aeneas gathers up an army of survivors and leads them to an escape by sea. In a scene of his leaving Troy, Aeneas lifts his aging father on his back and grasps the hand of his little son, who runs along by his side. He was physically carrying, protecting, preserving the past, one could say, and, in the same act, taking care of those who would live in the future. That, I decided Virgil was trying to say, was the duty of a responsible man, a leader.

The poem actually begins at a later moment in his story, at a climax of Aeneas' sea journey, the world crashing around him in a catastrophic storm. His fleet splits apart, some of his shattered ships and men sinking, some smashing into rocks and shore. Instead of his own ship landing where the *fata*, the fates, had promised him was his goal, on the shores of what we now call Italy, he finds himself stranded on the jungle shores of Africa, losing more of his men. "I've been deceived," he cries. He's ready to give up, craves to get out of this mission and its terrors and suffering. But he knows that his destiny, through the *fata*, has commanded him to get himself and the tatters of his army to Italy to start a new city. He's exhausted, discouraged. Aeneas has to go through a great struggle with himself to renew any kind of faith in the *fata*, in the voices of his destiny.

That puzzled and bothered me. If he knew he wanted to quit, how did he know he had to go on? If he lost faith in the *fata*, how did he know what his destiny was?

So Father Bermingham had to explain some confusion over the modern meaning of the word "fate." Today we think of fate the way the Greeks meant it: something that just happened that takes control of your life, something meted out to you, the piece of pie you were handed. It's not something you chose. Among the great Greek storytellers, especially Homer, heroes like Odysseus and Achilles are batted around constantly by predetermined accidents, obstacles they couldn't foresee and can't do a thing about.

The word *fatum* in Latin means something different. It means a *divine word*. All through *The Aeneid*, Aeneas gets the messages from Jupiter, the supreme god, through Mercury or others whose voices he hears in his head. They keep saying, You ought to do this, You've got to do that. (Today, people talk about a "voice within," or intuition, or "a strong feeling." Maybe they're saying the same thing.) Virgil keeps harping that Aeneas—that anybody—needs to have faith and trust in that *fatum*. It may confuse, it may bewilder, it may contradict and frustrate all of a guy's most precious urges. It sure as hell may seem illogical. But a *fatum* cannot be denied.

And that's where the deepest trouble is. Destiny, the *fatum*, the divine word, the inner voice, whatever you want to call it, tells you where you have to wind up and what you're destined to do, but it doesn't tell you how to get there or how to do it. Aeneas has to struggle and suffer—and make his own decisions. How he *acts* is not determined by fate. He listens, he considers. But then he must act out of free will.

Aeneas cannot choose not to found Rome. He's destined to create it. But he has to struggle with himself, inch by inch, hour by hour—play by play!—to figure out how to do it, to *endure* the struggle and torment of doing it, and take all the bad breaks along the way.

As I sat there, an impressionable twentieth-century seventeen-year-old, I wasn't really swallowing Virgil's rigid brand of fatalism. But I sensed him speaking to me with a broader and deeper kind of truth.

It was terrible that Aeneas' beloved city of Troy had to be destroyed. But what I absorbed as we read was that the founding of Rome had a cost. The cost was Troy's defeat and Aeneas' years of torment. Everything costs. No accomplishment comes without suffering. *Humanum est pati. To be alive is to suffer.* There are tears in the very nature of things.

Virgil wasn't saying something as simple-headed as "No pain, no gain." That implies you can choose between hurting and taking life easy. To Virgil, nobody gets to choose not to suffer.

And nobody is guaranteed a reward, a victory, in repayment for his suffering. The best man, the best team, isn't automatically entitled to win. The winds of fate can turn you around, run you aground, sink you, and sometimes you can't do a thing about it. You can commit yourself to accomplishing a goal, doing something good, winning a game. Just to make that commitment to something you believe in *is* winning—even if you lose the game. But for commiting yourself to winning the game, whether you win it or not, you always pay in tears and blood.

In some of the passages that touched me the deepest, Virgil looks straight into the heart of Aeneas. In the opening storm at sea, he figures everything he risked his life to save in leaving Troy is now lost. His mission seems impossible. He feels helpless and overwhelmed. He goes off by himself to tremble and cry like a kid. Then, somehow, he pulls himself together, knowing, even in his agony, that he can't spill his guts to the men he has to lead. Destiny has stuck him with being a leader, and he can't escape it.

The bravery, the picking up and going on, affected me, sure. But what got to me most in that scene was that Aeneas, the son of a god driven by fates, was, after all, a human being. His secret places were like mine. He might have had to put up a bold front as a leader, but he didn't have to hide his sadness and trembling from himself.

There was one more important thing that Father Bermingham led me to see in Virgil, and it made the deepest mark of all on the way I coach.

Almost everybody who's been to high school knows about Homer and his two epics, *The Odyssey* and *The Iliad.* Teachers often draw parallels between Virgil and Homer because their epics of heroes seem to have a lot in common. Of course, Homer was Greek and Virgil Roman; Homer was dead for seven hundred years before Virgil learned his alphabet. But there's a more important difference between them, which teachers don't always see, that helped shape my outlook on life—and on football.

To Homer—and, in fact, to most of the modern world— heroes are created through personal exploits and glorification—often through an ambitious drive for self-glorification. Heroes are superstars. In sports, the grandstands cheer them, and they throw their high fives up and slam the football down after a touchdown. Homer's hero Achilles, in his pursuit of glory, ends up destroying his men and his cause and rotting at the end into a kind of monster.

Aeneas, as Virgil created him, was a totally new kind of epic hero. Like Homer's heroes, he endures battles, storms, shipwrecks and the rages of the gods. But the worst storm is the one that rages within himself. He yearns to be free of his tormenting duty, but he knows that his duty is to others, to his men. Through years of hardship and peril, Aeneas reluctantly but relentlessly heeds his *fata* until he founds Rome.

Aeneas is not a grandstanding superstar. He is, above all, a

Trojan and a Roman. His first commitment is not to himself, but to others. He is bugged constantly by the reminder, the *fatum*, "You must be a man for others." He lives his life not for "me" and "I," but for "us" and "we." Aeneas is the ultimate team man.

A hero of Aeneas' kind does not wear his name on the back of his uniform. He doesn't wear Nittany Lions on his helmet to claim star credit for touchdowns and tackles that were enabled by everybody doing his job. For Virgil's kind of hero, the score belongs to the team.

Father Bermingham didn't have to lecture me on most of that. We were just reading, sentence by sentence, in Latin, and there it was, like a living experience.

For entertainment today, we flip the channel to *Rambo* or *Miami Vice* or even *The G-String Murders* and get caught up by the fight scenes or the shoot-'em-ups and the chase. But it's not the same kind of experience. Once a person has experienced a genuine masterpiece, the size and scope of it last as a memory forever.

5· Not-So-Divine Providence

I made the New York all-Metropolitan high school football team but, probably because of my unimpressive height and weight, the Paterno doorstep wasn't overrun with college scouts. Holy Cross came by to talk, but they wouldn't talk about George, who still had a year and a half to go at Brooklyn Prep. My father, wanting us to go to the same college, hoped to enroll us as a "package." Boston College, another Catholic school, went after George early on a football scholarship but wasn't excited about me, either for football or basketball. Fordham offered me a basketball scholarship, but only a partial one.

One day, Coach Zev Graham told me that an alumnus of Brown University, the Ivy League school at Providence, Rhode Island, wanted to talk to my father about paying tuition for George and me to Brown. In those days, it was legal and common for an alumnus to pick up the tab for an athlete who met admission standards. The mysterious benefactor, I soon learned, was named Everett M. "Busy" Arnold, a publisher of comic books. My father and I traveled to Brown, where the head coach, Charles A. "Rip" Engle, impressed both of us, and so did Mr. Arnold, who was taking care of a dozen or more other football players at Brown.

The offer created a real crisis for my father. The double "scholarship" for both George and me was exactly what he wanted for us, except for one thing. At that time bishops and priests were telling the flock that some well-meaning families had fallen into error, sending a son or daughter to any but a Catholic college, like Holy Cross, Georgetown, or Boston College. We had a special mass at Brooklyn Prep just to warn parents of the moral risks of a non-Catholic education. Some parochial high schools refused to forward transcripts of academic records to a non-Catholic college. During that special sermon, I felt a white-hot heat on my neck, and I wasn't the only one. Frankie Mahoney, another football player and a good student, had already decided on Brown, sponsored by the same benefactor. A boy named Brennan, our class valedictorian, who had the best mind in the whole school, was headed for Harvard and eventually for their medical school. My father sounded out several priests on our terrific opportunity at Brown. Without exception, they echoed the bishops and threw cold water on it. My father, a devout Catholic, wasn't the type just to ignore such opposition. In a last-ditch search for moral support, any kind of feeble support, he went to Father Bermingham, who wasn't even yet a priest.

"I'll give you my personal answer," the young scholastic told him in that deep voice. "In terms of what I know of your son, if I were in your place, I wouldn't be concerned about Joe going astray at Brown."

I think my father's mind was already made up anyhow. He took me to the monsignor to inform him of the decision. The monsignor said: "Well, Angelo, this boy's soul is in your hands."

I could feel the weight of that monkey on his back. My father walked silently and slightly hunched all the way home.

Later, Father Bermingham sat me down to explain the "facts of life" about a non-Catholic environment. He assured me (probably in a low voice) that I did not have to be automatically fearful of all non-Catholics. He said I'd be challenged, but shouldn't run from all thoughts and experiences that didn't line up with what I'd been taught. For stability, I should make sure to get to know some priests in Providence, and he gave me some material to read. Finally, we reviewed a few passages from Virgil that might fortify me through the dangers of being alone and vulnerable in a world of non-Catholic thought.

Whether in retribution or not I don't know, but the thunders soon crashed down. Six weeks after my graduation from Brooklyn Prep, the U.S. Army drafted me. Less than a month later, President Truman dropped the two bombs on Hiroshima and Nagasaki, suddenly ending World War II, but not improving my personal situation. The army shipped me from Fort Dix, New Jersey, near home, to Korea. Finally, a year later, I was discharged just in time to start at Brown in the fall of 1946. Meanwhile, George had caught up with me in his schooling. George became a Brown freshman the same day I did.

My uncle Freddie told me to be practical and to enroll in engineering, which I did. That lasted long enough (about a week) for me to discover that engineering had a lot to do with mathematics. I had a Greek mind, not a German mind. I switched to economics, partly because I knew that smart economists could improve the world. What I didn't know for another couple of weeks was that economics was a far-from-exact science—and boring. So I looked back at my extensive academic career and asked myself when I had my happiest hours. That was easy: studying those epics with Father Bermingham. I changed my major to English literature and never regretted it for a moment.

The Romantic period held my interest most. I'm a romantic. I dreamed then, and do now, about gladiators and knights winning battles. I like the movie *Patton*. George Patton, a tough-minded lover of poetry and epics, believed he was reincarnated, probably from a previous life as a Roman general. My kind of guy.

After hearing a lot from the priests at Brooklyn Prep about how a young Catholic should brace his mind against a heathen world, at Brown I sure got the other side. I had never come across the argument, until I heard it from some fellow students, that while Protestants go to church because they love God, Catholics go because they're afraid of God. And I'd certainly never stayed up, as I did in college, until three or four in the morning arguing against birth control and defending the infallibility of the Pope.

Those late-night debates didn't unbalance me even when I momentarily groped for moral answers. Father Bermingham had instructed me, after all, on where to find proper literature. I won't dishonestly claim that some of the outrageous Protestant doctrine I heard left me entirely uninfluenced. But I carefully acted as though none of it had the slightest effect. Those debates, after all, were a form of *competition*—and I was not about to lose an argument, whether I was right or wrong. In fact, winning or losing for Roman Catholicism wasn't the issue. I just wasn't about to let a Protestant think he was smarter than I was.

Nor was I the only one to mellow during that period of history. Not long afterward, Pope John XXIII himself started advocating the idea of ecumenism, saying that people of all religions have to accept and respect one another. A voice inside me yelled, "For crying out loud, what have we been waiting for?"

Word about a freshman on football scholarship gets around. He might be a desirable character to know. So I got invited to a cocktail party at a fraternity, my first invitation at Brown to anything. Nobody told me it was the fraternity of John D. Rockefeller, Jr., and God knows who else. In fact, I didn't have the slightest idea what fraternity life was about.

Drawing on my mother's careful teaching, I put on a nice shirt and my best white sweater. At the frat house I walked into a calm sea of blue blazers, sharkskin suits, and Harris tweeds. I knew I had blown something when all those cool-eyed faces turned toward me and my sweater, slowly, so as not to tip and spill their stemmed glasses that seemed to hold nothing but clear water, except for an olive in each. I heard somebody whisper, "How did that dago get invited?" My clothes scratched at my skin, and a chill surged down my insides.

Everybody was polite as I got through the dinner. I imagined each of them asking himself what to expect of a football animal. They never asked me back.

That party didn't hurt my life at Brown; far from it. But it made me angry. I still see and feel that room, those people, fingering their cocktails, studying me out of the corners of their eyes. I guess I had figured that life in the world was like life in Brooklyn. At home, if I ever felt I was better than another kid, it was because I could play better or think better—not because I *was* better. This time I caught a whiff of people who put themselves in a higher echelon for starters, without a contest. I soon understood, but never learned to accept, that in those days a typical Brownie instinctively needed to sniff out who your family was and how rich you were. If you were a football player who wasn't rich or from the right tree, you were admired and all that, but you never quite got free of the stereotype of the football player. (Right after World War II, the GI Bill enabled a lot of kids to get into the Ivy League sheerly on brains, without the traditional social background. Football players and athletes, among them, gravitated toward two or three fraternity houses. Those got to be called "animal houses." Maybe that's part of why I hate athletic dorms.)

In class, sometimes I got the feeling that some traditional Brownies simply assumed I wasn't as smart as they were—and didn't have to be. After all, I'd entered this good company on some kind of special terms, polluting the atmosphere with an athletic scholarship. But I knew I belonged in Brown or any other place I could show I was qualified to go. I was always determined to prove to those kids in class that I was smarter than a lot of them. Yet at the same time, I was always nervous in a discussion, always afraid I might slip and look stupid.

What I felt in those days from some Brownie snobs was exactly what I feel today from some people who clamp shut their white jaws in the presence of a black stranger, silently, eloquently, scarily expressing their superiority. Maybe being taken at times for a football animal was what sensitized me for a lifelong empathy with black people. And ever since that scalding moment of the sweater, I have known something about the subtle freeze a black person senses when he walks into a nice restaurant, the only black there, and the whole place gets slightly quieter.

People who sympathize (not truly empathize) with black kids in schools have helped create one of the worst and most perplexing problems those kids have to carry on their backs: all the special help they get as students. Necessary as much of it may be to make up for previous deprivations, every bit of special help adds to the constant drumbeat of a message that they're not as good as the next kid. On equal terms, says the message, nobody expects them to make it. So a kid sits in class scared to death to open his mouth—not because he isn't smart, but because he's not a hundred percent convinced he can make it. All those legal protections and special helps reinforce the doubts of his teachers as well as his own.

This is difficult to discuss out loud, even to think about. But it must be discussed out loud, looked at, thought about, be frankly debated. When we create special regulations to help minority students, we do it to help, and the feeling of helping makes us feel good. But the more I live intimately and daily with these kids and their lack of confidence, the more I see the sources of that lack—and the more I see these kids accomplish, expand, develop, flourish in a program that is designed to build confidence instead of tearing it down. And the more I think that no matter how we *think* we're helping these kids by giving them special help and protection, in the long run we're probably doing more harm than good.

* * *

Before long, I pledged at a fraternity, Delta Kappa Epsilon—known as the Dekes. Eventually, the Brown chapter elected me its vice president.

I didn't date girls much because I never had enough extra money. Nor was I drawn to cutting up. Some of the guys went out on the lawn of Deke House high on College Hill to drive golf balls clear over the courthouse roof below into downtown Providence. The moment they heard the wail of police sirens, they fled to the John Hay Library across the street, slumped over a table with open books, where nobody could tell them apart from the innocent grinds.

Our chapter was the first fraternity at Brown to admit a Jewish brother. His name was Steve Fenn and he was from Brookline, Massachusetts. Steve was an active, friendly kid who almost everybody liked, but some thought that letting in a Jew would destroy one of the last protections of tradition. The first time we proposed Steve, a secret vote produced two blackballs (only one needed to bar him). We urged him not to turn sour on the whole group just over those two votes. After talking to two guys we suspected of casting them, we felt we changed one, but were left uncertain as to who cast the other. In a later vote, I became convinced the remaining blackball was not cast by our second suspect. That probably meant the bigot, whoever he was, was scared silly of being found out.

The moment the vote was announced, I leaped up and said, "Look, I'm embarrassed to say this, but I voted the blackball. I want to withdraw it."

Sure enough, the guy didn't stand up to say, "Hey, no, it was *my* blackball."

Steve became a Deke.

Of course, in football, too, you often have to make split-second decisions like that. If you had more time, instead of obeying your split-second instincts you'd probably think and think, then come up with a cautious move that was dead wrong.

Sometimes at the table somebody would make some good-natured crack, in Steve's presence, about the Jew-boy or kike. Of course, everybody knew no harm was meant, and Steve smiled. Those moments always stuck me like a knife, just like those good-natured moments at Brooklyn Prep where I was the dago or wop, and I didn't stop hurting all day.

For my first two years of college football, our coach, Rip Engle, called on me almost exclusively for defense, mostly at safety. By my junior year, 1948, I began getting a reputation as an aggressive tackler, partly through the colorful reporting of the *Brown Daily Herald.* Against Holy Cross, according to the *Herald,* "Paterno nearly cut Don Davis, Crusader back, in two, with a vicious tackle on the opening kickoff in the second half." Vicious? Me?

That year, Engle also got to depend on me for punt and kickoff returns. I led the team in total yards for runbacks. My best game was against Princeton, when I ran back four punts and four kickoffs for 146 yards. We won 23–20.

In my junior year, Engle began thinking of me as a quarterback. Even more important, he began thinking of me. Rip Engle was then forty years old, soft-spoken and gentle, his prematurely gray hair, always adorned during games with a fedora, making him a perfect father figure. Nothing ever disturbed that gentlemanly image, except his sudden sideline outbursts of fretting, shouting, yelling, grunting, moaning, and flailing his fists in the air.

While using me fairly often on offense, Rip never let me forget I was in competition for the quarterback assignment with Ed Finn, a senior, and Walt Pastuszak, like me, a junior.

In my senior year, 1949, eight wins and only one loss made us one of the powers in the East. John Scott and I had been elected cocaptains, and I played double duty—as quarterback for Engle's famous wing-T formation while also playing defensive halfback. Rip let me call the defensive signals. I intercepted six times for 114 yards. That added up to fourteen interceptions for my career at Brown, returning them for 290 yards. Last time I looked, that was still a Brown record.

In the spring of 1950, after my senior football season, Rip Engle accepted an offer by Penn State to become its head coach starting the following year. Wanting to leave things in good order, he needed to develop my replacement, a promising new quarterback prospect named Dave Carter. Rip asked if I would take a part-time spring job coaching Carter while counting the weeks till my graduation. I was twenty-three. After spring practice, Rip took off for Penn State.

I enjoyed that spring, a kind of last diversion from the future that was quite clearly laid out before me. For the fall, I had applied to the law school of Boston University. Earlier, I had cockily set my eye on Harvard Law School, but was realistic enough to know I'd better get some advice about that. Brown had a vice president for student affairs, a wonderful man named Bruce Bigelow, who always seemed to know everything and made himself accessible to students. We trusted his judgment even though he was quite old—probably forty-five. He told me, "Joe, you might make it into Harvard. But how are you going to finance it?"

I said, "I'll get a job." Actually, Rip Engle had told me he was confident he could get me hired as a part-time assistant coach at Harvard or at Boston University.

"You're not going to be able to do Harvard Law School and hold a job too. Twenty percent of your class will be dropped before the second year. Even without a job, you'd have to hustle. If you must work, why not try some other place that's a little less competitive?"

I said I wanted to stay around Boston.

Boston University, he said, had a good law school, less pressured, and less expensive.

I applied there and was accepted. So everything was set—

until I got a surprising phone call from Rip Engle in Pennsylvania. He told me that his contract allowed him to bring one assistant coach. None of his assistants was tempted to the boondocks of the Alleghenies. Rip astonished me by asking me to take the job.

Penn State—at that time known as The Pennsylvania State College—had been a school of good football teams. In the 1920s, when Harvard dominated as the premier college team in the country, Penn State, coached by Hugo Bezdek, played them to a tie, then played in the Rose Bowl in 1922. The 1947 team, under Coach Bob Higgins, set two NCAA records that still stand. In fact, the records are so remarkable, they may stand forever. Opponents were held to an almost unbelievable average of seventeen yards per game rushing and the fewest average rushing yards per play—0.64! A lot of credit for that goes to the team's all-American guard, Steve Suhey.

My recollection is that the idea of becoming a football coach was new to me, although I've been contradicted about that. Dennis Booher, a Penn State sports historian who did his doctoral dissertation about me, has found copies of a publicity questionnaire that he says I furnished for the 1949 *Brown University Football Press Guide,* when I was twenty-two. My answers, he says, "clearly indicate that Paterno was considering coaching as an occupation prior to Spring 1949."

As I could have predicted, my father asked, "Is going to Penn State what you want to do?" Much as he loved the law and wanted me to follow him into it, when I said I wanted to give coaching a try, he gave me his blessing. My mother took a different stance: "A *coach?* You didn't have to go to college to be a coach!"

6· The Possible Importance of College Football

EUGENE McCarthy, the former senator and presidential candidate, is on my mother's side. After he lost his race, he said that running for president is like being a football coach. You have to be smart enough to understand the game, yet dumb enough to think it's important.

Robert M. Hutchins, the "boy wonder" chancellor of the University of Chicago back in the thirties, was on her side too. He became famous for closing down varsity football at his school. He said he had a better idea for preserving the flow of sports revenue and at the same time ending the exploitation of players. Why not convert the football locker room to a stable, fill it with prize race horses, blanket the horses under university colors, and let 'em run? The cost, both financial and human, would be far lower, and the university would bring in more money.

We football people often get roasted like that, and most often by faculties of some elite universities. Some argue that a commitment to first-class football distracts the university from its true mission: the education of our best young minds. Maybe they're right. But I'd like to return the honor—and the heat—of the roast. The large, once relatively poor state universities, like Penn State, with an educational mission for the many, didn't dream up big-time college football. That was done by the high-endowment, highbrow schools—Yale, Princeton, Harvard, Columbia, and the University of Pennsylvania. The father of American intercollegiate sports, in a sense, was a man who still symbolizes the purest tradition of higher education, Charles Eliot, the president of Harvard. Back in 1869, Eliot grew concerned about the drain of large numbers of upper-class students to European universities, especially to England. It had become classy to go abroad, where the educational institutions seemed to be more demanding, and the payoff to students, both socially and professionally, seemed to be greater. Worst of all for those like Eliot, who had to worry about declining enrollments, the word kept coming back that Europe was more fun. Our leading colleges couldn't change their curricula or their faculties overnight. But Eliot got the notion that one way American colleges might compete successfully was in offering more and better sports.

In 1869, Princeton and Rutgers played the first intercollegiate football game. In the 1870s, college sports became the rage. By 1880—in little more than ten years—the administrators of colleges began to get a serious vision of how sports might help them (although they sharply underestimated the phenomenon). A football team that could win games, attract spectators, improve student morale, and stir the pride of successful alumni, were good business. The management of teams and schedules, handled at first by undergraduates, became a serious occupation, and administrators took over. Alumni moved in to wrestle over those decisions and, in a wink of an eye, the paid profession of college coaching and athletic management was born.

The first university leader to envision the national attention and "image" possibilities of football was President William Rainey Harper of the University of Chicago, a school almost created full-blown with a large gift of money by an oil baron, John D. Rockefeller, but sadly in need of prestige and publicity. President Harper wrote to a football coach at Springfield College in Massachusetts—Alonzo Stagg—dazzling him with the idea of organizing a team to spend its vacations traveling the country in a palatial railroad car and playing other colleges. That was in the late 1890s, and Alonzo Stagg went on to become one of the legendary football coaches. Some of the best players transferred from one university to another, sometimes from week to week, if a competing school offered to pay them more.

College football got its first serious black eye in 1905, when the Chicago *Tribune* revealed that in that year the roughhouse game of football had killed eighteen players and seriously injured 159. President Theodore Roosevelt called a White House meeting of leaders from Yale, Harvard, and Princeton to "save the game by helping to eliminate from it all brutality and foul play." That meeting led to the formation in 1906 of an intercollegiate athletic association. In 1910, that group named itself the National Collegiate Athletic Institution, later the NCAA. Its task at first was to govern football and no other sport. By 1947, the NCAA had put itself in charge of issues in college sports that had probably never crossed the minds of its founders: definitions of amateurism, academic requirements for athletic participation, faculty control of sports, recruiting, scholarships and financial aid, broadcast rights.

Penn State, one of the early football schools, was part of those first moves to regulate college football, supporting rules of gentlemanly conduct and good sportsmanship as well as academic standards.

Why does an American kid want to play football?

I have a son who once had a terrible accident and we thought we were going to lose him. When he came out of it, the doctor who miraculously saved him said, "But don't let him play football." When I told David he couldn't play football, he cried for a week.

Today, as a graduate student, David motorcycles and sky-dives. I tell him, "You're driving your mother crazy. Don't you love your mother? There have to be other ways to fulfill yourself." He says, "Sure I love Mom, but I love motorcycles. I've got to live my life."

So tell me why my kid wants to skydive and ride a motorcycle and I'll tell you why a kid wants to play football. That's the way young people everywhere have always been. Boys want to express themselves competitively and physically.

I remember one day back on my street in Brooklyn, the Garrison Avenue gang came over. They said, Let's go see how tough the Eighteenth Street kids are. We had a fight. They went home, about twenty blocks away, came back with more guys—this time with bats. We never used knives the way gangs do today. The two gangs would swear and knock each other around, just a good, old-fashioned fight for the sake of fighting. They were mostly Irish—shanty Irish, we used to call them— tougher and more working class than our mostly middle-class Jewish and Italian neighborhood.

Boys crave physical competition in some form. Football channels the craving into a game that has to be played within rules and in an arena with a lot of people watching. And now that it's become culturally okay for girls to compete, girls want the same thing.

As a kid, I loved watching movies with Errol Flynn or Douglas Fairbanks, Jr., dueling and jousting in the medieval courts, where clarions with colorful pennants trumpeted the call to the contests and hailed the champions and a lady awarded her handkerchief to the victor. Just as I loved watching that stuff, today I love watching the medieval pageant in the football stadium: the colors, the precision bands, the plumed hats, the cheerleaders, the university president's box where the "king" sits and nods his pleasure. In September we melt, but we joust. In December, we can hardly grip the icy ball, but we joust. In rain, in snow, we suffer, they suffer, we're determined to win, they're determined to win, and the contest pursues its fate. (I don't like indoor football. It takes away an important uncertainty.)

Whether a team or a gang, the group needs the expression of that fire in them—through flags and bands and ceremony and pageant—or they'll find some other way. There are many different ways. Hitler knew that and channeled it his way. Wordsworth sat on a couch and, as he said, saw daffodils. But some kids need to do it physically. Where in the Bible is there a time without a war, great contests to establish leaders and heroes? Today, thank God, we can't just march off to war to show our valor. It's become too dangerous. After the next war, maybe the memorial statues will be of computer geniuses and scientists. Maybe General Patton, the poet soldier, is obsolete. We can no longer ask the question posed in *Henry V*, "Can this cockpit hold the vasty fields of France?"

Football, played seriously, is a tough and aggressive game. Right off, the very idea of physical aggressiveness bothers some people. One of the old objections to football was that kids had serious injuries. Every year a few kids died. Today, fatalities are very rare and hardly ever the direct result of football. The equipment's better, the coaching's better, the rules protect the players, and we do a better job in getting kids in condition to play. We know more about diet. In the old days, for example, we'd never give a kid water. It's amazing that more kids didn't die of heat exhaustion. Throwing water on your face was okay, but drinking it, we thought, slowed a player down, or some thought it was a sissy thing to do, and, above all, he had to be tough. Today, we always have a doctor at practice and at the game. When the heat and humidity hit certain levels, the kids drink water at will. Also, we're watchful to pull a kid out of the game, give him rest. Still, there are knee injuries and shoulder injuries.

Our object in playing hard is not violence but what we call *attrition*—hitting the guy, hitting the guy, hitting the guy, until he gets tired of getting hit. You just hit him so many times and so hard that he quits. If you're in better shape than he is, and if you're more committed, he wears down. To me, a bunch of kids going after each other as hard as they can—and within the rules—is not violence.

Rip Engle hated hearing anybody say that football was a violent game. He hated commercials for pro football that dramatized violent playing styles. In his day, defensive schemes gave rise to their own vocabulary. A "blood end" was a defensive man who lined up a certain way. A secondary back playing to the open field was called a "monster back." Rip would say, "I don't want to hear that word 'monster.' It doesn't belong in football." We puzzled over what to call him until Rip said, "Let's call him a hero." To this day at Penn State, even in our technical discussions in coaches' meetings, that roving back is "the hero." When we started that, Michigan began calling theirs the "Wolverine," and a few other schools adopted other names. Figuring out a name for the blood end took longer. After tossing around names for about two hours, Rip threw up his hands and said, "The next name anybody mentions is going to be it." I wasn't paying attention because I was hungry. I said, "Let's call up Fritz for a pizza before he closes." From that moment on, the "blood end" became "Fritz."

Many women used to express disgust at men pounding each other in football and crowds going crazy over it. Some still do. But now that the women's revolution has also created a revolution in women's sports, that's largely changed. When I first became athletic director at Penn State, I was condescending about women's new interest in competitive sports. I said, "This is a fad. Throw them a crumb. They'll go away and not ask for too much." I wasn't against women, or didn't think I was. But I didn't believe women really understood what competition meant. Then I discovered that women athletes are real competitors. I watched Gillian Rattray, our women's field hockey and lacrosse coach, an English-born woman who coaches in a skirt. I watched her coach a lacrosse game one day, watched her drive those women as they banged into each other with sticks, and I mumbled to myself, "Gad, I don't know whether I'd want my daughters to be playing that." Our Penn State women's basketball team competes for the national championship, one of its player-stars, Suzie McConnell, made the U.S. Olympic team, and they're a pride of a sports-minded university. Women's sports have arrived. They give women another way of feeling good about themselves. They've made it no longer necessary for women to feel that they have to be the support of men's glory.

We should have known this all along, even when women usually expressed themselves only through their husbands' achievements. Macbeth's wife urged him on, saying, "Hey, Mac, don't you want to be king? Get with it." Recently I watched a *Masterpiece Theatre* about Robert Scott, the English antarctic explorer. I was fascinated by the part Scott's wife played. She egged him on to become a hero. He was reluctant to risk the expedition, but she kept telling him he had a place in history. She said something like, "I want to marry you because I want to be the wife of a great man and the mother of a great son. Only a great man can give me a great son." Today, women compete for themselves—and have proven themselves under the full stress of competition.

When one of our major opponents comes up with a new coach and some great new players, and their football gets better, people ask, "Gee whiz, Joe, what are you going to do now?"

I say, "We just have to get better."

I welcome our opponents' improvements. When in some seasons we're way ahead of the pack, we get careless. Doesn't everybody? The human tendency, when the competition is better, is to get better.

As Americans, for fifteen years or more we've been worrying in the wrong ways about the Japanese and the Germans and all those other people who are racing ahead. We should be happy, not only for them, but for ourselves. They're making us figure out methods to shape up and make ourselves a still better country. The only enemy of American growth is the potential within ourselves to get lazy, slow down, get discouraged, quit. The genuine obstacles to our growth are potential failures within ourselves—failures of discipline, commitment, ingenuity, innovation.

Americans have been more ambitious, more inventive, better managers than people of other countries. Today, we're the same sort of people we have always been—successful and generous, too. We've cheered at the prosperity and progress of others—and our instinctive response has been to compete, to improve ourselves, and to work to stay number one.

I look around the highly diverse state of Pennsylvania, in many ways a miniature of all America. Like Texas and parts of California and Louisiana, we once grew rich on oil. Now it's gone. We were a great producer of coal. Not much left. We once dominated the world's production of steel. No longer. Yet today, Pennsylvania remains prosperous for one reason: New kinds of small industries and companies are creating more new jobs as old businesses shut down. Even more than where we live, that has been dramatically true in Silicon Valley and much of the West, around the Route 128 beltway of Boston and a good deal of New England, in the Research Triangle of North Carolina and throughout the New South, and in Phoenix and Albuquerque and the other boom towns of the desert.

No matter which industries age and die in our state, we still have our railroads, airline hubs, and interstates. We still have the natural beauty of green mountain ranges, rivers, and dairy pastures that make it a glorious place to live and work. We still have one of the most invigorating, yet temperate, climates in the world. We still have the abundance of water that is always an essential of economic success. Most of all, what we have is a great, experienced, disciplined, ambitious force of working people—in blue, white, and lace collars—who helped to build great industries of the past and can adapt to creating new ones.

What we need is someone daring enough to stop looking back and instead to look ahead on a foggy road to some new future—someone gutsy enough to organize us in striding toward a new, if uncertain goal. No nation has ever produced as many inventive or entrepreneurial giants as America, and they always arise when we need them. Eli Whitney, Jay Gould, Andrew Carnegie, the Wright brothers, George Westinghouse, Henry Ford, Thomas Watson, and, yes, young Steve Jobs.

Those individuals were the greatest coaches of all: the inventors, organizers, managers, and risk-takers who responded to competition and created new levels of competition.

Why should I fear other teams getting better?

Football has become our national game. The English let it all out for soccer and get rowdy. To Spaniards, bullfighting expresses something national and natural. As an American, I think bullfighting is cruel. You know in advance who's going to win, and it's not the dumb animal. In our game of football, the outcome is unknown, and we love that. Every country, every culture has a sport that captures and releases its special spirit.

We have a Catholic theologian here in Pennsylvania named Mike Novak, a kind of hero of mine, who writes extensively on sports as well as on theology. He wrote in his book *The Joy of Sports:*

"I believe that sports are not merely entertainment, but are rooted in necessities and aspirations of the human spirit. They provide an ennobling quality, a joy, that can lift us out of our own lives and put us in touch with the highest standards of excellence. They can inspire us to stretch our bodies and our spirits. Sports must be treated with all the intelligence and care and love that the human spirit can bring to bear. Sports at their heart are a special kind of reality, a spiritual activity, a kind of naturalistic religion, a tribute to grace and beauty and excellence. Sports help the athlete and spectator alike to keep the streams of the spirit running clean and strong."

Art and music and literature and philosophy and religion add to the quality of our lives. They help us understand our humanity. Without music and literature, without philosophy and religion, we'd have trouble knowing where we came from. We'd have trouble expressing ourselves across generations. They help us understand our humanity. And so does sport.

7· A Foreign Country

CENTRAL Pennsylvania, until the spring of 1950, was a foreign place to me: a land of roads curving uphill to sudden valley views, of tilted cow pastures and Amish farmers trundling behind horse-drawn plows, a country with nothing *natural* to see, like city streets, for which you had to travel to faraway Philadelphia or Pittsburgh. The isolated mountain borough of State College with a campus attached—population, 28,000, including about 10,000 students—was a cemetery.

Rip Engle and his wife bought a house next door to the campus, and they offered me a room. State College had one pretty good restaurant, a cozy, wood-beamed, antiquey place called The Tavern, but it was for professors and visiting parents, too expensive for me. Most evenings I ambled over to the American Legion post that served meals, had a bar, a television set (hooked to a mountaintop contraption called a "community antenna," later renamed cable TV, a Central Pennsylvania survival invention), and sometimes a lively customer or two, but not one of them a Brooklyn Dodger fan. The nearest major league baseball was in Philadelphia or Pittsburgh, enemy territory, and each almost two hundred miles away.

Football at Penn State was in something of a turmoil. Two assistant coaches, Earle Edwards and Joe Bedenk, had competed to replace their former boss, Bob Higgins, who had left a year earlier. Bedenk, who had been around since 1932 and picked up a lot of influential friends, got the job. Bedenk squeaked through his first season in 1949, winning five and losing four, which didn't look too good after Higgins had closed out his career with two triumphant years (9–0–1 plus a tie in the Cotton Bowl in 1947 and 7–1–1 in 1948). Bedenk gave the board of trustees notice before his first year was over and reverted for a year to his old job as assistant coach. But before doing so, he hired Frank Patrick and Sever Toretti at more money than the salaries of older assistants Al Michaels, Jim O'Hora, and Earl Bruce. So when Rip arrived, bringing only me, he inherited a staff of people who felt itchy with one another.

I wasn't Rip's first choice to come as "his man." Gus Zitrides, his veteran assistant at Brown, was. But Gus replaced Rip as head coach in Providence. Rip turned to Bill Doolittle, another Brown assistant, but Bill decided to stay with Gus. Finally, he settled for me.

Four years of the Ivy League, I now realized, had succeeded in making a snob out of me. While I imagined my Brown teammates and fraternity brothers crashing new worlds in graduate school at Harvard, here I was banishing myself—*voluntarily*—to this farmers' college in the boondocks, passing up—who knows?—a clerkship in the United States Supreme Court, a law partnership on Wall Street. After a few weeks, I told Rip, "I'm getting out of here before I go nuts in this town. You better start looking around for another coach."

But that fall, everything changed. A former Penn State guard and all-American, Steve Suhey, who was just starting to work his way through graduate school by helping Coach Engle as a graduate assistant, had just moved into a two-bedroom apartment with his wife, Ginger, and their baby son. Ginger was the daughter of Penn State's famous former coach, Bob Higgins. They invited me to rent their second bedroom.

The big change was that I moved out of the father-and-son,

all-football atmosphere of living with my head coach. The Suheys had young friends, mostly graduate students, some of them not even caring about sports. Without being too high-tone or intellectual, they felt going to school was important, a feeling I'd almost forgotten. They liked to talk about ideas and books and music and politics and the excitements of the world around them. They seemed to enjoy friendship. Most of them came from poor or middle-class homes, from farms, from steel and coal-mining towns as well as the suburbs of Philadelphia and Pittsburgh, places that couldn't be more different from Brooklyn. They were strivers. They liked people for the way they shaped their thoughts and for the things they chose to do, not for who they "were." They put on none of the snooty airs of Brown, where some guys around me went through college as an ordained privilege instead of a terrific opportunity, guys who almost never talked about school as fun.

These new friends and their enthusiasms stimulated me to sign up for a graduate English course on the Australian novel with a popular professor named Bruce Sutherland and another with Joe Rubin on Walt Whitman.

One of the best of my new friends was named Paul Litwak from Shenandoah, Pennsylvania, a graduate student in political science who shined with a certainty of making something of himself. Paul worked with me when Coach Engle got all his football players assigned to live on the top two floors of McKee Hall, and he appointed me the resident counselor, since I was the only bachelor on the coaching staff. The job mainly meant tutoring players who had academic troubles, as well as policing their behavior and habits. What a mistake! I don't mean Engle picking me or Paul, but the creation of a football players' ghetto. The players beefed about being fenced off from other students and from campus life, but at the same time they got the idea they were superspecial and entitled to special treatment.

Today, I tremble when I think of some of the high-energy

kids I had to contain in that dorm: Jesse Arnelle, later an
all-time star in basketball as well as football who became a
prominent San Francisco lawyer and member of the Penn
State board of trustees; Rosey Grier, later the all-pro lineman
of the New York Giants and Los Angeles Rams, who was to
suffer the fate years later, standing by the side of his friend
Bobby Kennedy, of wrestling down Kennedy's assassin, Sirhan
Sirhan and seizing his gun moments after the mortal shots.
Another was Joe Yukica, one day to become head football
coach at Boston College and Dartmouth.

One clique of those pent-up athletes took to playing poker
late into the night. I closed down the games, not as much on
moral grounds as in the interest of sleep. One night at 3 A.M.
I heard faint echoes of laughter and checked all the bedrooms,
which proved dark and peaceful. I located the game in the
shower room. That helped me convince Rip his social experiment was a loser.

During many of those nights, I wondered if I wasn't wasting
a piece of my life teaching kids a kid's game. By putting off law
school, was I evading my destiny? Then I'd come across some
student who was serious about his schooling and his life, serious
about how he approached the game, and that made it feel okay.
All the coaches who had groomed me were people of books as
well as teachers of the serious playing of games. Rip Engle
taught mathematics in high school before he taught football at
Brown. Zev Graham, my high school coach, was trained as a
teacher, and he also taught excellence in football, basketball,
and baseball. They were gentlemen doing gentlemen's work.
When Rip paced the sidelines at a game, he wore a topcoat and
hat. I never heard him swear. (Maybe that's why, when I slip
into a swear word, I get upset with myself. I don't allow any
swearing in my home. Anybody can use four-letter words. Why
not show you're different by not using them?)

Early in life, I discovered that once I feel close to someone
I don't give up the relationship easily, probably the result of

growing up among a lot of cousins and uncles and aunts. I started feeling close to some of those first kids I coached. I was only twenty-three; they were nineteen to twenty-two. So I'd talk myself into staying another year with them, and, naturally, by the time they graduated into the outer world, some new good people had come along. Then, one day, I looked up and wondered if I still wanted to go to law school. Or maybe I wanted to go, but it seemed too late. I was becoming pretty good at what I was doing, getting some recognition, even offers of jobs as assistant coach in other colleges and from the pro teams of Boston, Oakland, and Philadelphia. And then one day I heard myself ask, "Hey, wouldn't it be fun to become a head coach?"

While I don't remember just when I first imagined spending life as a coach, I remember feeling with certainty from the earliest days that I'm not going to coach a bunch of guys who just want to knock their opponents over on their rear ends. I was going to make sure, by God, that our Penn State football players were kids who were going to make it as teachers, doctors, dentists, lawyers, business leaders. I didn't—and don't—want any football animals around here, guys who want to play football and do nothing else.

With the other assistant coaches uneasy and unhappy, Rip began depending on me as his sounding board. I'd argue with him, sometimes fiercely. But that was okay because he knew I was loyal to him, no matter what. I think he also welcomed my lack of hesitation in challenging the other coaches. That had to be done, but it just wasn't Rip's nature to do it, especially when he was trying to develop their loyalty. I had the advantage of knowing how Rip Engle thought, felt, and acted about most things. They didn't, so they felt insecure, or at least watchful, until they got a handle on how to work with their new boss.

Maybe I should have hung back and respected their uncertainty more, but I was inexperienced in human relationships. I probably irritated the hell out of them as I overplayed my advantage. At meetings, I was a damn loudmouth, unable to keep quiet when things weren't going right. Some of the staff were physical education graduates. I argued with no hesitation that phys ed didn't belong as a college major. That, of course, did a lot for my popularity, especially since athletic teams were administered by the phys ed college at that time. I'm not talking about scrapping with my peers. I mean my seniors, people who had a lot of experience. It wasn't as if I'd arrived here with medals for success I'd earned someplace else. But I'd come from an Ivy League school and they hadn't.

From Jim O'Hora, my senior by twelve years, I always sensed a kind of big-brotherly tolerance. Bedenk, the self-deposed head coach, naturally had a harder time suffering Engle's youthful, headstrong protégé. We often clashed. Yet that staff worked together and got the job done. I think it was because Rip let everybody have his say until we discovered we basically agreed with him and with each other. I learned a lot about handling people from Rip, especially that people usually don't mind not getting their way, but they always resent not getting their say.

Even to Rip I was argumentative, cocky, frustrated. I wanted him to get rid of people, make new things happen faster. While I moaned and complained, Rip held to his own way, which, in the long haul, proved to be the right way. I got away with being the whippersnapper I was because Rip always knew my goal was the good of the organization, not to make myself visible for getting a better job and certainly not for going after his.

Sure, I was also full of ambition, but I knew that the only way to get to the top in coaching, if that's what I wanted, was through the success of the team.

Coach Engle had to redesign the playing style of the Nittany Lions, introducing the wing-T formation that we'd used successfully at Brown. After a shaky start of our first season in

1950, including consecutive humiliations by Army (41–7), Syracuse (27–7), and Nebraska (19–0), we found our footing and finished the season with four consecutive victories, a final record of 5–3–1.

By this time, in almost every waking moment, and maybe in my sleep too, I thought football, got a thirst for learning all I could about football. For hours every night, I watched game films, analyzing every mistake on both sides. Soon I knew the strengths and weaknesses of every member of our squad.

Rip Engle pried two hundred bucks out of the university to help four young assistant coaches make our way down to Dallas for my first football clinic. That's correct, mathematicians: fifty bucks apiece, and grateful for it. We drove through two days and a night in a single car to share one room at a hotel, where our midnight arrival was unforgettable. One side of the lobby was filled with a crowd of guys straining to hear the words of a heavy gent in an armchair who fielded questions, scrapped with skeptics, and made no bones about the true gospel. The self-confident oracle turned out to be Woody Hayes, a rising coaching star who had just surprised everybody with an un-beaten season at little Miami of Ohio and who everybody knew had been interviewed to take over as head coach at Ohio State. I completely forgot my sleeplessness and stood there till 4 A.M., lapping up every precious word.

Next day I roamed from one hospitality suite to another, at times with young assistants from other schools, including Don Shula and Bill Arnsparger, sipping free drinks as we thirsted to lay eyes on another—any other—famous head coach.

At a later clinic, in St. Louis, I remember stepping into an elevator followed by three guys wearing the unmistakable faces of Bud Wilkinson of Oklahoma, Frank Leahy of Notre Dame, and Wally Butts of Georgia. I couldn't believe my awesome luck. How I hoped they wouldn't know my destination was the third floor. One of them pushed the button for the eighth. I nervously hit "9" and hung back, ready to record in my head every word they said to repeat to my roommates. Actually, they didn't say a memorable word, but it was still an experience.

At Christmas break, I went home to Brooklyn and discussed my career with my father (not much with my mother, who I knew had already mentally placed me on the judicial bench, or at least standing in front of it, and was not about to consider alternatives). My father heard me out, asked a few questions, then said, not to my surprise, that if I was really having fun coaching, maybe I should stick with it.

"There's no money in it," I told him. "I'm only making thirty-six hundred a year."

He thought a moment and said, "I've never made any real money, but I'm doing what I want to do. I think that's more important than money. If you like coaching, son, stay with it."

Jim O'Hora had rapidly become my closest friend. He fought battles for me, defended me, even risked friendships standing by me. I know that some people stopped inviting Jim and his wife, Elizabeth, whom we called Betts, because they felt they would have to invite me too, and they didn't want me around. Jim would sit and listen to me while I poured out my heart. He would point out where I was wrong. He encouraged me to be patient. He was always patient about teaching me to be more patient.

After a year or so of living with the Suheys, my housing changed again—and, again, so did my life. Jim, Betsy, and their young child had just moved into a small home, and they rented me a room. It had an old iron bed, an orange crate for a nightstand, and a chest of drawers. Before long, a second child was born to the O'Horas and they moved me to a room upstairs that was unfinished. In 1955, my third year in their house, I got up very early one rainy morning to travel with Rip Engle and Ernie McCoy, our athletic director, to go to New York. As I sleepily poked my razor into a sink full of water, the whole earth flashed and blasted around me, smashing me against the wall. The wall was a sheet of flame. After I got hold of my senses I realized that lightning had hit our roof, setting it ablaze. Counting all my limbs and gaping into what was left of the mirror, I figured out that, by some miracle, I was okay. But the fire totally finished that unfinished room of mine, burned all my clothing and just about everything I owned.

The worst of it was that the lightning had smashed and melted down my collection of records. Losing those operas seemed like losing the closest member of my family. (I soon learned it wasn't. During that same year, my father died. I missed him more.)

Jim and Betts O'Hora and their children—who soon numbered three—got me through that year. They had become my new family. We ate together, went to movies together, shared secrets and the events of the day, and, when they built a bigger home, I moved with them. In that new house they built a room for me.

Jim took life as it came, having a talent for anticipating potential conflicts and harmonizing them before they happened, just the opposite of me. In a hundred years, I'd never learn to be easygoing like Jim. But the funny thing was that, as our friendship grew, he became scrappy and combative like me, just for the fun of the competition. We'd have a good time arguing about anything, but mostly football strategy, night after night, sometimes into the morning. We replayed games, evaluated players, invented new techniques and strategies. Jim coached the defense side, while my specialty had always been offense. So we constantly learned from each other—and since I was twelve years younger, I probably learned a heck of a lot more than he did. We celebrated together when our team won and shared the downer when we lost. But the downers never got us too far down. One of us would draw out of the other the basic attitude we shared: We'll go at it again, and next time we'll do it better. A good many years later, when I became head coach, I also became Jim's boss. But I never lost a sense of Jim as one of my important teachers.

Betts was good for me too. When everyone else was fast

asleep, I'd sit up in my room with a yellow pad, scratching x's and o's, inventing new plays and counterplays. Then I'd shove all those yellow sheets into my dresser drawers till they overflowed and spilled around the floor. From time to time, Betts would leave me a polite note: "Get this cleaned up or leave." So to her I owe my discipline.

I also owe to her my success as a world-famous toastmaster and spellbinding orator. During those early days, I got my first invitation to address a football clinic, at a meeting of coaches in Pittsburgh. I penciled out an outline and bought a tape recorder, which was a sign of how seriously I took that speech. I taped and retaped what I had to say until I thought it sounded pretty acceptable, then sprang the tape on Betts, who sent me to see a speech prof and debating coach named Pat O'Brien.

"That's really good, Joe," O'Brien said in faint praise.

With more anxiety than I wanted to let on, I asked, "How's the Brooklyn accent doing?"

"It's fine."

"You mean you don't hear it? I'm rid of it?"

He looked as though I was slightly nuts. "Why do you want to lose your accent? That's your charm."

So now I know why today I get more invitations to speak than I could handle in a twenty-one-day week. My Flatbush charm.

As with Jim, my relationship with Betts deepened in mutual understanding, except in one way. On rare occasions, I'd invite a girl home for dinner, and I'd cook some spaghetti. As any Italian knows, there's only one true way to tell if the spaghetti's done. You fork a couple of strands and heave it against the wall. If it sticks, it's done. Well, I stretched that a little. I like my spaghetti enhanced by small, firm meatballs. To shape and tighten them just right, in those days I also threw the meatballs against the wall. Betts didn't have an appreciation of that. She'd see subtle marks on the wall, the sure sign of a gourmet household, and go out of her mind over what she called the "grease stains." That's what can happen when you're not born of the right stock.

During one year of my comfortable arrangement with the O'Horas, when I was thirty-four, Jim one day opened an evening's conversation a little differently than he ever had before. He cleared his throat a few times and worked his fingers and asked me if I wouldn't like to sit down. I was sure he was going to tell me the facts of life. Which, in a sense, he did.

"You know, Joe," he began, looking out the window, "my father and my mother came to this country from Ireland. Later, one after another, my cousins came and each one lived in my parents' home. My parents always said it was wonderful having them. But then, after each of those relatives found their place in the way of life of this country and they were financially able to take care of themselves, my father would sit each cousin down and say, 'Patrick,' or 'Terence,' or whoever it was, 'now it's time for you to go out in the world on your own and set up a proper home.' "

I don't remember what he or I said next. I just remember that I got the hint and quickly found a little apartment. In June 1961, after nine years of living with the O'Horas, I set up my own housekeeping.

When Jim gave me that little speech, I had already met Suzanne Pohland, so it's absolutely not true that if not for Jim O'Hora's eviction notice I'd still be single.

As a freshman, Sue had begun dating one of our freshman football players, who I'll call Roy, and that's what led me to her. One of my football duties was to run the team study hall in two rooms at the top of the library. That was long before any school I ever heard of had a special study hall for the football team. Every day, when study hall ended, there she was, waiting for him. Roy, good-looking, a good athlete and bright, came from a troubled home and was not doing very well in his studies. One day during their sophomore year I asked Sue if I could meet her somewhere else to talk about Roy, and she said okay. When we did, I told her that Roy had been cutting classes. I also pointed out that we strictly observed a rule at Penn State that we would not call a prof about how a particular kid was doing because it might be taken as implied pressure to give the kid a break. So I asked Sue if she would keep tabs on Roy for me. If he cut a class or got a poor grade, I wanted her to tell me so we could help him by applying an ounce of prevention.

Sue and I met from time to time and discovered our mutual interest in English literature. Pretty soon Roy transferred to another school. Not having him to talk about anymore, I realized I was highly attracted to Sue myself. One night, Leslie Fiedler, the mischievous literary critic, gave a lecture on campus. I saw her in the audience, and we left together, getting into absorbed discussion of some of the provocative things he'd said. One of us got a little book of Fiedler lectures, and we lent it back and forth, reading one essay after another, and discovered we both enjoyed the competition of disagreement. In one lively argument, I remember we kicked around Fiedler's theory that Huckleberry Finn was having a homosexual relationship with Jim. I don't remember who was on which side. She was very bubbly and would say whatever came into her head, which I liked. I could see her smarts, especially when I went out to her house and saw what kind of leader she was among her roommates. In all our discussions, I don't think football or athletics ever came up once.

During the summer of 1961—I was approaching my thirty-fifth birthday; she was twenty-two—Sue took a job at the New Jersey shore. I rented a little house with my sister and her family in a neighboring town to be near Sue. She was already "pinned" to somebody else, but that didn't stop us from sitting on the beach, reading aloud to each other from Albert Camus's *The Stranger,* and talking about literature. Near the end of the summer, I asked Sue about that guy she was "pinned" to, and she all but said that, well, maybe the pin wasn't too important. I got around to asking her to marry me and she said she'd have to think about it. Maybe I'd picked up a little technique during all those years of recruiting high school football players, because by the end of the summer she agreed. That fall, Sue loaded her course schedule to speed her graduation. She won a fellowship to do graduate work in English at Brown—total coincidence—then decided not to go.

In bits and pieces, I got from Sue's conversation that her parents weren't crazy about our plans. I'm not sure what bothered them most—that I was thirteen years older than Sue or that I was an assistant coach of a football team. Her father was an architect in Latrobe, Pennsylvania.

We arranged that Sue and I would meet her mother at the famous bar of the Astor Hotel in Times Square, New York. After we gathered nervously, Sue's mother ordered a whiskey sour. She drained it down so fast I wondered what kind of crowd I was getting into. Later I learned that she almost never drinks.

Her parents persuaded us to wait until Sue's graduation the following December. We decided to announce our engagement on Thanksgiving Day—right after the Pitt game—and to schedule the wedding for January or February.

Sue soon began to learn the unpredictables of football life. First, the team got invited to the Gator Bowl to play Georgia Tech on December 30. That usurped all my attention between Thanksgiving and New Year's, which left no time to catch a breath before the recruiting season, which started right after the bowl game. Finally, on May 12, 1962, we married in a church in Latrobe. At first we planned a two-month honeymoon in Europe until I realized I couldn't afford it—I told her I couldn't take that much time—so we backtracked to a few weeks in Bermuda, which soon shrank to two weeks in the Virgin Islands, which shortened to ten days in Florida, until I proposed a week at Sea Isle, Georgia. The bottom line was we had a wonderful five days at Virginia Beach.

On the way down, I stopped off to see a recruit at Somerset, Pennsylvania, while Sue waited in the car. We lost him to Miami.

8· The Rookie Coach

I wish I had known in those early days what I think I know today about coaching. I don't mean about techniques and play selection and strategies. I mean about coaching in its first and highest sense.

A coach, above all other duties, is a teacher. Coaches have the same obligation as all teachers, except that we may have more moral and life-shaping influence over our players than anyone else outside of their families. When a kid comes from a family that is not strong, our influence can become foremost.

The job of a teacher of academic subjects is to implant facts, ideas, and ways of thinking, and so expand kids' minds. In teaching excellence in football, we have to reach the soul of a player. Football is played, above all, with the heart and mind. It's played with the body only secondarily. A coach's first duty is to coach minds. If he doesn't succeed at that, his team will not reach its potential.

Therefore, at the heart of our curriculum, as important as skills and tactics, are the purposeful uses of emotion, commitment, discipline, loyalty, and pride. In facing the realities of competition, a person learns the meaning of excellence and professionalism. Not only to an athlete but to any person, that makes a decisive difference in how he feels about himself.

More than just himself. A good coach helps a person make a difference in the world—in whatever he or she does. A good athlete learns the will and determination to come back after a tough defeat. An athlete absorbs that from the air around him on the bench, in the locker room, from good coaches, from good teammates. Where else does a school or does life *systematically* train that into a kid? What could be more valuable?

Plenty of people may laugh me off, but I look at my football players as the very best male students at Penn State. To make the team and stay on it, these players make a combined commitment to academic success, to intense athletic competition, and to extraordinary self-discipline. As coaches, we have to push kids—more correctly, make them learn to push themselves—to reach their potential. Those kids look to us for examples in struggling to learn poise, class, and the handling of adversity.

Coaches don't automatically provide those examples. Indiana University basketball coach Bobby Knight (a personal friend who I value) and baseball manager Billy Martin (not a personal friend, but somebody I admire for his competitive drive) don't always advance the essential goodness of sport. Yelling at officials, losing control of themselves are not compatible with excellence. When we're teaching kids, we have to represent the best in sport and, by doing so, the best in living.

If confidence and poise are essential to great players, they're at least as important to coaches. We cannot convince a football team that they have greatness in them unless they smell self-confidence in us. When Bear Bryant, among the great coaches of all time, walked out on that football field, self-confidence hung in the air around him like a fine mist. That was worth at least one touchdown for Alabama. Confidence was the secret ingredient of Bryant's greatness and of Lombardi's legend.

If coaches have to teach kids, older coaches have to teach kid coaches. As a young assistant coach, I had a lot to learn.

I was impatient with kids who didn't learn new plays *now*. If somebody had trouble mastering a physical technique, that was a little different, because I had always had trouble mastering techniques. But I never had any problem learning the mental part quickly, so I had no patience with anybody else who had trouble.

I'd look at a kid and see that when he was going to throw he had a habit of holding the ball lower than when he was going to hand it off or run, or his footwork was bad, or this or that was bad. He might make five or six kinds of mistakes and I wanted him to fix them all in one day. But I began to learn before leaving Brown, mostly from Rip and Gus Zitrides, to get one thing right at a time. Spend a couple of days with a kid on his footwork and get it right. Then go to the next part and get that right. They taught me to analyze a problem, put down a specific plan for how to get from here to there, step by step, in the time we had available. Time is our biggest enemy in football. You don't have time to say this may take a month, so we'll work on it for a month. If you've got three days to teach a kid how to hold the ball before he throws so that nobody can strip it away from him, you speed up the teaching and you get that one thing done.

The best teacher is not only the person who has the most knowledge, but the one who has his knowledge best organized and who knows how to state what he knows in different ways. If a student doesn't get it when you teach it one way, you've got to teach it another way.

In developing skills and techniques, every day they've got to get a little quicker. Today, you do this drill, you get quicker. Tomorrow, you do another drill on the same technique, you get still quicker. They don't see themselves getting quicker, and they don't see themselves become good football players. They just do. It's dirty work, hard work, like becoming a good ballet dancer, a good cellist, a good surgeon, a good Marine commando, a good writer. It's mastering details, day in, day out.

The other side of being a good teacher is sensing when to get off their backs, when to say, "Let's knock off today and have some laughs, and tomorrow we'll start all over again—from a higher plateau."

In learning how to get the most out of football practice, kids have to learn that they're going to be just as tired if they practice poorly as if they practice well. So they'd better use that hour and forty-five minutes to make themselves better. The theme every day has to be, Let's get better, let's get quicker, let's play more intelligently.

Sometimes a terrific player who becomes a coach doesn't get it straight that he's there not because he knows how to *do* it, but because he's supposed to *teach* it. I once had a guy on the staff who had just finished a career as a great kicker and punter. Everybody said, What a great punting coach he's going to be. This great kicker was the lousiest punting coach I ever saw. Why? He kept punting and thought it was teaching. He'd punt the ball ten times, then let a kid do it once. He should have kicked once, and let the kid do it ten times. Maybe the rule is that a coach shouldn't enjoy playing as much as he enjoys teaching.

Another important rule for a coach, especially a college coach, is that he mustn't waste his players' time. Kids have classes, studies, other things to do. That's why on the practice field I run from drill to drill, yelling and hollering, "Get this done, do that, keep it moving." We mustn't waste moments. Time is our enemy.

Eventually, through trial and error, I found out there are different ways to handle different people. So I began to be a coach. I remember saying to Rip one day, "How can that kid have such a different outlook on football than that other kid from the same high school, same football program? How can he be so gung ho to practice while that other kid can't get himself out of first gear?" Rip said, "Joe, the longer you're in this business, the more you're going to realize that everybody's different." I heard him say that, and it entered my head, but I still had trouble buying it until I had my own family. Then I saw for myself: same home, same parents, and look how different my own kids are.

I still hadn't outgrown my impatience with injury, nor really learned that while some injuries can be covered over by biting the lip, others can't. Worst of all, too often I felt smarter than people who knew more than I did. I still bite my own lip recalling the time our Penn State team physician in those early days, Dr. Al Griess, wanted to pull a player out during the second half of a game. We needed him and I thought he was well enough to keep playing. We had some lively words. Ed Sulkowski, our trainer, a long-term fixture around the team, stepped in to support the doctor's authority. I called Ed a name I shouldn't have called him. Ed, a former pro boxer and boxing coach, took a swing at me. Fortunately for both of us, Ed's cleats slipped and the punch didn't make contact. Obviously, I had no business either taking the position I did with the doctor or provoking the trainer with a personal insult.

Another terrible mistake I made has stuck in my head even more painfully. In the early sixties we recruited a terrific high school athlete—let's call him Don—from upstate New York. He was about six-foot-four, could really run, and we thought he'd be a great tight end. Eager to test how tough he was, we talked Rip into scheduling what we call a dive drill. With the whole team standing around watching, a blocker on offense comes smashing at a defensive man, trying to drive him away from the football.

Dave Robinson was the defensive player, Don the blocker. Dave was a magnificent athlete. When he didn't want to get blocked, our best guys, who'd been playing with us for four years, couldn't stop him. He went on to become an all-pro star with the Green Bay Packers. So everybody stood around egging them on: "Okay, Don. Let's see what you can do, Don. You can handle Robinson, can't you, Don?" And, meanwhile, "Yeah, Robby, let's see how tough he is."

So there we were testing young, talented, unsure Don in that medieval joust we absolutely knew he couldn't handle. When Don made his first go at the block, Dave just picked up all 210 pounds of him and literally threw him down. "Come on, Don. Let's go, Don. You can do better than that." They went at it again. Again Robinson just picked him up and threw him back down. Then a third time. Every time Don was thrown down, a piece of that fine young athlete's inner strength and belief in himself just cracked. The poor freshman, whom we had worked so hard to recruit, never showed up at practice again.

Don taught me a lesson forever: Don't confront a kid with an important challenge until he has a chance to succeed at it. When he has some success, give him a little more. That mistake helped me grow as a coach—but I wish to God the lesson hadn't been at the expense of a kid who might have enjoyed becoming a good football player.

The incident also illustrates why I dislike much of Little League baseball and youth football. No matter how they piously pledge otherwise, too many coaches who run those teams apply terrific pressure to win before kids are ready. For every kid who feels his oats as a winner, there may be a dozen who are made to feel like losers, wearing lifelong marks. Every kid needs time to build strength, have physical success, gain confidence in himself. Then a coach has a chance to develop him.

Even after I became head coach, I hadn't fully learned the lesson that a kid may have a legitimate reason for not playing 110 percent. We had a big, athletically talented, but sometimes undermotivated player named Paul Gabel, who's now a prison warden in West Virginia. I drove Paul hard, always trying to get out of him what I felt he was holding back. He frustrated me and I frustrated him, and I think he wound up hating both me and the game. I knew the kid had asthma. Maybe he didn't belong on the team, but neither he nor the team were helped by my pressing him beyond his limit. Later, Paul lambasted me in the Washington papers. He's been very apologetic about that, but he shouldn't be, because he was right. I think Paul understood that perhaps he hadn't made the complete commitment I was asking him to make and that I pushed him to make him better than he was. But I didn't allow for his legitimate health problem. I expected him to be like me when I was a kid. If I got hurt, I played hurt. But asthma is not the same as a hurt arm or stabbing your lip with your own teeth.

In my third or fourth year as a head coach—something like twenty years after I started coaching—I also finally learned to appreciate picking up an idea from somebody else, anybody else. Until then I was too sure of myself to listen to others, and I hurt myself as a result.

As at Brown, Rip assigned me to coach quarterbacks. While working with the quarterback he liked best, Don Bailey, I put my faith and hope in a rangy 195-pound recruit from Woodbury, New Jersey, a kid named Milt Plum. I tried to convince Rip that Bailey's hands were too small for a quarterback—smaller than mine, and mine are ordinary. More than once I'd seen Bailey go back to pass under pressure, elude his pursuers just fine, give his throwing motion a perfect follow-through. But you'd look downfield to follow the ball, and it wasn't there. It had dropped out of his small hand. That was one of the shortcomings I kept nagging Rip about, trying to switch him to starting Plum.

Milt was a fine natural thrower, but, as with many lanky throwers, his arm worked better than his legs, and he was easy to throw off balance. That frustrated the development of self-confidence and poise that are essential for a quarterback. Still, I persuaded Rip to start Plum for the opening game of 1954, against Illinois. Maybe the challenge was too much and too early, especially since Illinois had a couple of all-American runners whose names were to make football history, J. C. Caroline and Nate Woodson. For mysterious reasons that so often surround quarterbacks, our offense simply didn't get revved up behind Plum's okay technical proficiency. So Engle yanked Plum, put Bailey back in, and we upset Illinois, 14–12.

That game helped reform my attitude about quarterbacks. What counts most in the end is not the quarterback's technique or even his statistics, but the quarterback's impact on the play of the whole team, which doesn't analyze. A quarterback has to be judged by the final score. As the season turned out, behind Bailey we won seven games, losing only two, our best percentage since Rip and I arrived at Penn State. Bailey played in the postseason East-West Shrine game in San Francisco and was named the game's outstanding player.

I kept working with Plum on his footwork, on picking out his receivers, on his self-confidence, looking ahead to 1955 when he had to become our starter, ready or not, because Bailey was to graduate. In our first six games that year we broke even, confirming the mediocrity of both our team and our quarterback. If the electricity a quarterback transmits (or doesn't) to a team defies analysis, another imponderable is what happens when that current suddenly transforms. In our seventh game of 1955, all the teaching, drilling, and praying I had pumped into Plum miraculously fused with his natural talent. He took charge. His passes clicked. His confidence lit the field and charged through the team. We surprised the experts in the press box by slipping past Syracuse, 21–20, when we were scheduled to be crushed by them. On that day, Milt Plum became a star quarterback—and my first visible coaching success. He led us through a winning season in 1956, went on to a long pro career with the Cleveland Browns and the Detroit Lions, then the Los Angeles Rams and New York Giants.

During Plum's last season, 1956, I stumbled over a replacement who was not the passer that Plum learned to be, but who was a better all-around quarterback. The top-rated quarterback in Pennsylvania high schools that year was a kid named Jerry Eisman of Bethel. Everybody wanted him. If they couldn't get him, they wanted Ross Fichtner of McKeesport. One day, watching a film of Eisman in combat, my eye was caught by his generally unnoticed opponent, the Glassport High School quarterback, Richie Lucas. Lucas seemed to do everything right. I said so to Rip Engle, who responded cautiously, "Okay, let's go after both Eisman and Lucas."

The recruiting grapevine is as sensitive and hot as Wall Street's. My simple inquiry of Glassport's coach got the rumors flying that Penn State was after Lucas, and that put the kid on the map. So we had to lock horns, particularly with Pitt, not only for Eisman and Fichtner, but Lucas as well. In each of their hometowns, I kept running into my Pitt counterpart, Vic Fusia, who later became head coach at the University of Massachusetts. Vic and I enjoyed pasta in the same circuit of restaurants, so we became good friends, which didn't interfere with our rivalry. I visited Glassport so often that I was able to give up on restaurants. Whenever Mrs. Lucas heard that "that nice man from Penn State" was in town, she set a place for me. In the hottest of the competitions, for Eisman, my partner, Earl Bruce, and I came out the winner—temporarily. He soon changed his mind and went to the University of Kentucky. Fichtner declared for the University of Miami, then switched to Purdue, where he eventually became a Big Ten All-Star. Lucas chose Penn State.

By 1959, Rip Engle, an artist at understatement, didn't hesitate to hail Richie Lucas as "the best all-around football player in the country." The Harrisburg *Patriot-News* one day called him "Riverboat Richie" because of his free-wheeling, rowdy motion while calling signals. Quick-minded Jim Tarman, our sports information director, photographed Richie in a striped shirt, gartered sleeves, and a derby, while displaying a royal flush. Jim renamed him the "Riverboat Gambler" to publicize our crossing the Mississippi for our opening game at the University of Missouri. The name stuck. Richie completed ten out of eleven passes for 154 yards and also led the team in rushing. We beat Missouri, 19–8, and won our next six games, including our first victory over Army in sixty years. Then we lost a heartbreaker to Syracuse, 20–18, because of our failure at two extra-point kicks and a two-point try. We went on to roll over Holy Cross, 46–0, but fell badly in our final game to Pitt, 22–7.

Those two defeats didn't stand in the way of my biggest thrill since coming to Penn State: working the sidelines of a nationally televised bowl game. It was the first Liberty Bowl match, in Philadelphia's Municipal Stadium. We were invited to face Alabama and their much-publicized first-year coach, Paul "Bear" Bryant. In a thirty-mile-an-hour frigid wind, we survived, 7–0, helped by a forty-yard run by Lucas.

Richie Lucas was slightly outvoted for the Heisman Trophy by Billy Cannon of LSU, but he won a landslide as all-American first-team quarterback in ten polls. He played two years with the Buffalo Bills, then returned to Penn State to become an administrator in our athletic department, and he is now assistant athletic director.

In the late 1950s, I began getting offers from professional teams to become an assistant coach. My old backfield coach at Brown, Weeb Ewbank, wanted me to join him at the Baltimore Colts. Nick Skorich, a former Pennsylvania high school coach who had advanced to running the Philadelphia Eagles, invited me to his staff. Another offer came from Al Davis, then the coach of the Oakland Raiders. Boston College talked to me about becoming its head coach in 1962. Those offers were good for my soul, but even then I knew they weren't what I was looking for.

One job I thought I did want—and went after—was head coach at Yale when Jordan Oliver resigned in 1962. John Pont, who had built a good team at Miami of Ohio, got it. But in 1964, when Pont left Yale to go to Indiana University, Yale came after me and offered me the job.

That was a tough one. Rip Engle had often said the Yale job was one of the best to be had. I had been at Penn State for fourteen years and was no less ambitious than I'd been when I began, although a lot more level-headed, with a sense of what would work for me and what wouldn't. The thought of having Yale and its influential alumni as a constituency was enough to go to anyone's head. On the other hand, Yale, like other Ivy League schools, had given up its interest in developing outstanding, nationally-ranked football teams. I understood why, and even agreed with its goal of putting education first. But I also believed, as Rip did, that the two goals didn't have to oppose one another. By aggressively recruiting the right kids, excellence in football and emphasis on discipline could serve the cause of excellence in education and in life. Penn State's tradition of clean and aggressive football, deepened by Rip Engle, seemed the right place to bring off "the grand experiment." Still, Yale was a temptation. I went to Rip and Ernie McCoy, the athletic director, and decided to play this high card I'd been handed. I knew that Rip had it in mind to quit within a few years. I said I'd stay if I could have assurance that when Rip retired I would succeed him as head coach. Rip and Ernie said that to the degree they could assure it, I was the front runner. Rip underlined his endorsement by giving me the title Associate Head Coach.

But what about Eric Walker, our president? He'd make the decision. If it was to be "no," I wanted to grab this opportunity at Yale. Rip urged me to go directly to see Dr. Walker, got me on his appointment pad, and, in fact, went with me.

The president's cordial greeting was memorable: "What do you want to talk about?"

"I've been offered the head coaching job at Yale. Before I decide, I want to know what my chances are for Rip's job when he retires."

Dr. Walker looked me straight in the eye, both sternly and warmly. "If you're good enough, you'll get the job. That's the only thing that's going to count."

I understood him perfectly. There was no doubt in my mind that over the years I had become good enough. I turned down Yale.

9· Head Coach

MY first year as head coach, which should have been one of the happiest of my life, was the darkest. Of our first five games in 1966, we lost three, including a humiliation by Michigan State, 42–8, then a crusher by UCLA, 49–11. The third loss was the worst of all. Everyone expected us to beat Army. We failed even there, 11–0.

At UCLA, worse than the beating was the way their coach, Tommy Prothro, ground our nose into it. Near the end, when they were way ahead, he called for an onside kick. That would have made sense only if he were behind one touchdown or less with seconds to go. The kick, naturally, caught us completely by surprise, and they did recover it—and did score their unneeded additional touchdown. We felt like naked jerks 2,500 miles from home, and I the exposed head jerk.

I remember walking down the field with Mickey Bergstein, our radio broadcaster, to a postgame interview with him. I said, "Mickey, I'm going to get that son of a bitch. If it kills me, there's going to be another day."

The second we went on the air, Mickey asked, "Do you think Tommy Prothro was trying to run up the score?"

"Oh, no," said suddenly nice-guy, humble-pie Paterno. "I think Coach Prothro had something he wanted to try out with his team."

That instinctive answer wasn't some gentlemanly protection of Prothro. It was to hide my dark side. Also, I think I was frantic to cover a fear that after sixteen years of working and waiting to be head coach, I wasn't going to be able to deliver, that I might not be as good as I wanted to think I was.

The burden that I imagined was all mine to carry alone was that Penn State football, which had a glorious past, had slumped into mediocrity. In the previous year, Rip's last, he had broken even, five wins, five losses. Before that, 1964, he squeaked by with six wins, four losses. I was headed for a first year as tepid as Rip's last: 5–5. No worse than Rip's, but still I felt totally responsible. Success was something for me either to bring off or fail at, as though nobody else had anything to do with it.

As though that wasn't depressing enough, I saw and felt, firsthand for the first time, how scary some fans can be. Hate mail and vile, abusive phone calls invaded my home daily, startling and bewildering Sue more than me. The most artistically despicable of the letters came from, of all people, a medical doctor in Stroudsburg, Pennsylvania. I wish I'd kept them to quote.

What had gone wrong? What was I supposed to do to set it right?

I had worked the team hard in practice, pushing them to reach for their limits, even beyond, with absolute concentration on football. Reaching beyond, in fact, was at the heart of what I was after. It still is today. A framed quotation on my office wall displays my favorite lines from Robert Browning: "Ah, but a man's reach should exceed his grasp, or what's a heaven for?" Beautiful sentiment, right?

Well, beautiful sentiments don't always work. I must have driven those kids to reach too far beyond their grasp. The squad began muttering behind my back so loud I couldn't help but hear. They had played well under Rip Engle who had formed them and played well for me as Rip's assistant. Now they were unhappy with their overeager new coach.

Maybe those letters were what made me lose perspective.

But one morning I woke up with my head and eyes suddenly clear. My approach had been totally wrong. First, I had become too concerned with making sure I didn't look like a duplicate of Rip Engle. How could that false goal advance the team's pride in itself, its pleasure at its own growth? Maybe worse, I had become too concerned with my own record—expecting *them* to protect *me* from a losing season.

I was consumed with wanting to be successful. I don't mean as successful as Rip—or any other Penn State coach of the past, or, for that matter, anybody else in the country. I didn't see why I should leave room in the number one spot for sharing with Bear Bryant or Vince Lombardi or anybody else. I hated losing, hated the idea of settling for number two. It didn't help me a bit to understand, as I did, that I probably absorbed my shame of losing from my mother, who had sent us to a prep school my parents couldn't afford and who would never tell anybody that she got up at four in the morning to iron our shirts so we'd look the best in school. Nor did this drive that hounded me come from anything she overtly taught. Kids don't learn much from "teaching." It came from what she *did*—the example she set, the way she lived. That's what education is really about.

Sure, you can ask, what's wrong with drive? Demanding of yourself the best results is commendable—if you're that good. But I wasn't that good.

I was caught up with racing like hell down the wrong road. The road was called Success. It was called Winning. It was called Don't Lose, No Matter What. I didn't yet know that there was a different route with different scenery called Excellence. And if I did know of that other road, I wasn't yet ready to appreciate its difference.

Waking up that morning, I heard Rip's voice reciting one of his important principles: "Always remember: This is *their* team, not ours."

I had started out, headstrong and insecure, with an attitude that the players better do it my way, or else. I had become so demanding that everybody was unhappy: the players, the assistant coaches, all the staff, the fans, and, as a natural consequence—me. I had to look for new answers, and not in new field strategies, nor in new plays or assistant coaches. First I had to look among the kids. Talking to individual players, I didn't have to look long before finding I had forgotten to remember my father's constant question: *Did you have any fun?*

At practice, I loosened up a little, not going for the last turn of the screw, not forgetting to sprinkle on a little kidding and joking and, especially, deserved praise. Something relaxed and lightened. We did lose two more games that season, to Syracuse and Georgia Tech, but lifted ourselves to breaking even, at 5–5. More important, we became a smarter group of people, coached by a more sensitive newcomer.

That was the beginning, but only the beginning, of understanding a thought that had helped carry another coach from my old Brooklyn neighborhood to St. Cecilia's High in New Jersey to the Green Bay Packers. Vince Lombardi once said: "Coaches who can outline plays on a blackboard are a dime a dozen. The ones who *win* get inside their players and motivate them."

No matter how often fans may say, "Yes, I know," I have observed that most fans don't know, and really don't want to know, the importance in football of attitude: of clear focus on a goal, of psyching up to attain it, of sustained discipline, of systematically building self-confidence—of each player *taking personal responsibility for his own play*. Maybe most people can't afford to let themselves know, for the same rules apply to winning at life. If they really understood those rules, many people would have to change their own habits of attitude and discipline—and that's hard. It's much easier to watch television to detect tricky plays and clever field strategies and blame everything that goes wrong on the quarterback and coach.

*   *   *

But, make no mistake, field strategies count, too.

The 1967 season really began for me just hours after spring practice ended in May and the last player boarded his bus home. For sixteen years I'd waited for the outside chance of becoming head coach. Suddenly I was in the job—and surely on the way out if I didn't perform some kind of magic with this mediocre hand I'd been dealt.

I had to start the fall by winning football games and didn't have a squad of great athletes to win them with. Especially, I didn't have great defensive athletes. No matter how often they say about warfare and chess that a great offense is the best defense, that simply doesn't hold true for football. If anything, a great defense that stays on the attack is the best offense. A great defense is the only way to control a football game and to win a championship. A great offense, in my experience, has to obey one principle above all others: Don't lose the ball in a turnover. In considering the next offensive play, in most situations our first question is, What's the chance of fumbling? What's the chance they'll intercept? If the risk is high, I'm likely to decide to do something else. Hang onto the football. That rule is not very fancy, and it doesn't always excite the customers, but it's a winner.

To go a step further, if the first source of football success is defense, the second is kicking, and the third is offense. I don't expect every coach to agree with me on that order of importance, but let them play their game, and I'll play mine.

So in that summer of 1967 I had to find a way of playing great defense *without great defensive athletes.*

Crazy? Maybe. But that was the imperative—no other choice—that stared me in the face. If I wanted to survive as a coach, I knew I had to do something radical. I had to do no less than rethink, redesign how a football team ought to play defense.

In my crowded little home in the Park Forest section of State College, I locked myself in an upstairs hideaway. From six in the morning until eight or nine at night, seven days a week, I sat up there at an old cheap desk working feverishly, making diagrams with x's and o's on hundreds and hundreds of sheets of large ledger paper. My wife, two little daughters, and son hardly saw me for all the weeks of the summer, except for visits to the dinner table. If I went down at all, I'd gulp my meal in twenty minutes and bound back upstairs—no time for her, for them, for anybody. Thank God for Sue being so patient a wife and mother.

I was just frantically determined not to be a failure. If that took twenty hours a day, I'd work twenty hours a day. Nothing in my earlier life allowed me even to imagine being a failure.

After throwing hundreds of scrap sheets away, I wound up with so many ledger books of those big ruled pages, you'd think I was the Collector of Internal Revenue.

The two toughest running plays to defend against in college football are the quarterback sprint-out—when the quarterback, taking the snap, tries to run outside the defensive end, either to pass or to run the ball himself—and the option play. In the option, the opponent's quarterback may fake a handoff to one of his backs or may skip the fake. Then he or a blocker attacks our defensive end. Depending on what our defensive end does, their quarterback will either pitch the ball to a halfback or, if he sees that halfback covered by our defensive end, the quarterback will run the ball himself.

Because a good quarterback—a good passer under pressure as well as a gifted runner—is a quick, accurate observer, anticipator, and thinker, a defensive end also has to be a superior athlete: big, fast, also with quick, accurate eyes, and very smart. He mustn't get fooled by the option and must get past two two-hundred-pound backs trying to block him. As soon as he shakes off the tight end, he must widen his range immediately to get the quarterback coming around the corner. A defensive

end needs great balance. Like a good quarterback, he has to be
good at everything.

Our inexperienced defensemen simply didn't have that kind
of talent.

That was why I had to work out a system of defense that was
different from anything going on in football. Since my guys
could not fulfill that description, it had to be a system that they
could handle. Second, it had to keep the other team confused
and disarmed. That doesn't mean I was looking for a gimmick
or clever trick. A trick might work for three plays. I needed
something that might take three years for other coaches to
figure out—truly a new *system*. The hard part about that was
testing a new system that summer—on paper, with nothing but
a pencil and eraser—against every possible running play and
passing play, testing both the system and my defense players.

If the other side's offense was stronger and faster than ours,
it could break what we call our "contain." Once getting outside
our perimeter, past our defensive end, it would be free to make
a quick choice, either to run or throw.

The only way to contain our opponents with reasonable
certainty was to add one man to our line of scrimmage. I had
to position that extra man to play wide enough so that no
matter how fast their quarterback was, and even though my
defensive end was not very fast, my guy was positioned to
contain the quarterback absolutely. The heavy cost of doing so,
of course, was that I'd have a backfield of only three instead
of four. Yet their deployment had to give them full flexibility
to handle pass defense, an option-play breakthrough, or anything a good quarterback might get away with.

So: If I do that, I have to give up this. If we give up this,
how do we handle them if they decide to do that? I couldn't
say, for example, "When I move my end wide, their ball
handler won't get *out*side, but he can run *in*side all he likes."
When I position a man to cover outside, I have to ask, How
am I up the middle? If we're shaky, we've got to do what we

call "stunting": We line up one way to tempt the opponent toward a hole, but with a quick move at the snap of the ball, we're ready for him.

Okay, their quarterback is not going to get outside my defensive end. He's not going to run the option. I've got enough stunts and blitzes so they won't run inside. I'm getting comfortable with my defenders who aren't all-stars in speed, weight, natural talent. All I absolutely require of them is that they be tough competitors. Great.

But I've used eight guys to accomplish that, where other teams use seven. I've spent an extra man to go after the quarterback *before* he acts, and I have one less man in the backfield to defend *after* he acts if he manages to get the ball out there.

That's what brought me to what we called a "rotate coverage," just one of the ways in which I had to rethink the conventional strategies of the backfield.

In rotate coverage, the three guys in the backfield would spread out and watch the quarterback. If he tried coming to our left on a sprint-out or option, our outside guy on that side would immediately come in to handle him. The middle man of the three, the safety, would shift to the left to back him. Then the third guy, from the far side, would shift over and play safety.

The idea was standard in baseball: When a batter hits a ground ball through the infield or a line drive sharply to left, the center fielder instantly shifts to back the left fielder in deep left and the right fielder shifts to cover center for a possible bobble or rebound off the wall. Right field goes largely uncovered because nothing's happening there. Similarly, if the quarterback moves to throw or sprint around to his right side, our "right fielder" races in toward the line of scrimmage, either to stop a short pass or to stop a run. The "center fielder" runs like crazy to get behind the "right fielder," ready for a deep pass or if the runner gets through. The "left fielder" shifts to cover center. Of course, this being football, not baseball, we can't completely give up covering "left field," so one of the eight men up front has to drop back to play "right fielder"—up to a point. He can't really back up deeply, but that's okay, so long as we pressure the quarterback to throw the ball fast. Then no offensive receiver has time to get behind that guy of ours on the right.

With eight guys on the line, we could surely put that pressure on the quarterback, especially when one of those guys made the quarterback "pull up"—forced him to stop and look. If he tries to run outside, we throw him for a loss. A run through the middle, he gets crushed by a crowd. He's trapped. So he's got to stop short behind his own blockers to look for a place to get rid of the ball. He's forced to throw inside our defensive end, under terrific pressure. We make him play *our* game—from inside the trap created by our extra man. When the quarterback has to get rid of the ball fast, he usually can't throw it deep, so our limited coverage out there is fairly safe.

Obviously, we couldn't do that play after play. So I worked out what we came to call "half coverage." Let's say the ball is placed on the hash mark on the offensive team's left side. Most plays start on the hash mark, because most plays end at or near the sideline. That gives the offensive team seventeen yards of playing room to their left, thirty-four yards to their right. That wide part of the field is much more dangerous for us, because it allows much more room to operate. So, as soon as the ball is snapped—not earlier, when our defense "reads" the quarterback, but at the moment of the snap—our back covering the big, fat, open side of the field rushes toward the line, just as he would have done in the rotate coverage, on the assumption that the quarterback is going to come to him. The "center fielder" immediately sprints to back him up and play a zone—playing for the football, not for a particular man. The "right fielder" plays man-to-man to cover totally the one receiver usually assigned to get back there. What is not ideally covered is the zone up forward. So we're announcing to them, "You want to pass? Go ahead and try. But you'll have to make it a short pass. If it's good, you'll get eight yards, no more." The best part was that that defense required exactly the same formation as the rotate coverage. It confused opposing coaches trying to figure out what we were doing—and made it easier to train our kids.

We had still another coverage: The three backfielders just stay out there and each covers his own field against passes, ready for an interception. Of the eight men in our line— remember the offensive team is geared to facing a seven-man line—four of them, the two ends and two tackles, have absolutely no pass responsibilities. They just go for the quarterback and the ball. The other four either play for a run, or fall back into the short zones, depending on how they read the offensive formation and the quarterback's eyes.

All of those formations look exactly the same until the snap. Furthermore, the eight guys up there give us many more stunting opportunities. But since we are playing our line wide to handle the option play, we create weak spots inside and have to stunt very intelligently. Furthermore, the stunts had to harmonize with our coverage. Mapping that out took a lot of the summer.

The hardest thing to teach in that new plan was not the rotate coverage or the half coverage, but the idea that we could cover all the receivers man-to-man while playing only two safeties to handle all the deep passing. Today you see it as standard in pro football. It's called a two-deep zone defense. As far as we know, that concept started at Penn State, during the summer of 1967, from those ledger sheets.

This involved a new technique of how to play man to man. With four guys on the line rushing, we had five guys covering each of the five eligible receivers man-to-man, plus two more playing deep for long passes in a two-deep zone. We'd play a receiver just as tight as could be, run right behind him playing follow-the-leader, never letting him turn and get inside. Our defense man would never make any attempt to see the ball, just let the other guy stay a little ahead, following him close. A lot of people thought I was nuts, saying we were going to let him beat us to the first step, purposely trailing him, purposely letting him outrun us. Then when he turned, our man turned. That put us in front of him, underneath the ball. I didn't have to worry about the deep pass because we had that two-deep secondary, the "center fielders," out there. We called that the "short man coverage." To my knowledge, nobody had ever covered in that way. Today most coaches and teams do it. In the pros, it's what they call "bump and run."

After working out the principles of the plays, I had to figure lengths of hypotenuses between sides of triangles and whatnot to develop mathematical rules of where to place those men in the secondary. If the quarterback got the ball on the left hash, and if the guy you assume is the receiver is x yards from him and will be able to run y yards deep, I had to figure out just where my "left fielder" had to be, if he was of equal speed, to meet the intended receiver at twenty yards deep and prevent a completion. Then I figured out that the "center fielder" had to be as distant horizontally from the "left fielder" as the "left fielder" was downfield from the potential receiver, and so forth. All those rules had to be worked out without bodies. It was like drawing up any kind of battle plan and war-gaming the possibilities of response without being sure of what's actually going to happen. You look at something that makes you uncomfortable, you struggle with it and change it, over and over, until you think you have every contingency covered.

Then I had to figure out how I was going to teach it. I had to develop a terminology for all the possible actions; also ways to drill the three rotators to react quickly and take proper positions and to drill linebackers in suddenly leaving their accustomed positions to cover in the backfield. For each move I needed clear, learnable rules so my players could instantly respond.

Execution of plays has to be better than good. It has to be perfect. In a game of about 160 plays, only three or four are going to make the difference in the outcome. You never know from moment to moment when those three or four are going to happen. Every player has to bust his butt on every single play, so that when each of those three or four game-turning plays is suddenly happening, it happens to be turning your way. Winning or losing depends on that and on little else. Put another way, the team that wins is the team that makes the fewest bad plays. The best player is the man who makes the fewest individual mistakes. So we've got to keep spending time on fundamental movements and techniques. The minute you take for granted, say, your tackling and you spend less time on tackling drills, your tackling will fail you, and so will your blocking. You will lose a football game.

"Practice doesn't make perfect," as that great sayer of football things, Vince Lombardi, once said. *"Perfect* practice makes perfect."

A team can absorb, practice, and perfect only as much and as fast as its slowest learner. Coaches make a mistake when they say, Let somebody else worry about a kid's brains, I care only about his athletics. Football is a game for quick minds, quick readers, and quick reactors. The minute we play a kid who can't learn quickly, can't absorb the complexity of some plays as well as his teammates, the whole game plan has to be narrowed down. (In the championship game of 1986 against Miami, we could not have executed some of the things we did in our secondary coverage if we didn't have bright kids whose minds were quick enough for the instantaneous adjustments.)

A game plan should include only as many plays as you can practice well. More than half the time, a coach brings a game plan that is too big and fat, with too many offensive plays, too many defensive plays. We struggle to practice all of it and leave too much of it not practiced well enough. In a sixty-minute game, you can't afford to have a single play that is not practiced to perfection. That is far more important than razzle-dazzling the opponent with clever surprises.

Then I had to sell my system to the staff. They had known me for sixteen years as one of their own, an assistant coach. But now, after a single season of near disaster as head coach, springing this? Yet until I had it all mapped out on paper, there had been no way to prepare them for this safety man, who had played *here*, now playing *there*. Or for why I thought he could handle it, and this is the rule he'd follow, and here is the technique he would use.

They were skeptical, uneasy, said it looked okay in theory, but— Their reputations, their pride as winners, were on the line, too. They had no experience with a scheme like this. Nobody did. That included me, except that my head was filled with it. I insisted that with our players we couldn't afford just to squat and read our opponents' offense formations. We had to surprise, adjust on the move, and attack, attack, attack.

The coaches asked, "But can they do it?"

I said, "We gotta do it."

Every day required a pep talk. Then they began to see, I think, how much work, thought, and figuring had gone into this. When one of them asked a question, I had the answer. When another asked, "Supposing they do this," I pulled out the ledger sheets and had a response. It was all written down: the rules, the terminology, all thought through and laid out.

To sell the plan to my coaches and players, thank God I was young enough to go out there and demonstrate it myself. I taught it to the linebackers. I say this not to brag, but to indicate how hard it was to teach something that nobody had ever done or seen before. I coached every position on defense in those new schemes until every staff coach understood them and could teach them and until every player could play them like a master. Once they caught on, the coaches were simply great.

Here again, my fate took care of me. Not only were we playing with a new defensive concept, but, without my knowing it, our new young players would have the perfect physical abilities to make the new defense work. Their talents and the plan, in combination, led to shaping two of the greatest defensive teams in college football history. In the first year of the plan, 1967, we were good. The greatness was achieved in 1968 and 1969. Mike Reid and Steve Smear were perfect for what we wanted to do at defensive tackle, as were John Ebersole and Gary Hull at defensive end, Jim Kates and Denny Onkotz at inside linebacker; Jack Ham, Pete Johnson, and Mike Smith at outside linebacker; as well as George Landis, Paul Johnson, and Neal Smith in the secondary. I mention these people because, no matter how proud I may be of a coaching innovation, the players have to execute it if it's to win football games. On D-Day, no matter how the generals mapped out landing plans that were elaborate, detailed, and precise, once the troops were on the beach, pinned down by enemy fire, young leaders among those young fighting men had to find the courage, the will, and the trained assurance to stand up and shout, "Let's go! Let's get out of here!" Or the whole expedition would have had to swim back to the boats—if they could.

10· Okay, This Is the Chapter You've Been Looking for, the Chapter You Probably Bought the Book for, Dealing with the Most Talked-About, Most Gossiped-About, Even Most Smirked-About Mystery of My Life, and Some Nervy People Even Ask Me About It to My Face, Point-Blank, as Though They Have a Right to Know. Okay, for Readers of This Book Only, and for the First Time in Public, This Chapter Now Openly Confronts and Demystifies the Question Why Do I Roll Up My Pants When I Pace the Sidelines? —and Why Those White Socks? —and What's the Story on Those Whale Pants?

THE rolled-up-pants thing was Sue's doing.
Back around 1964, or maybe '65, when I was assistant coach, I came home from a game and Sue said:
"You did it again. Every week the same thing."
"Did what again?"

"Got your pants muddy."

"So let's get 'em cleaned."

"I just got them cleaned. Do you know what it costs to dry-clean pants? Do you know how much money you make?"

What I knew was I owned one good pair of pants, and I believed in wearing my best to games, and every Saturday morning they were clean.

I said, "What do you want me to do?"

She said, "Roll 'em up or something."

So I rolled them up.

Nobody paid any attention, including me—until the second and third year I was head coach and we started winning football games. Then everybody started noticing *everything,* and talked about everything and wrote about everything, and made everything matter.

One day I tried not rolling my pants up. People yelled at me and catcalled and accused me of jinxing the game. So what could I do?

Oh yes, the white socks. That came later.

In the old days I used to wear good dress shoes to games (just as Rip Engle did) because I believed in that too. The good dress shoes got ruined by the mud quicker than the pants. So I began wearing football shoes.

Now, anybody who's ever worn football shoes knows you can't wear them with thin dress socks. The leather is thick and heavily seamed and it chafes through thin socks. So I wear thick white athletic socks.

Do I have to draw pictures? If I also roll up my pants, what's there to see?

Right. Black shoes and white socks.

That's the whole mysterious story.

Except for the other mysterious story of the whale pants.

Which didn't happen till many years later, but let's settle the details right here and now.

The summer before we won our 1982 national championship, I took my family down to the New Jersey shore. Pacing the sidelines on television *and* being irresistibly handsome, even though partly disguised by shaded glasses, is a disastrous combination. That was the year I became a Household Face. One afternoon my daughter Mary Kay and I were walking down—or trying to walk down—the main drag of Stone Harbor when, just one more time than I could stand it, some total stranger threw his arm around me like some old buddy, as though he owned me. I usually don't mind people stopping me, in fact, I sometimes enjoy it, except this guy was too much on a day that had too many. So I signed that one more autograph the guy didn't need for the nephew he probably didn't have and told Mary Kay to go get the car and pick me up right there at the curb as soon as she could. Before another tourist could assault me, I ducked into the nearest seaside souvenir store to hide.

"Can I help you?" the eager storekeeper asked.

"Sure, sure. I'll take these." I found my hand clutching something, *any*thing, on the counter. What I grabbed turned out to be a pair of khaki pants dotted with big blue whales.

"Hey, you're Joe Paterno!" he yelled, and I almost leaped under the counter. "I went to Penn State myself!"

"No kidding. Wonderful." No place to hide. I shoved the pants and some cash at the guy.

"Hey look, we usually don't hem these things to fit, but for *you,* Joe—"

"No, my wife'll do it. Just wrap them up."

Thank God, I heard Mary Kay blowing the horn.

One warm Saturday morning the following season Sue handed me a pair of pants to wear to the game—khaki pants with blue whales.

"What's this?" I asked.

"Your other pair got lost at the cleaners."

I wore them.

The players kidded me. The officials laughed at me. The cheerleaders cheered me. Next day, one newspaper had a head-line, WHALE PANTS LEAD LIONS TO VICTORY.

Off and on, I wore them, mostly because Sue handed them to me, and soon the whale pants began getting applause from the crowd. One day a male cheerleader asked if he could borrow them to wear the following week. He did, and the crowd went crazy.

I don't specifically remember the guy returning my whale pants, although I don't want to imply any accusation. All I know is that sometime later the Penn State Art Museum asked if it could auction off my whale pants in a big fund-raising affair. "Sure," I said. And that's when I discovered they were gone.

I don't care a heck of a lot about clothes, but has anybody seen my whales?

11· A Grand Experiment

WITH the same enthusiasm the coaches taught the new defense, the young players practiced it. I mean the *young* players, who could hardly wait for the seniors to graduate so they could compete to replace them in the starting jobs. But those seniors? They weren't buying. Maybe they still felt senior to their new head coach and weren't buying *him*, let alone overtroubling themselves to learn his whole new harebrained way of playing football.

After that first dismal season of winning five and losing five, I said to myself, "Start counting your days in this job. Those seniors are not going to get better. And those sophomores have never played college football, so they're really freshmen."

We opened 1967 against Navy, not a strong team, and let them sink us by a hairline, 23–22, with a touchdown pass in the final minute. Our team played the shabbiest football game I had ever been part of. We gained a total of 378 yards, not bad, but gave the Navy a horrendous 489. The players just went through motions; no commitment, no intensity, just flat. In fact, when I had to send in some sophomores to replace injured seniors, the young ones played with more eagerness and intensity than their elders, which made me all the madder.

I knew I needed a drastic change—but what change? On the long, downcast bus ride home that night from Annapolis, the crazy thought entered my mind of dumping almost the whole crew and starting from scratch with fresh kids. But that seemed too crazy. Too risky. I might come out a terrible loser.

But I was *already* a loser. I suddenly just knew—I had to let go of my obsessive fear of losing and commit myself to risks. I can't remember all my thoughts that night, but I know what I work to instill in my teams and coaches today, and the thoughts come directly from that night: Practice as hard as you can. Work toward perfection. Then, when you go out there to play, when you see an opportunity, chance it. Go for it. Don't be afraid of it. Reach beyond yourself. Reach a little beyond reason. If I was afraid to take a big risk that might lose our next game, I'd never know if I had what it takes to be a coach.

After the long ride, as I slunk into my house, Sue was on the phone with her architect father in Latrobe. He had called to soothe her—or me—about the loss. At that moment, I learned something about Sue's spirit.

"Only a game!" she let loose. "Dad, if one of your houses fell down, how would you like it if I said, 'It's only a house'?"

After a long period of moping silently, I muttered to Sue, "I've got to find out whether I'm a coach or not a coach. I've got to get rid of those guys. Can't win with them."

That scared her. She thought I meant the staff, the assistant coaches—our friends for years.

No, the problem was the players, I growled. In fact, the real problem was *me*. I needed to develop my own way of coaching, and I had to do it with a fresh squad that I could make my own.

Next Saturday, in a night game, we were to face Miami, a really strong football team. September nights in Miami are hot as a steambath for football. Every coach in the country knew that visiting teams wilt in Miami. The Miami team, used to the hothouse, counts on it. Our sophomores had never played there. So instead of flying to Miami on Friday night, I bunked the team at an airport hotel at Pittsburgh, flew out early next morning, then kept them all day Saturday in air-conditioned rooms near the Miami airport. Finally, in air-conditioned buses, we moved to the Orange Bowl, Miami's home stadium. The kids never realized how hot it was until they got on the field. After the opening plays, I sent in a couple of eager, inexperienced sophomores to replace a pair of going-through-the-motions seniors. Next down, I sent in two more and pulled out two more. Nothing anybody would notice. Before the first quarter was over I had almost a whole new football team of kids out there who'd scarcely played in a college football game: Kates, Smear, Onkotz, Pete Johnson, Paul Johnson, Neal Smith, all of whom were soon to become stars of Penn State football history.

We won that night. Ted Kwalick, now in the Hall of Fame, and Bob Campbell played a remarkable offensive game. Our new defense, which our new kids played as if razor-honed, just plain flabbergasted and bewildered the Miami squad. The score was 17–8.

I don't think anybody outside my coaching staff realized then or later how a crew of raw, eager sophomores had just snuck in, two by two, and taken over. "Sophomore linebacker Jim Kates was all over the field against Miami," reported our hometown paper, the *Centre Daily Times.* "He led the Lion defenders with eight tackles and two assists, while Steve Smear, another sophomore, was in on nine tackles."

The following week ended what might be called an era. We lost to UCLA again, this time in a 17–15 squeaker, but a far cry from the 49–11 of the year before. Our next game, at Boston College, began the historic Penn State streak of thirty-one games without a loss, including three bowl games, that didn't end until Colorado upset us in our second game of 1970—after my Sophomore Wonders had graduated.

I can't think of a stronger argument than that 1967 Boston College game for the primacy of defense in winning at football. "Although Boston College quarterbacks Joe DiVito and Mike Fallon set a new school record with 394 yards in passing," wrote the *Centre Daily Times,* "the game was strictly no con-

Top: Joseph V. Paterno, still young enough to need lots of coaching. With father and mother, 1927.

Middle: The brothers Paterno, at rest (as rarely). George (*left*), and Joe.

Bottom: Father Thomas V. Bermingham, who, as a young priest at Brooklyn Prep, became such a vital influence on the schoolboy Paterno.

Joseph V. Paterno

K.B.S. 1, 2, 3, 4; Sodality 1, 2, 3, 4,
Secretary 4; Student Council 1, 2, 3, 4,
President 4, Vice-President 4; Class Officer, Secretary 1, 2, President 2, Trea-
surer 3, 4; Book Club 2, 3; Football 2,
3, 4; Basketball 2, 3, 4, Captain 4;
Junior Varsity 1; Baseball (Freshman)
1; Intramurals 1, 2, 3, 4, Captain 3, 4.

Left: Among Brooklyn Prep's best, class of February 1945, a star in
football, basketball, baseball—and book club. *Right:* Posted briefly
to Fort Dix, New Jersey, a smiling Paterno hears the sound of
an honorable discharge coming up—and a shot at Brown.

The brothers at Brown—handing off, Joe (*left*) to George. Joe was no
faker, even then.

There was a gentlemanly—and winning—tradition at Penn State, even pre-Paterno. Here, the young assistant coach with the head coach who brought him along from Brown, Rip Engle.

Left: A young coach silently surveys the field.
Right: A slightly older one offers a mild suggestion.

Betts and (Coach) Jim O'Hora, who took in the new assistant coach as a boarder for a few weeks—except that the man who came to dinner stayed on...and on...and threw meatballs at the walls.

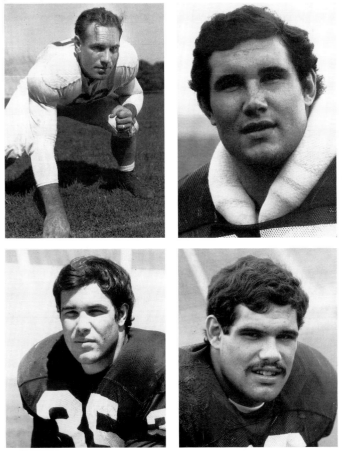

A Penn State football dynasty: the Suheys. (*Top left*) Steve (All-American, 1947; Pittsburgh Steeler, 1948–49); sons (*top right*) Matt, running back; (*bottom left*) Larry, fullback; (*bottom right*) Paul, linebacker. Important Missing Person: mother Ginger Suhey.

Penn State football *moves (left to right)*: Jim Kerr (14), Pat Botula (81), Dick Hoak (41), and Rich Lucas, quarterback.

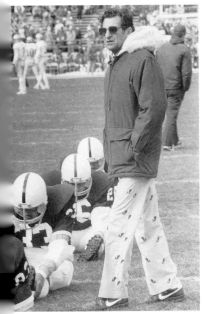

A COACH'S LIFE
The coach, too, must practice, practice, practice...plus spend endless hours on the telephone...which could cause a man to break out in pants with whales on them.

At the core of it is football, the playing of the game, doing your best, striving for excellence.

Top: Defensive back Harry Hamilton (17) returns an interception.

Middle: Quarterback John Shaffer (14) prepares to hand off.

Bottom: Curt Warner (25), now a Seattle Seahawk, shows his brilliant collegiate rushing form.

ACTION

Top: The great receiver Kenny Jackson (82) makes a leaping catch in traffic.

Middle: Number 10, Matt Bahr, kicking accurately, as usual.

Bottom: Number 49, Jim Coates, finds a respite in the end zone.

QUARTERBACKS
Quarterbacks have included *(top)* John Shaffer (14), *(bottom)* Todd Blackledge (14), behind center Mark Battaglia (59) and tackle Pete Speros (56).

(PENN STATE)

Mike Cooper.

RUNNING BACKS
Some running backs have run straight into football history.
Top Left: Curt Warner (25).
Top Right: Lydell Mitchell (23).
Bottom: D. J. Dozier.

John Cappelletti (22), Heisman Trophy winner, 1973.

(PENN STATE)

THE MANLY ART OF DEFENSE

Paterno believes that the best offense begins with a good defense. Here, a few of the defensive greats:

Top Left: Standout defensive tackles—the aptly named Steve Smear (76), and Mike Reid (68), later to become an outstanding pianist and Grammy award–winning composer.

Bottom: Heisman Trophy winner Herschel Walker of Georgia vs. the Penn State defense.

(PENN STATE)

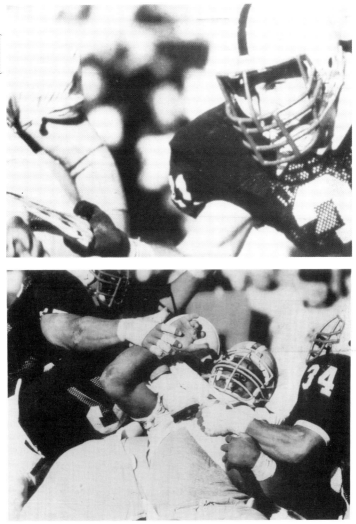

Top: Shane Conlan closes for a tackle.

Bottom: Pitt's Craig Heyward is stopped by Bob White (34) and friends.

A coach who spurns winning-is-everything coaches spawns others who win by the book.

Top: Joe with Dick Anderson, Rutgers.

Joe with George Welsh, Virginia.

test and was over 12 minutes after it had started . . . The Lions, cashing in on two fumbles, an interception, and some great defensive play by sophomores Steve Smear and Dennis Onkotz, stormed to a 43–8 halftime lead, then added another 7-pointer in the third period, to account for their biggest one-game point explosion since 1959 . . . The other Penn State TD's came on a one-yard plunge by another sophomore, Charlie Pittman . . . [who] played well, picking up 71 yards on 16 carries . . . For the second straight week Smear came up with a topnotch performance on defense, credited with nine unassisted tackles, three assists, and a fumble recovery."

The final score of our streak-starter was 50–28, which reminded me of my basketball days.

Those Sophomore Wonders topped their season with a convincing 42–6 victory over their archrival Pitt and an invitation—my first as a head coach—to the Gator Bowl. Florida State held us to a frustrating 17–17 tie, but our best years were ahead.

By the time of the Gator Bowl, even though other coaches hadn't yet figured out what we were doing, word had spread that Penn State was sure as hell doing something on its defense that was working.

Some of the magic, of course, was that we had increased the proportion of brains in the old recipe that had always called for mostly brawn. Suddenly, football was not as much a game of one team's biggest guys beating up on the other team's biggest guys. It became more a game of intelligent, well-trained players making fast decisions and staying coordinated. They had to read what was going on, quickly and accurately, and had to react with their minds as well as their bodies. They had to be in the game emotionally. During our next spring practice a high school coach attending one of our clinics watched our kids and told my brother, George, what impressed him most: that players resting on the sidelines didn't just watch the action or pace. They *talked* with one another, intensely, going over what their assignments and responsibilities were. They were in the game with their minds, not just their muscles. And they were in the game as a team, not as individuals. Everybody had a vital role in a system larger than themselves, and each player owed it to all the others to know his assignment, to execute it precisely, or he'd mess up everybody's cause.

That 1967 summer of work in my upstairs hideaway made a living for me for four good years, at least. Our opponents could study film until their screens wore out, but they had trouble finding clues to what our defense was going to do next. In about the fourth year, opponents began to catch on to what we were doing. But not before we had some of the greatest years in the history of Penn State football. Coaches from other colleges throughout the country visited Penn State to talk about our new system. Dartmouth and Georgia Tech paid Jim O'Hora and Frank Patrick to visit and show them elements of the defense.

I was glad that not everybody wanted to adopt my invention. Chuck Fairbanks at Oklahoma, for example, put it down as too unorthodox. Thank goodness not everybody agrees with me that you've got to be unorthodox in college football. You just can't keep doing the same thing all the time and keep winning. Besides, once word gets around that a coach is "unorthodox," he gets everybody worried. An opposing coach then warns his team, "Now watch out, they may do this, they may do that." When that coach and his players get caught up in worrying about all the unexpected things you might do, they're just not going to be properly prepared for what you *do* do. And anyhow, trying new things keeps my mind stimulated and protects me against boredom.

That Miami game was a turning point for me in other ways, too, and less happy ones. Late that night, as we waited to board our charter plane, Jim O'Hora and I strolled around the terminal replaying the joys of our victory when I saw something that stopped our conversation cold. I looked again and sure enough: Two of our best players were standing at a not-too-visible spot of the airport bar, each fingering a glass of beer. They saw that I saw them.

"You're in trouble," I told them. "You know that you're never to be seen standing at a bar."

Naturally, they protested that they were having only one, that they were coming down after the great game, that nobody around here knew them.

Never means *never*, I said. Nobody on the squad could possibly have the faintest doubt about my rule: We don't want a Penn State football player to drink in a public place. A beer or two may not hurt anybody, but as soon as a player has a bad day, the word will fly around town like lightning, "That guy blew it because he drinks." He throws a bad light on the entire team, putting every member under suspicion. Furthermore, impressionable students, some of them young, see our football players, hear about them. Football players are public figures, watched and talked about. Also they're role models. I reminded the two guys of the one loophole in my rule: You can sit down with your folks privately and have a glass of wine. You can even have a couple of beers on a Saturday night—in private, with personal friends. That won't make you victims of hearsay. But if I see you standing at a public bar, you're in trouble.

So now, these two kids had forced the decision on me.

One of them had previously got himself in a minor jam with the police. It made a mention in the paper.

"You're gone," I said. That meant for good. Off the team. To the other I said, "This is the first trouble I know about. You get one more chance, but you're suspended for the next two games."

On Monday evening, the captains, Tommy Sherman (now an assistant coach at Virginia) and Bill Lenkaitis (later with the San Diego Chargers and for eleven years with the Patriots and now a dentist in Massachusetts), came to see me. The whole squad was meeting at that moment, they said, and had sent the captains to tell me that they felt the penalties were too harsh. They wanted me to take the first guy back and lift the suspension on the second—and they wanted to return to the meeting with my changed decision.

There are moments in the life of a manager when his ability to maintain control teeters on a hair. He can only manage with the consent of the managed, unless he's a prison warden. On the other hand, he can only manage by unambiguous assertion of authority. Those are opposites, in a sense. If the manager, who sometimes has to choose in a split second, chooses the wrong one of those two, his effectiveness is finished.

"Go back to your meeting, and I'll be there myself in five minutes," I said.

The sentence was harsh, I said to myself, but the rule they had broken was perfectly clear, defensible, and necessary. The morale and support of the entire squad hung in the air. If I backed off, the message was clear as a bell: I'm afraid of you guys. Ignore this rule. Ignore any rule that itches as much as this one does. And if there's a rule that itches less, try me on that, too.

Five minutes later, that squad room was a tableau of sullen, hard faces.

I looked around, eye to eye, then talked. "A rule that protects us all was broken. The decision I made was the best one for all of us. I have no choice but to stand with it." Faces stayed frozen, waiting. I couldn't read them. "If anybody here can't live with it, go. Right now. If you stay, you do it my way, the right way, living by the rules. If you decide to stay and do it that way, we'll have a great football team. I'm going to walk out of here right now. A minute later I'm coming back in. Whoever's here, that's who we're going to play with."

As I walked bravely out of there, imitating John Wayne the best I could, my knees were shaking. In the promised minute,

I returned. Every frozen face that was there during my first visit was still there, although still frozen.

I was sorry to lose that kid I had dropped, although I didn't regret dropping him. He was an unusually good football player—and a good person. But he'd set himself up to become an example, and I had to make him one. He went on to become a successful veterinarian. The suspended squad member, also a fine player I hated to lose, even for a couple of games, spent five good years in the National Football League and is now vice president of a stock brokerage firm.

Despite that tough decision, which subtracted from the euphoria of the Miami game and added a touch of reality to it, I felt really good about our team and our prospects. Since those early days, we've had a lot of successes. But after enjoying them, we have to put them behind us. None of them assures us of what will happen in the next game or the next season.

Yet after Miami, after that 8–2 season and the Gator Bowl invitation, maybe I allowed myself a dream or two of how triumphant the next season might be. But the thought never crossed my mind that we were laying the groundwork for a program that would stay successful for the next twenty years. Maybe that winning season came too quickly and suddenly. Maybe I had the heady idea I had conquered the secrets of winning at football. Maybe I already felt that just winning for its own sake left a certain emptiness. Whatever the root of it, some unsatisfied itch in me required looking ahead to a next challenge, maybe something bigger that seemed more significant.

Something made me itch toward a different kind of goal—not football that puts winning first, but first-class football played by students who put first-class lives first. Maybe I wanted to re-create at this more-or-less ordinary state university, for these kids of more-or-less ordinary farm and working-class family backgrounds, something like the excitement that

made most days at Brown University wonderful for me—the
books, the bull sessions, the sense of wonder and anticipation,
all that and football, too. I keep saying "maybe" because I can't
clearly recall how the dream was formed. It was born slowly.
I don't remember just when or how it got started. I just know,
because there's a record of it, that I talked about it before that
season was over with a writer named Bill Conlin of the Philadelphia *Inquirer* in October 1967. He quoted me thinking out
loud:

"I'm thinking in terms of a Grand Experiment. It sounds a
little corny, I know, but it's that kind of thing for us because
we intend doing it with people who belong at Penn State.
Everybody assumes if you have a great football team there have
to be sacrifices in the area of [academic] standards. People tell
me it can't be done without sacrificing standards. They tell me
I'm daydreaming." The Grand Experiment, I said, was to see
if we could "play good football in the best league possible, with
people who belong in college, and who kept things in perspective. Look, I want these kids to enjoy football. But I also want
them to enjoy college. I want them to learn art and literature
and music and all the other things college has to offer. There's
room for it. College should be a great time. It's the only time
a person is really free. I don't want my players just tied to a
football program."

In the next several years, some wonderful things happened
for us on the football field that I would not have dared predict.
We rose to the top. There's an oddity about college football
not generally shared by any other sport: It brings more fame
and prestige to a guy who doesn't play—the coach—than it
does to anyone who imperils his bones on the field. Okay, I
accepted that curious gift. Gladly, in fact, because I wanted to
put it to good use. I dedicated the next five years not only to
winning football games, which we did in good measure, but
to codifying the Grand Experiment into some new rules of the

National Collegiate Athletic Association that I hoped would govern—or at least influence—college football everywhere.

With the help of many other coaches, we won some of those rules. More important and more difficult was getting all schools and all coaches to respect and live by them. But that gets us a little ahead of our story.

12· About Winning and Losing

PEOPLE today ask if I go along with Vince Lombardi's idea that winning isn't everything, that "it's the only thing."

I do believe in playing as though it's darn near the only thing. But then I never forget to remember that the other coach and the other team are going for the same victory, that they can't control all the winds and the tricks of fate that may decide the game and neither can I.

One day back in the days of Brooklyn Prep, Father Bermingham and I were talking about Aeneas and his supreme god among gods, Jupiter. More specifically, we were looking at whether divine will can control the free will of a true hero.

Father Bermingham said to me, "You know, the founder of the Jesuits, Saint Ignatius, said we should live by a maxim that seems like a paradox. He said, 'Always work as though everything depended on you. Yet always pray knowing that everything depends on God.'"

Over the years, that dynamite thought has exploded to something larger and larger in my life. It means to me now: Never be afraid to accept your own limitations or the limitations of others. Accept that we're all pretty small potatoes. Yet always know how great each of us can be. I never forget to remember that there's a higher power playing the biggest game of all—and that we small potatoes are only playing football. Yet I never forget to remember the first part of that maxim: Always work—or play—as though everything depends on you.

In a football game, I want my players to feel that we're demigods, able to do wondrous things. I don't worry because the other coach is ahead, or he's playing with fewer injuries, or he has some other advantage. Correction: I *do* worry about all those things, but those worries spur and stimulate me. I feel most alive surrounded by other people's doubts, when all around me it seems my forces are on the verge of collapse.

Certain scenes from Virgil's *Aeneid* still live in my mind: scenes of a whole army getting it in the neck from every side, bloody and broken, all but routed. Then enters some bold hero, maybe Aeneas, maybe somebody else, posting himself at the head of his army, raising his sword in a call to action and, lo and behold, everybody rallies and transforms. The army is born again. The great leader and his men take on the enemy one-on-one, turn the day around, and win it. That kind of image excites me.

When we played Pitt in 1981, they were ranked number one in the country, just going around slaughtering everybody. We were listed about fourth or fifth. Some of our alumni in Pittsburgh had me to lunch the day before the game, all anxious and worried. I felt good. I promised them, "You're going to see one great football team tomorrow." They couldn't understand my confidence—and I couldn't explain it.

Next day, their quarterback, Danny Marino, dazzled us. After the first quarter, Pitt led, 14–0. Next day, so I was told, Ross Lehman, head of our alumni association, wisecracked, "Joe said there was going to be *one* great team out there today. He didn't say which one."

That was one of those days I just enjoyed being behind. I pulled all my guys together on the sideline and said, "Hey, we're gonna win this game. You just believe we're gonna win it." At third quarter, I said, "Hey, you guys, they can't play that well. We just play our game and we're gonna win it."

They never scored after the first quarter. We won, 48–14.

I talk to players the way I did that day only when I really

believe it. I tell young coaches, "Whatever you do, if you don't have confidence, forget it." And I mean real confidence. I'm not talking about putting up a courageous front. If you don't really believe it, stay out of your locker room because the kids will smell it. Unless I believe we're going to win a game, that there's no way we can lose it, I don't want to walk into a locker room. I believe that prophesies fulfill themselves, but only when they're rooted in genuine belief. If your mind and will are really focused on an outcome, you can almost compel it to happen. Sure, that sounds spooky to some people. But I know it's true. I know the power of concentrating your brain, your whole body, your whole nervous system, your adrenalin, all your will, on a single goal. It's an almost unbeatable concentration of force.

Notice I hedged. I said *almost.* I can think of two things that may get in your way. First, if the coach pacing on the other side is every bit as focused and determined as you are, and if he has resources comparable to yours—a strong team with strong determination—the outcome for you may not be the winning score. But you *win.* You'll bring out the very best in yourself and your team. And there's nothing in a game that feels greater than that.

The second thing that may frustrate you is simply that the fates may play tricks on you: a sudden gust of wind, a lousy call by an official, a pothole on the field and your ball carrier stumbles. It just wasn't your destiny to win that day, and nothing's going to change that. But you can still win—by knowing, really knowing, that you stretched yourself to your best.

So, yes, against the tricks of fate I hedge. But then I hasten to repeat: Focus on your intention, and you'll make it happen almost every time.

There are days when I don't feel that focused will, and on those days we usually don't play very well and may lose a game we didn't have to lose. I feel that certainty of winning only when I know that we've done all the preparation—when we've practiced intelligently and thoroughly.

In 1982, the year following that Pitt game, we were on the verge of beating Nebraska when they scored with only one minute and eighteen seconds to go, taking the lead. During our final possession, Penn State's Mike McCloskey pulled down a sixteen-yard pass from Todd Blackledge at the edge of the two-yard line, completing our last-hope first down. In the final seconds, a second-string tight end, Kirk Bowman, snatched another from Todd, and we won.

A lot of Nebraska players and fans screamed about that last first down, but the officials didn't pick up what those screamers thought they saw. Sure enough, films later confirmed that Mike's foot came down an inch or so out of bounds. But the game was long over. A quirky "wind" had gusted in our favor, and the other side suffered a shipwreck.

Those gusts of fate blow both ways. In the 1978 Sugar Bowl, with a national championship at stake, just before the halftime break, an Alabama receiver hauled down a pass in the end zone. We never recovered from that touchdown and lost, 14–10. Again, it took the films to show later what really happened. The kid didn't properly catch the football. It hit the ground and bounced into his arms. The official, who saw it from an awkward angle, declared it a catch—and a score. We were struggling for our first-ever national championship. We were a great team and knew it. Alabama was a great team and knew it. Well, I didn't go home crying, "The officials lost our game." It was a great struggle, and an official made an honest but wrong call. It was one of the breaks of life, not to be confused with failure. We had lost our victory—but not our excellence or worth. The call didn't make the struggle of either team any more or less valiant. I didn't cry about my loss—and Tom Osborne, later in '82, didn't cry about his. That's one reason I have a high respect for Osborne.

*   *   *

Some people talk of "hatred" to describe what one team feels for another just before a game begins or during the intensity of playing it. I don't like hearing that word. Sure, in every earnest game there is an aspect of *you against me* and *I want what you want and you want what I want.* In order to make the blood run before the kickoff, you've got to say, with as much acid on your tongue and in your heart as you can find, "You guys, you're *Pitt,*" or "You're *Notre Dame,* with the stingiest and shabbiest locker room for your visitors in all of big-time football." As coach I have to say, "That's Lou Holtz over there, and he wants to be better than I am." So when I look across at the opposite bench just before kickoff, I'm sure a certain kind of unfriendly running of the blood is part of it. It's the same as when I'm driving happily somewhere, and a car suddenly cuts me off. I'll hiss, "You stupid jerk," then blow my horn and charge past. Then I find the other driver is a sweet old lady, and there goes that halo of Nice-Guy Joe Paterno.

In a game, you want to let those feelings stir a fire, but you don't want to become a victim of it. You don't want it to diminish your humanity or let you forget what you want to get out of this game. You're in this because you enjoy the competition. You want to play against the best, so remember to be grateful that they're very good.

To me the word *competition* is related to the word *compassion.* The more you pit yourself against the other guy and he pits himself against you, the better you understand each other because you're both struggling for the same thing in the same way.

I try to teach my kids this: As long as we compete the very best we can, we then have to accept that some we win, some we lose. The trouble begins when you think you've got to win all your games, or you've got to win eight of them or some other set number to make a season successful, or that you must be number one.

But something worthwhile is lost when you have a chance

to be number one and you don't try, or when you back away from risking the race or from asking kids to see how far they can stretch themselves. If you do go for it, yes, you may miss. We can't all be number one or be number one all the time. God knows, at Penn State we're not number one very often. But we really have come to believe that we have a chance every year to be number one. We go for it with the best and the most that we have, and therefore *we're always winners.*

Success to me is not winning *a* game. Success doesn't require, say, an 8–3 season or better. When Aeneas left his city of Troy which had been defeated and destroyed, his army waged war and endured hell, year after year, suffering storms and shipwrecks and pestilence, terrible elements they couldn't control while fighting battles they tried to control. What has made that drama last for two thousand years was not the temporary wins and losses, but the courage, the determination to endure, rising above the tricks and treacheries of fate to survive and create a new city. The epic is not about the victory, but about the glorious struggle. It is not about the success, but about the human striving that made it possible.

Many people, particularly in sports, think of success and excellence as though they are the same. They are not.

Success is perishable and often outside our control. In contrast, excellence is something that's lasting, dependable, and largely *within a person's control.*

If I've said to my squad once, I've said it a thousand times in the years I've coached: "I hope the other side plays well. I hope they play to their limit, because if they don't, there's no fun in beating them." We want opponents who make us play better than we think we can play.

In sports, in business, in politics, we all know of people who are very successful and who try to keep other people down. In football, they'll work angles or even cheat to get a recruiting advantage, or recruit players they don't need just to keep them off opponents' teams, or try to "play the officials" instead of playing the game. In contrast, I always think of Sandy Koufax. When the Dodgers played where they belonged—in Brooklyn, in Ebbets Field—Koufax was a pitching star among stars. As Tom Boswell of *The Washington Post* has pointed out, Koufax was known for going out of his way to spend time with new pitchers, always trying to get them up to their best level—if possible, to *his* level. He never feared or resented anybody else's success. People who truly excel don't fear or resent excellence in others. People who shoot only for success, however, always feel threatened by other people's success.

Success is measured by what others think: by whether they ask for autographs, buy tickets, stand up to applaud and cheer, reach for magazines because some celebrity's name is on the cover. Excellence is best measured by the achiever.

Every now and then Bobby Knight calls a meeting of his basketball team to hear a talk about excellence by one of his Indiana University colleagues. The speaker, talking about the burning ambitions of his young days, recently told the team: "It wasn't important to me, nor did it ever become important to me, to be recognized as number one or number two. Rather, I always tried to do the maximum with what nature gave me. The important thing is never who watches, or whether the audience cheers or not. If I know that I have done well, whether they like me or not is not important."

The speech, as reported in the *NCAA News,* was not by a seven-foot rebound snagger, but a bald, slightly stooped man who makes crowds cheer by—brace yourself—playing classical music on a cello. Janos Starker, after many years as first cellist of the Chicago Symphony, now travels the world doing solo concert tours and teaches music at Indiana. As a young kid, Starker told Knight's athletes, he was forced by his parents to take cello lessons and practice, practice, practice. Some days he wanted to run away. "But then one day," he said, "I realized I loved music. I realized I couldn't go through a day without thinking, doing, or making music. Anybody who can go through a day without wanting to be with music or hear music or make music isn't supposed to be a musician."

I've challenged my squad often with a similar powerful thought, long before I ever heard of Janos Starker: If you want to be a national championship football team, every single day of your life you've got to do something that challenges your body and that teaches you more about the game. Every single day. If you're not ready to commit yourself to excellence, there are too many really fine football squads in this country that will prevent you from becoming number one.

Something in me demands control of detail from top to bottom. A football coach is at the pivot of a big "business." That business is not just about winning games. While winning is a crucial part of it, winning won't matter much if the business isn't also successful at selling tickets, at keeping fans excited so season tickets remain in great demand, at getting on television and winning ratings so networks can sell spots at fat fees. Some fans would rather not understand that, but I love them anyway for loving our team. I have to understand it.

If I'm coach, the service a fan gets when he orders tickets is a reflection of my football team. If the ticket office is dirty or the clerks and secretaries are rude, that's a grubby reflection. The sportscaster and technical capacity of the TV coverage, the skill of the director at switching shots and ordering instant replays, those are all reflections on my team. The items advertised, even though the commercials are not sold by our organization, are a reflection. Our product is football, yes. A winning team when possible, an exciting team, yes. But more than that. As people buy a luxury product, whether it's football at Penn State or in Green Bay, a lovely object of Steuben glass, or one of Lee Iacocca's dashing cars, they're also buying a mystique. What every employee does contributes to it, and any employee can mess it up just by the way he or she answers the phone.

Sloppiness is a disease. Nobody ever built a great organization just worrying about the big things. It's the little things that give you the edge. If the equipment man in the locker room doesn't check his equipment properly, the player senses it and the sloppiness gets into his bloodstream and the disease spreads. And the most difficult thing is to find people on every level who understand that and who are completely committed to detail and to standards of excellence.

I know at least two guys in pro football who rose to where they are because they understand it. One is Al Davis, owner of the Oakland Raiders. He came out of Brooklyn and went to Syracuse. He became an assistant coach and an all-time great recruiter at The Citadel, a brilliant competitor in every way, who finally got lured into professional football and became head coach of the Raiders. While I was still an assistant at Penn State, he wanted to hire me away, apparently because he'd heard about my intensity and perfectionism, which was driving a lot of other people nuts. He wouldn't take no for an answer, upping the ante until he offered to triple my salary, promised me a courtesy car, a beautiful house in a San Francisco suburb, and whatnot. I finally had to say flat out, "Al, I don't want to work for you. We're two of a kind. You're an impossible perfectionist who's got to have his way, and you know I've got to have my way. We'd be fighting all the time."

The other is George Allen, coach of the Washington Redskins, a man so intense that to some people I must seem sleepy. During spring practice in 1976, he called and asked, "Joe, can I fly up there and spend a day watching you?" That was flattering but worrisome because he always made a nervous wreck out of me. As always, George showed up with a stenographer's note pad in his hand. "Why did you do this after that? Why'd you do that for only ten minutes? Why do you keep the strength equipment at that end? How come you have that painted green?" And at times I'd have to answer, "There may have been a reason, but I can't remember it." And he kept taking notes, notes, notes.

Soon after that visit, I was out in Oakland and had lunch with Al Davis. "You know, George Allen drove me bananas," I told him. "He kept moaning about assistant coaches who wouldn't do this or that, and I couldn't figure out why he was badmouthing them to me."

"You know what his problem is, Joe. He's looking for guys just like I'm looking for guys and you're looking for guys who have his kind of intensity. It's frustrating when you can't find people who understand what commitment is. Even if you're willing to settle for a little less commitment."

Al was reminding me of a maxim: A good manager's first need is controlling who his people are.

I'm not sure just when, how, or why, but I started becoming aware that we weren't just winning games. The kids winning them were starting to feel they were better as people than they ever thought they would or could be. Not just as football players. As whole people.

Such feelings hadn't hit me in the undefeated year of 1968. That year for me was about surviving—surviving by winning. By 1971 and 1972, I began to see more clearly, more specifically, how an emerging Penn State style of football was enriching these guys far beyond just winning and losing games. It had to do with pride; it had to do with caring about their teammates as people, as a community. It had to do with love.

When the squad gets together, sure, we talk mostly about technique and plays. Sometimes I praise their week of practice. Sometimes I scream my head off about the costs of being sloppy, of not thinking, of caving in. But we also talk about what it takes to make a difference, about not being afraid to risk making a difference—on the field or anywhere else. We remind ourselves of the kind of team we are: not a team of *I*'s and *me*'s, but a team of *we* and *us*. "We are Penn State," we chant, to remind ourselves of our special symbols: those black shoes, those plain uniforms with no glitter and no names. A Penn Stater doesn't have to let the whole world know, by putting six Nittany Lions on his helmet, that he made six big plays. When he scores a touchdown, he doesn't dance and go berserk in the end zone. When a Penn Stater goes on that field he *expects* to make a touchdown.

I say to them what Joe DiMaggio, noticing our uniforms, told me. His manager and coach, Joe McCarthy, ran the Bronx Bombers, the greatest Yankee team there ever was. They, too, stuck to black shoes when everyone began discovering whites; they stayed with their plain, traditional pinstripes when other teams switched to designer colors. Joe McCarthy told his players: "You are champions. You are New York Yankees. Never let it out of your mind. Always take your time walking off the field."

Sometimes we speak not only of pride but of something deeper still. People are surprised when I say that one of the things we talk about in a locker room is love. I just cannot adequately describe the love that permeates a good football team. Who knows, maybe part of it is what I once heard one of my players remark: "We grow together in love—hating the coach."

Before we run out on the field for the game, I lead the team in the locker room, kneeling down and together we say the Lord's Prayer.

To gather a team around you just before a big game, to look at grown men huddling close to each other with tears in their eyes, each one taking the hand of another on each side until every body and every soul in that room is connected, each pledging to give and to expect the best, each becoming part of all the others—to look into those strong faces that say "If we can only do it today"—to be there is to see and touch and be touched by people who have joined a cause that they have made bigger than themselves. If they can do it here, they will be able to do it anywhere.

This is hard to explain, but just before a game I have a need to touch the players—physically touch them. I need to do it to assure each kid that I know how hard everyone of us has worked and that the game and its outcome belongs to all of us. I'm not the only one. Several of my coaches, notably Ron Dickerson and Joe Sarra, circle the portion of the locker room where their particular players are sitting silently, psyching up, and they touch every players' hands, as though not to do so is to risk their entire commitment. That special moment shares an awareness that we've made a lot of sacrifices, endured a lot of physical pain, and now we've got to go out and get this thing done before 85,000 people, maybe 35 million people watching us on television. But I'm not sure that the bigger number makes a difference. The moment has come when I've got to depend on them, and they've got to depend on me and on each other or we can't get it done.

Something about that moment goes back to the epic poems. Great warriors and heroes in those poems cry, not over their own wounds, but over those of their opponents who died. Every game symbolizes the tragedy—the cost of every victory is that somebody's got to lose.

A few years ago the television producer of *60 Minutes* sent Harry Reasoner to spend three or four days with us to see if what people say about Penn State is real. They urged me to let them into the locker room before the game. I had never let any media people in and held firm with CBS, but relented for after the game. We won that day. CBS put on the air the few moments of those mud-stained, aching, happy players kneeling to say again softly, "Our Father who art in heaven . . ."

At least a dozen letters sailed into me—I don't know how many to CBS—sneering, "Enough's enough. How sanctimonious and phony can you be?" I don't know what to say to those people.

The prayer asks to forgive *us* and forgive *them*. There's no *I* or *me* in it. Of all things, we are not praying to win. I would be embarrassed to pray to win. My mother has always prayed for us to win, and I believe Sue does, but I can't and never have. Even in a clutch situation, I hear some part of my mind say, "Hey, God, let's make this thing work," but I catch myself. The idea of God taking my side in a football game embarrasses me.

13· Undefeated, Untied, and Unchosen

THE shortest way to get some of the feeling of 1968 is simply to read the scores—slowly, one at a time, with savor:

First there was Navy. 31–6.

Then Kansas State. 25–9.

Then we traveled to West Virginia. 31–20.

On their home ground we settled our score with UCLA. 21–6.

In our third straight away game, Boston College gave us a heady day. 29–0.

On Homecoming Day, Army reminded us we can never let up running scared. They scared us. 28–24.

Miami behaved. 22–7.

Maryland gave us a holiday. 57–13.

Pitt treated us to our highest score since 1947. 65–9.

Finally, Syracuse came through to give us an undefeated, untied season. 30–12.

The strong backbone of the greatest team I had ever been part of was its defense. The names are now a roll call of Penn State heroes: Mike Reid, Steve Smear, Jim Kates, Dennis Onkotz, John Ebersole, Jack Ham, Gary Hull, Pete Johnson, Paul Johnson, Neal Smith, and Mike Smith. Our halfbacks, Charlie Pittman and Bob Campbell, led our offensive punch.

Chuck Burkhart at quarterback did his job without much publicity, except for constant denunciation of him as "erratic" and not capable of leading his team to greatness. Burkhart (now president of a Schenley-owned company) never lost a game in which he started as quarterback all through his high school and college playing career.

There's something about quarterbacks that makes some fans and writers lose their mental balance. Unless the quarterback is a popular superstar, if the coach leaves him in, some fans insist they want him out; if the coach pulls him out, those fans think the guy should stay in. In a ground game, the coach should have called for more passes; in a passing game . . . you've got it.

Erratic? Burkhart? I stay with "erratic" guys like that—consistently—because what they do consistently is lead teams to win football games.

Since the 17–15 loss to UCLA in our third game of 1967, we had now won seventeen straight games by the end of 1968, except for a tie with Florida State in the Gator Bowl. Yet week after week, a big Penn State victory came up as a surprise and a sensation. The sportswriters and sportscasters heaped all kinds of praise on us but couldn't quite bring themselves to credit us—or any college in the East—with having a great football team. The "experts" couldn't get their eyes off the Big Ten, the Big Eight, the Southwest Conference, the Southeast Conference, the Pac-10.

"Well," went one of the excuses, "Eastern teams don't play as tough a schedule as those conferences." That, of course, was baloney. I was determined to prove it was baloney—in the Orange Bowl, where we were chosen to face Kansas before 77,719 spectators.

Kansas had lost one game, yet we were rated the underdog. That's one example of why I don't think much of sportswriters' polls. Ohio State, also undefeated, ranked ahead of us in both the Associated Press and United Press International polls, because we were from the "weak" East.

* * *

As I look back at that Orange Bowl game, I think what won it for us was our secret weapon—so secret that even I didn't know it was used until later. To explain, I have to shift the scene.

In Flushing, a kind of suburb of Brooklyn, my brother, George, was watching the game in his apartment with two women—an Australian he was dating who knew next to nothing about football and cared less, and with my mother, who knew at least that it was important that her older son always win no matter what and who couldn't possibly care more.

Less than two minutes before the final gun, when we were losing by a touchdown, my mother began pacing and wringing her hands, "My poor Joe, my poor Joe." George looked up and was astounded to see my mother crying big real tears.

"Mom," George protested, "don't be selfish. He's won seventeen games in a row. He's got to lose sometime. That's a great team he's playing."

"I can't watch. I've got to go and pray."

She reached into her pocketbook for her rosary beads and locked herself in the bathroom.

Next thing George knew, Chuck Burkhart, enclosed and threatened by gigantic Kansas defensemen in our own territory, heaved the football out of the well. It rose and lobbed like a mortar shell. Bobby Campbell, materializing out in the backfield, hauled it down a few yards from the goal line and held it under a smashing tackle. A couple of more plays, bang, bang, and we scored.

We trailed by a single point, 14–13. A good kick would now tie the game. Naturally, I decided to risk going for two—and a clear victory. We decided to try a rollout pass. It failed.

The game was lost.

Wait.

Like a heaven-sent flame, a yellow flag rose from the jumble of players and landed big as life. Against *them. Kansas had twelve men on the field.*

We get another shot!

The ball was moved halfway to the goal from the three-yard line. We ran off-tackle—and this time won the game, 15–14.

My mother, in the bathroom, heard George scream. Her face still running with tears, she ran out, got the news, and exclaimed, "You *see?*"

George soon told a luncheon crowd how my mother won the Orange Bowl game in Flushing. It got into *Sports Illustrated*— and our secret weapon was no longer a secret. Art Rooney, Sr., owner of the Pittsburgh Steelers, who grew up in a family that produced a priest and two nuns, sent me a telegram: I'LL TRADE MY BROTHER AND TWO SISTERS FOR YOUR MOTHER, EVEN UP.

Sure enough, Ohio State beat USC in the Rose Bowl and the newswriters confirmed them as number one in the nation. Our victory over Kansas made us the only Division I team that played eleven games and won them all. Yet we wound up rated number two by the AP and number three by UPI.

For the second year in a row we were awarded the Lambert Trophy, signifying the Eastern championship. Though glad to win it, I couldn't help looking at that trophy as a kind of consolation prize for the second-class citizenship of Eastern teams. But then came a far bigger thrill. The coaches of the nation voted me Coach of the Year, which led to an unforgettable bit of education from an expert.

At the Coach of the Year banquet, a marvelous, big-league affair thrown by Eastman Kodak, I was seated next to the nearest thing we had to a god of football, Bear Bryant of Alabama. Wasting no time, Bear took charge between the fruit cup and the salad:

"I hope you're going to renegotiate your contract."

I said I didn't have any contract.

"Why not?"

"Well, I just got tenure."

He peered queerly at me. "Tenure?"

"Yeah. The Pittsburgh Steelers just offered me their coaching job. I turned it down. But I went to our president, Eric Walker, and told him I was the only head coach he'd ever had that didn't have tenure. So he gave me tenure and made me a full professor."

"Full professor?" His peculiar glare was hard to read. Getting back on track, he said, "Now here's what you ought to get in your contract." He named a sum of money that was so incredible I don't remember it.

I had started as head coach two years earlier at $20,000, so I guess my routine raises had brought me to a shade more. But I didn't tell him that.

"Your contract should be for five years, and you ought to be able to roll it over."

I had no idea what rolling it over meant. Although I felt a little naïve and foolish, I appreciated his interest in me, a newcomer, and he didn't let up:

"You ought to have a car and you ought to have the country club."

"I don't play golf." I don't think he heard me, because he was preparing to drop the big one.

"You ought to have two hundred tickets—season tickets."

"What would I do with them?"

"The way you're going, you're going to have good football up there. I know enough about Penn State to know that people are going to be fighting to get into that stadium. You've got to have two hundred good tickets. That's going to give you the power to do whatever you want with your program and with yourself."

Naturally, I understood what he was saying. But what he was urging didn't feel right. The discomfort was not from a difference in scruples, only style. Maybe I didn't fully understand then a coach's potential power in a college, in a community, among alumni and financial angels, and that he's got to use that power effectively or he's not serving the program he was hired to run. But I was beginning to sense that he's got to gather that power and use it in a way that fits his personality.

If a team needs facilities as a condition of success, the coach needs the power to get them—and needs to use it. If a coach has a bad year and needs protection from those ready to chop off his head without asking questions, he's at an advantage if he's surrounded by a friendly force of important alumni. People like to be around a winning coach. Not just alumni, but politicians, journalists, influential businessmen, and, believe it or not, even some celebrity professors who swing a lot of power inside a university. The more successful a football program (or any kind of program in a university—athletic, academic, research, or anything else), the more it needs friends and supporters to help it survive and move ahead in an environment of extreme competition for dollars, for physical space, for equipment.

To the coach who can collect some of that power by controlling a stack of hard-to-get football tickets, I say (literally) more power to him. Paul Bryant, born to an old-time Southern style of politics, had, out of his genuine generosity, a natural sense for giving favors, but then turning them into power. He could get summer jobs for his players with just a phone call because he'd established many small, flattering, accommodating relationships. What he put to work wasn't raw power, but a personal charm that made people want to do what he wanted. If he wanted a new building or a new policy on grades, people did what he wanted not because they feared him, but because they wanted to please him.

I know now (and probably knew then) that a coach who builds into his contract a couple of hundred tickets on the fifty-yard line, as some coaches make sure they do, would find mysteriously that he'd never have to pay for a meal downtown. He could pick out three or four suits of clothes a year and not look at the price tag because it wouldn't apply to him. He'd never get a dentist's or a doctor's bill. People love him. A guy calls up and says, "My wife's brother is coming in with his family from Seattle . . ." or "I got a special customer coming in from New York and he's a Notre Dame alumnus. I just need to take him to the Notre Dame game." I get requests like that all the time, day after day, all season. I just don't want to get involved in that kind of thing. That's why, to this day, I have never put in my contract that I want x number of tickets.

I have no clue that Paul Bryant ever used his tickets for any kind of direct personal gain. But even at that banquet table, inexperienced as I was, I knew I couldn't be the Bryant kind of charmer, or play the ticket game, or the favor-and-IOU game. On extremely rare occasions, Sue and I have entertained somebody we weren't sure we liked, because we'd been persuaded that we could turn our hospitality into some big gift for the university. But far more often, when Dave Gearhart, our development director, has asked me to go see somebody and put a touch on him, I've said, "Dave, I don't like that guy and I'm not going," or, "I was nice to that guy once and had him to my house. Even if it means he doesn't give the money, I don't want him in my house anymore."

I have tried to develop a different way of gathering power to protect Penn State football. I try to win football games. Doing so has given me power, and I work it for all it's worth. Without it, we'd have no chance of continuing a first-class program and a winning team.

Make no mistake. I don't claim that my way is morally superior. There's nothing necessarily unscrupulous about making important friends for the football team through supplying good tickets. I just feel more at home with my way.

After that Orange Bowl victory, recruiting became far more productive—and easier. Sure, schools compete for recruits with claims that their academics are stronger—or weaker and less demanding—or that social life is merrier and the girls are prettier, or that the coaching is better, or that the kid is "guaranteed" to play first-string in his freshman year, or almost anything. What counts most with great high school athletes more than any other single attraction—and studies have demonstrated this—is the high school kid's dream of playing in a national championship game. Also, the kids' high school coaches glow when their former players make it big, which they're far more likely to do on a winning team. As we became better known as winners, we became all the more attractive to the ambitious player who also wanted to take his education seriously. Our recruiting slowly but surely moved toward allowing us to select the best players—and the best students among them—instead of chasing after them and selling on bended knee. We developed depth charts that were rich with young, smart, eager, and trainable football talents.

The second development was some success I had not only in evaluating our recruited talent, but in *re*evaluating. Too often a player gets stuck too early in a defensive or offensive role and into a particular position. A high school player isn't formed yet, sometimes isn't even fully grown, when a high school coach, who may not have experience, types the kid and trains him in a role. Maybe a kid with great potential as a running back or linebacker may be cast as a tackle simply because the high school coach needs a tackle. I began spending a lot of time observing recruits for agility, speed, aggressiveness in attack, ability to catch under pressure, throw under pressure, and what have you. When Jack Ham showed up as a big 198-pound freshman in 1967 after playing offensive guard in high school, we converted him to defense, as a linebacker, because we saw his talent for it. He turned out to be the first player I coached who wound up in the Pro Football Hall of Fame—as a linebacker. John Cappelletti arrived as a linebacker. John played defense at first because we had Lydell Mitchell and Franco Harris as running backs. He won his Heisman Trophy for starring as an offensive runner, as a tailback. Mike Reid, our defensive tackle who made the all-pro lists, arrived from high school as a fullback.

*   *   *

My fear was that after that dream season of 1968 the team would be too eager to win. That's when a great team tightens up—and starts losing.

To make matters tenser, our 1969 schedule put us against six of the country's finest quarterbacks and two teams that led the Big Eight Conference (Colorado and Kansas State). "We'll need momentum sustained week after week, preparation styled for each opponent, and toughness to take each game as it comes," I said in a preseason statement for the press.

But we also had something new going for us. It's hard to put a finger on just when and where it crept in, but it has since become not just a roar from the stands but the essence of our play: *We are Penn State.* I continued in that statement:

"We've developed our football to the place where pride is the ingredient working for us—the pride of our alumni and students, the pride we have in ourselves. A lot of people have worked hard to build our program from the dismal thirties when we were losing to small college teams in Pennsylvania, to a place where playing on a Penn State team means something great . . . we're close to number one and our incentive is to stay there."

14· Grab-Bag Champions

O N the night of September 19, 1969, our team bedded down in a motel in Bowie, Maryland, twelve miles from Annapolis. Next day, we would open our season, playing Navy, shooting for our twentieth consecutive game without a loss. From the moment our police escort arrived Saturday to clear our path through the traffic jam of 28,796 spectators, the third largest crowd in the Navy stadium's history, I should have known the season was destined to end in chaos and comedy.

A single sedan from the Maryland State Police casually appeared at the motel curb at twelve-thirty. For a two o'clock kickoff we'd normally be well settled into our locker room by then. We'd have sampled the water fountains, laid out our extra rolls of tape, be at least half dressed under layers of pads and jerseys, moping privately in the active, silent work of psyching up for combat. But not this day. When the cop car arrived, its driver at his radio began tuning in to the latest intelligence about the state of traffic, and he took his time negotiating with his headquarters about a scenic route for leading us to the battlefield. I finally had to shout a reminder that we had come for a football game and that we didn't plan to play it at the motel. The driver, suddenly alerted, started not only his car but his siren. We swam into a sea of motorists, but by then the sea would not part for us. We drifted until all traffic, including our buses, stopped dead. Ahead lay the bottleneck of the College Creek Bridge. The whole student body of midshipmen had just begun marching across, bound for the stadium, and tradition dictated that everybody, everything in town stops for them. Even the opposing football team.

As we finally approached the stadium, the middies were still marching through the main gate—the same gate we were scheduled to drive through. So our resourceful single-car police escort, switching to an audible play, end-ran us to a distant gate, where our team climbed out of the buses and walked halfway around the world, through clusters of ticket holders, some jeering, others autograph-seeking, to our dressing rooms. We got there at 1:25, giving us ten minutes to dress for the hastiest of pregame drills.

Maybe staying concentrated on the game isn't all that important after all. Flustered as we were, we did win that day, 45–22.

Actually the 1969 season couldn't have progressed better as, again, the scores summarize. Our first two games pitted us against two of those superhuman Western Conference teams that, as any sportswriter could tell you, we of the frail East couldn't match:

Colorado: Our defense overwhelmed Bobby Anderson, a Big Eight star quarterback, sacking him for twenty-eight yards, letting him net only five, and allowing him to connect on only eight of twenty-six passes. 27–3.

Kansas State: I put in a number of second-stringers after a 17–0 half, and we let a couple of touchdowns slip through. 17–14.

Syracuse: a more genuine squeaker. 15–14.

Ohio University. We really hit our stride. 42–3.

Boston College. 38–16.

Maryland. 48–0.

Pitt. 27–17.

North Carolina State. 33–8.

When writers in Big Eight country came to sum up the 1969

season, what impressed and excited them most? That Big Eight teams rolled up a 6–0 record in their games against Big Ten teams. But, unless I missed a clipping, they never once brought themselves to mention that Penn State, of the unmentionable East, beat all three Big Eight teams that it met in 1969, including vaunted Kansas in the Orange Bowl the previous January.

Ohio State appeared again to have a clear grasp on the writers' votes for number one. Dan Jenkins of *Sports Illustrated* got so starry-eyed he suggested that the title game ought to be played between Woody Hayes's first offensive and defensive teams. That was before their last regular game, when Michigan knocked off the Buckeyes.

We were rich with attractive invitations and choices for bowl games. The Orange Bowl wanted us back, where we would meet the Big Eight champs. If I'd had my way—and the players theirs—we would have played Ohio State. But that was not in the cards, because the Big Ten champion automatically goes to the Rose Bowl. By the time Michigan toppled them, our choice had been made.

At the time we had to make our decision, Ohio State, then still undefeated, was rated number one. Texas, undefeated, was rated number two. Penn State, undefeated, was rated number three.

Here's how our decision was made:

I wanted the experienced kids on our team to vote on where we would go. First I called in some of the black players—Lydell Mitchell, Charlie Pittman, Franco Harris, and a few others. This was at the peak of the new civil rights awareness, and I wanted to hear them out first about any choice among Southern cities. We had at most five black players at that time out of ninety or so squad members. They didn't want to go to the Cotton Bowl. More specifically, they didn't want to go to Dallas, where John F. Kennedy had been shot. Six years after that terrible shock, Dallas still stirred horror in many Americans. The revulsion seemed particularly strong among young black people who linked gun-loving Dallas with the lingering racism that had once been taken for granted throughout the South. The other players seemed sensitive to what their black teammates wanted, but if the majority wanted to go to Dallas, I believe Mitchell, Pittman, and the others would have accepted that too. (Two years later we played Texas in the Cotton Bowl. The whole team, including the black players, found Dallas a wonderful city.)

In a vote we took on the Sunday before the Saturday announcements of bowl pairings, almost everybody, it turned out for reasons I didn't expect, wanted the Orange Bowl. The previous year they'd played a good football game there and had had a great time in Miami. That choice would probably pair us against Missouri.

The following week the Ohio State loss to Michigan lifted Texas to number one in the polls, and we rose to number two.

That meant a Penn State–Texas face-off in the Cotton Bowl would have been for the national championship! Darrell Royal, the Texas coach, had urged me, both in public and private, to "hold out" for the Cotton Bowl. Then even Royal admitted that Missouri might be our strongest possible opponent, even though they had lost one game. They were certainly the strongest offensive power in the nation. The Missouri offense had smashed Michigan's celebrated defense. But whether Texas or Missouri was the tougher test, nobody could know without a playoff.

Trying to identify America's best college football team still left one unexpected—and preposterous—complication.

Texas still had one game to play in its regular-season schedule—against Arkansas. And who introduced the complication? Of all people, a great football coach who, by this time, was no longer the coach at Oklahoma but a broadcaster for the ABC network, Bud Wilkinson. Wilkinson took it upon himself to *announce*—unilaterally and on the air, naturally on ABC—

that the Texas-Arkansas game was to be the national championship match! By no coincidence, the game had long been
signed and scheduled on ABC. Just in case the "announcement" didn't take, Bud, as good a promoter as he had been a
football coach, had a strong secondary—or backup plan. He
was a personal friend as well as physical fitness adviser of
President Richard Nixon. Bud trumped up a number one official *trophy*—and had no trouble getting Nixon to agree to
present the "trophy" in the Texas-Arkansas winner's dressing
room—naturally, for all the world to see on the ABC telecast.

Sure enough, after the game, Richard Nixon, America's
leading self-appointed athletic authority, grinned into the cameras and "crowned" Texas number one.

By that time, however, word had penetrated the White
House that the great commonwealth of Pennsylvania—with a
governor from the President's own party, Raymond Shafer—
was about to blow the world's largest fuse over the affront.
The White House quickly saw a smooth way out of that one,
however. The President announced, right there in the dressing room, that, at a later time, he would present a plaque to
Penn State for having the longest winning streak in college
football.

The blood-curdling nerve! In his Solomon-like presidential
wisdom, Nixon *favored* us with an honor that any idiot consult-
ing a record book could see that we had taken for ourselves,
thank you, without his help. After Sue cooled me down, I
decided to express myself formally with a controlled, written
statement:

> Although I have heard nothing about a President's plaque, it
> would be a disservice to our squad, to Pennsylvania, and to the
> East to accept such an award, and, perhaps, to Missouri, which
> just might be the nation's best team. Because I had to baby-sit
> during the Texas-Arkansas game [our son Jay had recently ar-
> rived], I missed the President's final remarks, but it would seem
> to me to be a waste of his very valuable time to present Penn

State with a plaque for something it already indisputably owns—the nation's longest winning and unbeaten records.

By the end of the season, four Penn Staters made all-America teams on defense: linebacker Denny Onkotz (his second year of selection), tackle Mike Reid, halfback Charlie Pittman, and safety Neal Smith. Reid won fifth place in votes for the Heisman Trophy, the highest for any lineman. He also took the Maxwell and Knute Rockne awards and the Outland Trophy as the best interior lineman in the country.

Our Orange Bowl game against Missouri shaped up as the irresistible force meeting the immovable object, a classic test of offense versus defense. Missouri, champions of what experts had come to call a superconference, the Big Eight, a team that had averaged 450-yard gains in its ten season games, was slowed down to 175 yards on the ground and 117 in the air. Missouri's quarterback, McMillan, completed ten passes—but his teammates caught only three of them. We intercepted the other seven, setting an Orange Bowl record and tying the record for all postseason bowl games. McMillan had the good grace to say the next day, "I've never seen a defense like Penn State's . . . They always rushed four men and forced me to throw before I was ready. Seven men were in their pass coverage . . . They covered my men like blankets." After viewing the films, Coach Dan Devine, who said his staff had put more time and effort into this game than any of their previous five bowl trips, called Penn State "the best defensive team I've seen in twenty years of college football."

The final score, reflecting the preeminence of defensive play, was 10–3.

After the game, our exultant Nittany Lions tossed Governor Shafer into their shower.

Oh yes, Texas beat Notre Dame in the Cotton Bowl. That left them undefeated. Having beaten Missouri, we were undefeated.

The pundits and the pollsters still rated us number two.

*   *   *

Throughout the world of sports—*all* sports, college, amateur, Olympic, professional, any other kind you can think of—champions are determined on the field of play. They rise by knocking off previous champions or knocking off challengers, until a champion comes out undisputably tops.

That's true in every sport I can think of—*except one.*

The exception is big-time college football.

Even in lower divisions of college football, champions are crowned on the playing field. Teams with the best records in each geographical district of each division (or playing level) of the NCAA meet in the postseason bowls that don't get on national television: the Stagg Bowl, the Grantland Rice Bowl, and others, so that one team wins the flag as division champion.

A playoff to determine an indisputable champion among first-line college football teams has been a subject of argument for years. The desire for a playoff has been so often expressed by so many, and opposed by so many others, you'd think it would be hard to have one.

With a little planning, it would not be hard to accomplish at all. But everybody knows how some people in power tremble over the prospect of change.

The chief opponents of a playoff are not coaches or athletic directors. They are the bowl managements themselves. College athletic departments don't have much to do with controlling postseason matches. The big bowls support management organizations of their own. They take in tens of millions in ticket sales. They multiply that several times over through television contracts. The networks, in turn, must recover their costs plus a profit by huge sales of commercials to some of the biggest advertisers in the economy. Bowl managements fear that a system of true playoffs would ruin the economic attractiveness of their games.

Playoffs will come. The more that televised bowl games succeed in making football fans out of more Americans, the more these fans will demand a clear and rational system for choosing a real champion. The present system of bowl games should—and surely will—be a solid part, a foundation of play-offs. The bowls don't have anything to be afraid of.

The best and easiest way to launch a playoff series would be right after January 1, just as the present bowl games are completed. Few people have any serious gripe with the way bowls now pick their participants. Nobody questions that the best teams get to compete. When we played Miami in 1986, nobody seriously doubted that our Fiesta Bowl game pitted the nation's two strongest teams against each other and that the contest would produce an authentic national champion. But far more often the season results in frustrating guesswork—a sportswriters' poll of the kind that named Texas as national champs in 1969 and that arbitrarily rated Penn State number two. There was no way of anybody being satisfied.

When you look at the relatively small number of top-rank teams that come out winners of bowl games, a panel of coaches and sports journalists, helped if necessary by computer calculations of who beat whom during the season, could name, almost without controversy, the four top contenders for the national championship. Undefeated teams of the top NCAA division, of course, automatically would be candidates. In the extremely rare instance when more than four are undefeated, the panel would select the four, just as they do in basketball. More often, only one or two would be undefeated, and the panel would have to choose two or three from those who lost only one. That would present no serious problem.

The problem is that bowls are afraid of losing the good thing they now have. The opposite is more likely: With a final playoff, they'd be better off. Today, one bowl game usually grabs the main national attention. Everybody knew that the 1986 Fiesta Bowl would produce a recognized national champion, either Miami or Penn State. That was so again in 1988, when Notre Dame played West Virginia, again in the Fiesta Bowl.

In all the other bowls, the invited teams were just playing. If a true playoff followed those games, virtually every bowl game would be an important qualifying contest.

On the first weekend following the first full week after the bowl games, the four contending teams would clash in a pair of semifinals. What a television double-header that would make! Then, next weekend, the national collegiate championship finals. For audience and enthusiasm, the game, after a few years of buildup, could rival the professionals' Super Bowl.

And you know what's a most appealing part of it? The players wouldn't have to miss classes. Colleges are on Christmas vacation until mid-January.

Obviously, what I'm presenting here isn't a detailed blueprint. If it were, somebody would find some minor flaw in it and try to close off further exploration and discussion. This is a broad approach and a plea for more people to get behind a simple system—any kind of reasonable, fair system—to establish a playoff for a real college football championship.

My guiding principle here is love of competition—competition on the playing field, not competition for somebody's good opinion. I don't want somebody *deciding* how good we are. If your team beats us, you're better than we are. But don't tell me—or have the President or anybody else tell me—you're better than we are and then not want to play us to prove it.

I know of some coaches who don't want a playoff. Under the present system, they say, maybe ten coaches come out looking good. (Get the assumption? The purpose of college football is to polish and shine the reputations of coaches.) Why should most of us wind up beaten and only one guy come out a winner?

Or some will say, "A playoff would create too much stress. Who needs it?" Football games are stressful, sure. That's the best part about them. That's what makes a game a peak experience. Why is a guy who would say that coaching football?

The Syracuse coach, Dick McPherson, once said to me: "I love coaching. The only time I don't love it is on Saturdays."

I couldn't believe what I heard. I said, "For crying out loud, Dick, Saturdays are the best part of it."

Maybe I'm different. Maybe I'm crazy. But I *live* for fall Saturdays.

15· Quarterbacking in Black and White

T HERE were mornings I'd wake up, suddenly remember, and have trouble believing it: We had played thirty consecutive games over three seasons without a loss.

What load of special fortune had dropped on us to make that possible? One answer was obvious: Just go down the list of the early 1970 National Football League draft. Count the good news—and the bad. Recite the names of great people who had brought us glory—and who we were about to lose to graduation.

In the first round, Cincinnati snapped up Mike Reid. In the third round, Saint Louis took Charlie Pittman, and the New York Jets claimed Denny Onkotz. In the fourth, Steve Smear joined Baltimore, and the New York Jets picked John Ebersole. In the seventh, Dallas named Don Abbey, and in the eighth and twelfth rounds the Washington Redskins took Paul Johnson and Jim Kates. In addition, we lost Neal Smith, Pete Johnson, Tom Jackson (now head coach at the University of Connecticut)—and Chuck Burkhart, our baby-faced quarterback who had been taunted incessantly by writers and fans as a guy who couldn't pass and couldn't run. Just as some writer had said about me in my playing days, all he did was think— and win.

Coaches of pro teams eventually lose their players to smashed knees, crushed discs, aging, and arthritis. College coaches lose them to the bittersweet of graduation.

To some coaches, graduation is disaster, the enemy. All the things I believe in force me to celebrate graduation as achievement, as victory. But a secret part of me weeps inside at commencement. Like any professor, I hate to see those kids leave their dependence on me. Like any father, I hate to see them leave home. Like any coach, I hate to lose those players.

As hours crept toward the fall, and the first game of a whole new team, our fans sent up a rising excitement of expectations and hopes. They wanted our string of victories to go on—and on, and on. I had no quarrel with that. Second, they wanted me to name our new quarterback. They wanted no more "mistakes" like Chuck Burkhart. The fans wanted what fans always want in their quarterbacks—a razzle-dazzle passer, a rubber-band-loose runner, an emotional body linguist, a bright quotable quipster for the after-the-game press conference, a ladies' man, and a man's man. They want a sparkling jewel. A superstar who carries the team on his back. They want a Homeric hero.

If the quarterback falls short of all-purpose perfect, and if the coach has to choose between athleticism and leadership, his choice tells a lot about what kind of coach he is. There's no doubt the superstar quarterback will excite the fans and juice up the box office. The other kind—a leader—is a nerve center, the energy source, the field commander of the team. He will probably contribute more in the long run to building a great team and to winning games. But that contribution may be less visible, certainly less flashy. He is a man not primarily for the fans, but *for the team*. He is a Virgilian hero.

Burkhart had been a knowledgeable, quick-minded, leadership-oriented kind of quarterback who lifted the confidence of the entire team, helped make everybody a better player, and who got razzberries from the fans who didn't understand football enough to appreciate his contributions.

For the 1970 season, I had to choose a quarterback from the

young guys coming up behind Burkhart. Our number three quarterback, John Hufnagel, a sophomore like Burkhart, had been recruited from Montour High School in McKees Rocks, Pennsylvania.

Then there was Bob Parsons, a six-foot-three-inch junior from Wind Gap, Pennsylvania. He shot a pass like a cannon. Problem was, Parsons worked a five-day week—terrific Monday to Friday. On Saturday, he was no better a passer than Chuck Burkhart and not nearly as effective a leader. (Parsons later had a great pro career with the Chicago Bears—as a tight end *and* a punter.)

Finally, there was Mike Cooper, a bright senior from Harrisburg who had been Burkhart's number two for two 11–0 seasons, including two Orange Bowl victories. Mike's passing and running were good, although not record-book stuff. But he had something extra, not always visible in the stands or the press box. Maybe it arose from a burning ambition that drove him: to become a college football coach.

To make my choice, I had to grapple—no matter how I preferred just to ignore it—with one added complication. Mike Cooper was black. The world of football, including college football, had not taken the radical step of opening the door to black quarterbacks. Well, nobody ever said out loud the door was closed. But it had not been opened. From the earliest wisps of public speculation in the annual game of Who's Gonna Be Paterno's Quarterback?, I could tell I was bound to lose. If I picked Cooper, it was because he was black. If I picked Parsons, it was because Cooper was black.

The problem itself stirred emotions in me that I wanted to exclude from the decision. I remembered times I'd come home from school smarting because some kid had called me a wop or something equally affectionate. I sensed the hatred in the word and couldn't understand what I did to make someone hate me. My mom would sense my pain and eventually pry out of me what had happened. She could have incited me against the other kid, as some parents do, or she could have taught me to swallow the bitter taste, letting me fester in a growing self-doubt and self-contempt, as the world so often instructs kids to do. Instead, she turned my tears into pride. She'd sit me on a kitchen stool to listen while she recited her memorized list of all the great Italians and their exploits: Michelangelo, Leonardo, Garibaldi, Columbus, Toscanini. She'd go through all of them, planting them forever in my head and in my life. Then she'd add: "Remember, every knock is a boost."

That's why, in the late sixties, I identified strongly with black kids. It was a time when hatred against blacks was coming out in the open because of the civil rights movement. But it was also a time when black people were asserting and demanding their right to full citizenship and full humanity. I often said to friends at that time that I wished I were black. Maybe some people thought I was some kind of overdramatic or sentimental bleeding heart. What they didn't get about me was that I always feel my best and highest when I have a cause, when I have something to fight for, when I'm behind in the score and there's barely enough time to pull off a win. Being black and insisting on being fully a person was a cause.

I did have one escape hatch if I wanted to use it. I could start both Cooper and Parsons alternately and let public opinion shake itself down and decide (which is one way to abdicate being coach). But I had always been, and still believe in being, a one-quarterback coach. If I wasn't going to pick either of these worthy guys based on color, I wasn't going to straddle both to avoid the issue of color.

A final point to consider: As backup, Cooper had had two years of close practice, and some game play, with two outstanding sophomore backs, Franco Harris and Lydell Mitchell. They were the new core of a good new football team.

I decided to start Cooper.

In our opener against Navy, as though the scoreboard couldn't break an old habit, the numbers kept rising for us till we won, 55–7. Cooper completed six of ten passes for 109 yards. Two of his passes scored touchdowns and Mike scored a third himself on the run. After we safely led, I relieved him with Parsons, who convinced me further that Cooper was the right choice. That final score made us look further invincible, even without our stars of past years, and maybe I was starting to believe it myself.

Next Saturday morning, we awoke at the University of Colorado to meet the team we'd handled the previous year, 27–3. Sue, who had come on the trip, rose before I did, threw open the hotel window for her first sight of the Rockies, and just about shrieked, "Have you seen those *mountains!*"

Those mountains were not kind to us. All we seemed able to win that day was the opening coin toss. Colorado intercepted Mike Cooper's first-play pass and scored a touchdown within two minutes. We got flattened that day, 41–13. In our locker room, we heard something that for some of our kids was a strange and shocking experience: the roar of celebration from the other team's room. Some of them looked stricken, humiliated, fallen into some pit of disgrace. I hated the feeling, too, but I had to remind them that losing is the flip side of winning. "Listen to them," I said in a little locker-room speech I still remember. "Let them have their glory. We've had our share."

There's a range of feelings that goes with wins and losses. At Colorado that day, I, too, felt jolted, taken by surprise. When I get beaten, I often get angry: angry at my coaching staff, at my players, and, if I can find the slightest excuse to, at the officials. I get angry at the breaks that might have gone against us. Then I get angry at myself.

I hate to lose. God, I hate to lose. Ever since those kid days of stickball in Flatbush, of boxing my cousins in Coney Island, of my mother insisting, *expecting,* that I be the best, I have never learned how not to hate losing.

Yes, I know, I preach a lot about being willing to lose, that there can be valor in losing to a better opponent. Yes, I know it seems contradictory, inconsistent, maybe even hypocritical.

I'm sorry about that. The world is a more complicated and ambiguous place than I wish it were.

I'll say it again: To win right, you cannot be afraid to lose. But God, I hate to lose.

Those kids in that locker room that day, because they hadn't lost in a long time, and some of them had never lost, now had to feel and find out just how miserable it is. Maybe it was necessary for their complete education.

And maybe I needed a refresher course myself in one of the prices a coach pays for losing. Next day, all day, back in State College, Sue took incessant calls from fans who wouldn't name themselves, who demanded to talk to me, who called her a liar when she said I wasn't home (I was on campus studying films for our next game against Wisconsin), and who wanted me to know I had lost my touch, and who demanded that I listen to their prescriptions for getting back on the road to winning now that we had that disgraceful losing streak of one.

The education, as it turned out, was far from complete. Next week, Wisconsin battered us, 26–9, and, two weeks after that, Syracuse reminded us, in a way we wouldn't soon forget, just how vincible we were: 24–7. To make matters worse, Cooper was not playing well. The pressure on him was more than he could handle at that time, and more than I knew how to handle, in light of what followed those losses.

What followed? An outburst of expression so painful and embarrassing, I had to fight myself not to turn sour and bitter against Penn State and its alumni. I had to remind myself every day that a few are not the many—that to judge many by a few is bigotry.

My telephone at home—which was listed in the book then, and still is today, so that players or recruits can reach me in an emergency—rang day and night, cauterizing the ears of Sue, who usually answered.

"Is the nigger lover home?" one caller demanded.

Another seethed at her, "You tell that son of a bitch we're going to get that nigger."

In recalling it, I have to remind myself again that this was at the peak of the civil rights movement, when many, perhaps most, Americans had broadened their acceptance of minority people in new roles. In sports, they had fully accepted black players in baseball, in football, in basketball. But in baseball, for example, a black third-base coach or manager was still unthinkable. And in football, blacks had won the right to play, mainly because so many blacks played so well. But a quarter-back has to *lead,* and blacks had not yet won *that* right. No matter how many times I said, "Cooper's a good quarterback—give him a chance to prove it," the calls kept coming. Mike was black. These haters were not going to forget it—or let me forget it.

Many of the calls had the sound of long distance, but what hurt most was that more than a few sounded like they came from State College, which, by this time, had become a beloved place to me.

Letters poured in, too, in numbers I had never received, nor ever expected to. Many of them, anonymous, of course, were just as ugly as the calls. And many were signed. They were well-meaning attempts to advise me, to help save me from myself. These respectfully, politely, referred to "the Negro," cautioning me that I'd hurt the team or hurt Penn State. The players, so these volunteer experts advised me, wouldn't coop-erate with, wouldn't accept the leadership of, a Negro quarter-back. Then I felt worse when I learned that a lot of the hate mail was going directly to Cooper himself.

During the Syracuse game, played in our home stadium, Cooper was booed by our own fans. Not by the majority, thank God, far from it, but by enough voices to break Cooper's heart, and mine. Minutes after the defeat, Sever Toretti, our chief recruiter and former coach, was crossing the crowded parking lot to his car when he heard a beered-up tailgater bellow across the field like a hog-calling contestant, "Paterno's got to get rid of that nigger at quarterback," Tor charged the fan, spread-eagled him across his car hood, and regained his good sense just as he was about to smash the fool's bones. Tor quickly switched to the weapon of enraged words, and I'd like to have heard them.

The disgraceful minority led me to do things that normally I might not have gone out of my way to do. In a later game that season, when we were well ahead, I happened to notice four of my best offense players, all black, sitting together on the bench. The four were Charlie Pittman, Franco Harris, Lydell Mitchell—and Mike Cooper. I really liked all those kids, and the more I got letters, the more I wanted to defy the bastards who wrote them. I asked Pittman, "How do you think the brothers would like it if I put all four of you in the backfield together?"

In those days, an all-black backfield would be noticed, in fact, was unheard of.

Charlie said, "You're kidding."

I said, "The heck I am." I sent them all in and felt like turning to the crowd and giving a traditional Italian full-arm gesture that some of them wouldn't forget.

I left that quartet in for a series, and they played their hearts out.

Yes, I do believe in staying with one quarterback. But sometimes I have no choice but to switch around until I can pick the best one to go with. Whether due to the special pressure or because his talent fell short, Cooper just wasn't steady enough. I put in Parsons to relieve Cooper, but he didn't come through. Finally, faced with our first losing season since 1938, I transferred Hufnagel from defense to quarterback. Suddenly he blossomed, turned the team around, and racked up a few quarterback records as we won our next five games for a 7–3 season.

We went on to win sixteen games in a row led by Hufnagel.

When I stopped playing Cooper, those hate letters, by this time numbering about two hundred, stopped too. Now they started coming from the other side. The new letters—about a hundred—called me names for "caving in" to the racists. Letter writers on both sides were too deeply trapped in their prejudice or their "raised consciousness" to accept that I had made a football decision, not a political decision. In my view, callers of both stripes were racists of two different kinds.

Sad to say, Mike Cooper graduated without understanding or accepting my decision to relieve him. At least I don't think he did. I think he felt that he'd played better than I thought he had and that I'd forsaken him under that public outcry. I still think that Mike, in the back of his mind, feels I gave in to the racists. He never said so, but I saw it in a changed attitude.

I'll never know whether Mike's potential was drained by the sear of that terrible spotlight. I do know that he graduated with a bad taste for Penn State, although he deserved to leave feeling the buoyancy of a successful letterman. After graduation, he became militantly active in civil rights issues in Harrisburg. One day a civic leader there, besieged by protesters, called me to ask, "Can you do me any good with Mike Cooper? Can you get him to back off?"

I said I couldn't. First of all, in the particular local school issue that involved him at that moment, I thought Mike was right. Second, I wouldn't try even if I thought he was wrong. He had a right to say what he wanted to say.

Mike Cooper, who had the ability, the intelligence, the discipline to make it as a coach, gave up that ambition. I've always wondered if those harassers—who imagined themselves friends of Penn State, and, more ironically, of mine—were responsible for derailing him from his goal.

A lot of change and a lot of progress came out of that period of our history. But like everything worth doing, it came at great cost. Much of the cost was in the craziness that took hold of some people's heads on every side of the rampant racism. One night, about a year or two after Mike's graduation, I got an emergency call at home from one of our players, the kind of call that requires that I keep a listed telephone number. The player told me that a teammate, who was black—let's call him Eddie—had just been charged by a young woman, who was white, of raping her at a party. First thing next day, I talked to Eddie in my office. He denied the charge. A couple of other players, white kids, came to see me. They said they knew the young woman as a football hanger-on known to be someone to avoid and that she had "led him into that room."

The following morning, I called Eddie in and said, "I'm going to put you off the team until we get this thing straightened out. It's not a judgment of you, but it's for your good and everybody else's good."

Next thing I knew I got a call from someone who identified himself as an official of the NAACP in Philadelphia. I have no idea if he thought he was calling in his official capacity, and I would not hold that fine organization responsible for his conversation. I remember the call as though it were tape-recorded in my head:

"I want to let you know that I can appreciate your wanting to protect that white girl, but we want you to know that you're going to have to put Eddie back on the team and play him."

"I can't do that," I said. "We have certain rules on this team. Eddie has admitted being out after hours and admitted drinking in a public gathering. That breaks team rules, without regard to the alleged rape. And until we get it cleaned up—"

"Listen, you mother————. I got people in high places. You better play him."

"You'd better stop and think about this."

"Don't give me that. You think you're going to protect that little white bitch at the expense of one of our people. I'll get your ass."

"One more word like that and I'm hanging up."

I got the one more word and hung up.

That caller, presumably acting for his NAACP chapter, arranged a lawyer to defend Eddie against the young woman's charges. I went to see her parents in a nearby town, hoping to save them, their daughter, and my player from embarrassment, telling them that witnesses had come forth to contradict her. They pressed anyway. In court, Eddie was exonerated.

The craziness hit me from another direction one night when one of our great former players dropped by to see me. His kid was on the squad at the time, but I wasn't playing him much. The former star said I was playing another kid ahead of him because that kid was black and that "everybody knows" I favor black players.

The visit—and the claim—stunned me. He'd hardly started his car outside when the phone rang, and I began to think I had been trapped in a nut house. The call was from New Jersey, from the mother of a kid who was a backup at the same position as the ex-player's son.

"The only reason you aren't playing my boy," she told me with no uncertainty, "is because you love playing black players and because you promised [the ex-player] that, if you played any white, you'd play his kid."

I had been head coach for almost ten years, but still wondered: Does anyone ever say, This guy's honest and tries to be fair? That he's trying to do the best he can? Or that his first consideration in choosing players is to try to win games?

Now, another fifteen years or so have gone by. I don't wonder about those questions anymore. I have had to learn just to shut them out.

16· A Heisman with Tears

AFTER rolling up our socks and winning our last five games of 1970 for a 7–3 season, we streaked through 1971 with ten successive victories. The scores gave us that (dangerous) invincible feeling again:

Navy, with four touchdowns by Franco Harris. 56–3.

Iowa, Lydell Mitchell ground-gaining 211 yards. 44–14.

Army, Mitchell running 161 yards and scoring three touchdowns all in the second half. 42–0.

Syracuse. 31–0.

Texas Christian, with our net gain of 632 yards, including four more touchdowns by Mitchell. 66–14.

West Virginia. 35–7.

Maryland, a five-touchdown game for Mitchell in which he ran for 209 yards. 63–27.

North Carolina State, with four more Mitchell touchdowns. 35–3.

Pittsburgh, in which Mitchell not only gained 181 yards, but scored three times to set an NCAA season record of twenty-five touchdowns. 55–18.

Only one hair-raiser was tucked in there, against Air Force, 16–14.

Winning streaks like that are always dangerous. For our eleventh and final season game against Tennessee, we flew to Knoxville feeling fat and secure with an invitation in our pockets to play Texas in the Cotton Bowl. That was a game President Nixon two years earlier had made a "must" for us.

We played the kind of game against Tenneessee that we were famous for making other teams play. We fumbled, and Tennessee ran the goof for a seventy-six-yard touchdown. We punted, and they returned it for a forty-four-yard touchdown. We passed, and they intercepted and ran forty-three yards for a touchdown. Instead of forcing their mistakes, we made our own. Final score, Penn State 11, Tennessee 31, breaking our streak at fifteen games. We staged that whole sorry spectacle on the national ABC television network.

I was embarrassed, angry, and soon let the tyrant in me leap out. Not bad enough that I let it escape, I let it leap against, of all people, Franco Harris, who was fighting his own demons. Injuries had nagged Franco most of the season, keeping him out of a few games. That no doubt drove him quietly frantic as he had to sit on the bench watching his backfield partner, Mitchell, having a season of fun.

Our run-in occurred a few days before the Cotton Bowl, when Franco showed up late for a practice. It happens that Franco and I were victims of two powerful quirks. He had trouble arriving for meetings and practices on time, and I couldn't—and still can't—stand anybody being late, especially when it holds up the team. (My coaches tell me they set their watches by "Paterno time"—five minutes early.) So I chewed out Franco in front of the whole squad.

If you've been hearing those ugly whispered rumors that sometimes I rant and rage when my players goof up, you better pay attention. It's part of the special charm I bring to my work. Naturally, my ear-splitting voice and the veins around my temples that bulge to the verge of bursting are really under perfect control, and I rage only for good cause and only when it will bring desirable results. Ask anybody.

Well, I felt Franco had given me good cause. Besides, I wanted my less experienced kids to witness that my demand of discipline goes for everybody. Maybe Franco found it harder than I thought simply to rise above his time-management problem. Maybe he was smarting over those lost opportunities caused by his injuries. Maybe he wanted to test me or challenge me or even defy me. I don't want to read his mind. Whatever the cause, at next day's practice Franco showed up three minutes late. After the previous day's scene, that simply was not tolerable. I told him—out loud, for all to hear—that he would not start against Texas. It hit the team like a bolt. And he didn't start against Texas, although he did play after we were well ahead.

Looking back, I think I handled that wrong. Instead of popping off in front of the team that I felt he had offended, I wish I had held my peace, met Franco privately later, and tried to dig out what was bugging him. A legend has made the rounds that I later nurtured some grudge against Harris, or he had one against me. It is not so. I admire the great human being he is. To Franco's credit, maybe more than mine, he didn't brood over his embarrassment. After the season and his graduation, we kept in touch with each other and still do now, and Franco has helped us in our recruiting.

At the Cotton Bowl, for the first time in eighty games Texas failed to score a touchdown. We beat them, 30–6. Sam Blair, reporting in the Dallas *Morning News*, wrote:

"Penn State stormed through, over, and around the Long-horns . . . When it was over not a soul was making jokes about the so-called eastern style football which the Lions supposedly play . . . Rarely, if ever, has a good [Darrell] Royal team, supposedly operating under normal strength, been subjected to such a licking."

A year and a half later, when Penn State seniors invited me to give their commencement address—and after the White House and President Nixon had all but drowned in a national scandal—I made my debut as a commentator on public affairs. "How come," I asked in my speech, "a President who knew so much about college football in 1969 could have known so little about Watergate in 1973?"

As the 1971 regular season ended, so 1972 began: our opponent again Tennessee and again on their home field. The game became a landmark in Penn State history, for a reason few would have predicted.

The worst thing about returning to Tennessee was the challenge of mounting an offense without Lydell Mitchell and Franco Harris, both now graduated. That was balanced, however, by the astonishing development of John Hufnagel, who I now considered the best college quarterback in America.

Maybe what happened was, just as on our previous visit to Knoxville, our eyes were affected by an overdose of orange. When people visit State College for the first time on a football Saturday, they often walk bug-eyed through a world that all seems painted blue and white. But orange is brighter than blue. When you see enough of it, it's almost blinding: orange ties, orange jackets, orange pants, orange miniskirts, orange shoes; orange ironing boards in department stores, orange bowling balls in the alleys. Bartenders wear orange vests. Two and a half hours before kickoff, Orange fans are already out in full force waving orange pennants and pompons, screaming, chanting, and stomping in the stands, believing in their team. Anybody who doesn't think that stuff counts just doesn't understand football. For our return match, the stands turned orange with the largest crowd, 71,647, ever to witness an athletic contest in Tennessee.

Thanks to the interceptions and fumbles we presented as gifts, Tennessee rolled up twenty-one points in the first half, while our score remained round and empty. Then, in the first evidence that our graduation ceremony had not destroyed us, John Hufnagel, backed against his own goal line, adjusted his sights and heaved a grenade to Jimmy Scott, a sprint champion, who ran it for seventy-nine yards. Huffy hit eleven more receivers out of twenty-five attempts, totaling 190 yards. In the third quarter, Doug Allen smashed an Orange fullback so hard the ball sprang loose and we recovered on their twenty-two-yard line.

That was the historic moment that John Cappelletti, a junior at tailback, launched Penn State's most famous career of power running. He carried the football six times in a row, finally planting it mere feet from the goal. Then Bob Nagle lobbed his body over a pileup for our second touchdown. In the final quarter, each team reached the end zone again, Cappelletti showing amazing strength in powering our drive.

So, at the short end of 21–28, we lost the second in a row to Tennessee. Worse still, the Volunteers had now blocked us from undefeated regular seasons twice in a row. But that was the game that raised the curtain on the Cappelletti era of Penn State football.

The next few weeks were a demonstration, for anyone who doubted it, of how runners are helped by good passing and of how passing helps good runners. At West Point, Army tried to cover the new threat of Cappelletti by diverting some pressure from Hufnagel. As a result, Huffy threw twelve completions out of eighteen and ran the option for seventy-one yards. We won, 45–0. Next week Syracuse decided to concentrate on Hufnagel, sacking him often enough to limit him to five completions. But that effort freed Cappy to gain 163 yards on the ground. We confounded our rival, 31–0.

That brought us to West Virginia, home of some of the scrappiest, most earnest football, and some of the wildest fans in the world of sports. A visit to Morgantown is not an English gentlemen's polo match. As one of our kids said after the game, "We were given a ten-minute standing boo when we came on the field—before we did anything."

The Mountaineers' characteristic jumping and yelling started with justification right at opening kickoff. Their Kerry Marbury returned it for 101 yards! As the crowd went crazy,

his ecstatic teammates almost pounded Marbury into a meat-
ball. That could have intimidated and slowed us. But Cappelletti methodically took the ball thirty-four times and rammed
for 158 yards. Meanwhile, Hufnagel completed seven passes
for 165 yards and optioned for 64 more on the ground. We
went home with the game, 28–19.

In leading us through a 10–1 regular season, Hufnagel, who,
you remember, got his try at quarterback only after Cooper and
Parsons fell short, completed his senior year, 1972, as a Heisman candidate and a leading character in the book of Penn
State records. For passing in a single game, he set the yardage
record (against Pitt, 329), for a season (2,195 yards in eleven
games) and most passes completed (123). Altogether, he col-
lected ten records for passing and others for the number of
offensive plays and total offense yardage for a game, a season,
and a career.

Cappelletti's greatest year still lay ahead.

The television drama widely advertised for the Sugar Bowl
on the last day of 1972 was a showdown between John and
Oklahoma's all-American, Greg Pruitt. That drama was canceled, however, when a flu bug shot a high temperature
through Cappelletti on the morning of the game.

As though compensating for the loss of his offensive power,
three times our defense stopped the Sooners cold within one
yard of the goal. But we couldn't contain Oklahoma's strength
forever. They scored in the second quarter on a seventy-seven-
yard drive that culminated in a twenty-seven-yard pass. Then
Oklahoma scored a second touchdown that may not have been
a touchdown. We fumbled a punt in the last quarter, a decisive
moment that blew our chance to seize control of the game.
They passed from our eighteen-yard line. A Sooner dove for the
ball on the one and plunged into the end zone. Up in the press
box, the public address announcer said a TV replay (not official
in college football) showed that the pass was caught on a

bounce. Two New Orleans newspapers reported it that way. Our kid nearest to the play, Gregg Ducatte, protested the catch. But the nearest official declared a touchdown. I wasn't able to see the play at an angle to second-guess the official.

Would Cappelletti have made a difference in that game? Of course. But nobody can say any absent player would have changed the result. What broke my heart was that a coming star who had gained 1,117 yards during the season had to miss this chance at a great day.

The strangest turn was yet to come. Information soon came to light that two Oklahoma freshmen who had played had been academically ineligible, their high school grades allegedly having been doctored. The NCAA hit Oklahoma with a two-year probation, then shocked the sports world with an order that forfeited all of Oklahoma's games in which the two freshmen played. That included the Sugar Bowl game.

I put out a statement and used it to get in a sideways lick against a practice I have always opposed: letting freshmen play in varsity games. Yes, at rare times I've been forced by competition to play a freshman myself. But if I had my way, none of us would be permitted to play a green kid who should be concentrating on learning to study and how to live in the strange new world of college. My statement said:

> It's a shame a great effort by an Oklahoma football team has to be marred by an inexcusable recruitment violation such as this incident. However, our players and the Oklahoma players know who won the game. Perhaps the irony is that if freshmen were not allowed to participate, recruiting irregularities would have come to light before their participation caused another embarrassing situation for intercollegiate athletics.

To this day, the Sugar Bowl lists Penn State as winner of that game. The players on both sides know who got the higher score, and we continue to list Oklahoma.

* * *

We sailed through 1973, rolling over Stanford, Navy, Iowa, Air Force, Army, Syracuse, West Virginia, Maryland, North Carolina State, Ohio, and Pitt—our third season without a defeat or a tie in eight years. Near the season's end, when the Army game was clearly going in the right direction, we played more than eighty Penn Staters, every healthy body wearing blue and white, and we piled up 607 yards for a score of 54–3. At Navy, we used our starters for hardly more than half the game, holding the score down to 39–0.

Against Maryland, Cappelletti carried the ball thirty-seven times, a Penn State record, and he gained 202 yards. That was the game that started the boom for Cappelletti as a Heisman candidate. Next week, against North Carolina State, we were losing at the half, 14–9, but a twenty-four-yard touchdown run by Cappy helped tie it at the third-quarter whistle, 22–22. With six minutes to go, we were locked again, 29–29, when Cappy broke through for a twenty-seven-yard touchdown, his third of the game. Altogether, he ran 220 yards in forty-one carries. Against Ohio University, Cappy tore into the end zone four times, locking up our 49–10 victory.

I can't think of a year when picking a champion by poll was more absurd than after the 1973 season. Before our New Year's night meeting with Louisiana State University, Notre Dame had upset Alabama in the Sugar Bowl, 24–23. Also, Ohio State had beaten USC in the Rose Bowl, 42–21. Those two winners plus the winner of our Orange Bowl game all had an argument for proclaiming themselves national champs.

So when we won the game against LSU, 16–9—for a season record of 12–0—naturally, the creative minds in the postgame press conference produced the creative question: "Who's number one? Who's number one?" I had no idea where we'd come out in the AP and UPI polls of writers and coaches. But I was prepared with a creative answer:

"I just held the Paterno Poll. I did it in our locker room. Our players voted Penn State number one. It was unanimous. That is official."

In fact, based on that official locker-room poll, I soon presented "national championship" rings to our players and coaches.

The unofficial polls—AP and UPI—differed with us. They voted Notre Dame the national champion. Undefeated, untied Penn State came out fifth behind Ohio State, Oklahoma, and Alabama.

Another poll, indisputably official, brought our team a matchless honor. John Cappelletti won the Heisman Trophy, the most valued in the world of college football. He was the first ever to win it for a Pennsylvania school. He also earned the Maxwell Award as the best college player in America. Those trophies made Cappy the grand marshal of a parade of great Penn State running backs that preceded and followed him: Charlie Pittman, Lydell Mitchell, Franco Harris, Lenny Moore, Curt Warner, Matt Suhey, Booker Moore, Jon Williams, D. J. Dozier, Blair Thomas. Mark Markowich, an outstanding blocker on that 1973 team, tells best what made Cappy great: "We knock people down and when they get up, Cappy comes by and knocks them down again."

The high spot of the annual Heisman dinner at the New York Hilton, sponsored by New York's Downtown Athletic Club, should have been the presence of Gerald Ford, an ex–football player who had recently been appointed vice president of the United States. But there was no competing with a drama that surrounded the young man being honored. As a Heisman winner, Cappy was a symbol of toughness, physical superiority, determination to dominate under pressure, all those traditional traits of athleticism and maleness. Yet Cappy brought no false display of machismo, being strong enough to show his vulnerability instead. He began with tributes to his teammates, his parents, and others along his way. Then he said that he wished the award could go to someone in the audience—his eleven-year-old brother, Joey.

"I'd like to dedicate this trophy to the many who have touched my life and helped me"—John's voice now heavy and uneven, choking back tears—"but especially to the youngest member of my family, Joseph, who is very ill. He has leukemia. If I could dedicate it to him tonight and give him a couple of days of happiness, it would mean everything to him. For me, it's a battle on a field, and only in the fall. For Joseph, it's all year round. I think this trophy is more his than it is mine because of the inspiration he has been to me."

My face almost bursting from the pain of restraint, I looked around. The vice president sat there all flushed. His eyes, I thought, glistened. Everybody else in the room was fighting runaway emotion. The master of ceremonies got up and I wondered what he'd say—what I'd say in his spot. All he could get out was:

"John Cappelletti, you're something else."

Bishop Fulton J. Sheen had to say a benediction. I couldn't imagine Bishop Sheen at a loss for words, ever. What he said, on that special moment's notice, was not your average, everyday benediction:

"Maybe for the first time in your lives you have heard a speech from the heart and not from the lips. Part of John's triumph was made by Joseph's sorrow. You don't need a blessing. God has already blessed you in John Cappelletti."

Afterward, we attended a reception in a penthouse of the Hilton. Bill Sullivan, the Patriots' owner, was there. This was almost a year after our aborted negotiation.

"Are you still happy at Penn State?" he asked.

"Do you see now why I couldn't leave?"

He responded, "Yes, I think I do."

At least I had that clue that I'd left Sullivan with no hard feelings.

On April 8, 1976, a little more than two years after that banquet, Joseph Cappelletti died. In 1977, the Cappellettis were the subjects of a TV movie, *Something for Joey.* John went on to a good career with the Los Angeles Rams and the San Diego Chargers, retiring from football in 1985 to go into the construction business in California.

17· License to Hunt

I N 1985, it seemed the whole football world was after a linebacker named Quintus McDonald from Montclair, New Jersey. In the end, we got him. But in getting him I could have lost my hunting license.

Each year the NCAA designates the first day on which a high school player may sign a binding "letter of intent," declaring his choice among colleges offering him a football scholarship. When the 1985 "signing day" arrived, Quintus had not made up his mind. A week later he called Fran Ganter, our offensive coordinator, who had been tracking him on the recruiting trail. Quintus said he was sorry, but he had narrowed his choices to U.S.C. and U.C.L.A. Disappointed, Fran tried to call me with the bad news, but failed to locate me right away. While Fran kept trying, Quintus called him again. The player had now made up his mind—and was coming to Penn State!

To minimize the chances of another mind-change, Fran and I climbed into a car at the first gleam of dawn and headed for the McDonald home more than four hours away. En route, Fran tried to remind me that I couldn't go into the home for the signing. An NCAA rule forbids the presence of a head coach. The rule was designed to protect coaches from the wishes of perhaps a dozen recruits in a dozen far-flung places all wanting to be seen with the coach on television on the same day.

No, no, I told Fran, that rule didn't affect us. It applied only to "signing day," not to a delayed signing like this one. I *knew*, because I had been on the NCAA committee that devised it.

A few days later, a Pennsylvania newspaper reported I had broken the NCAA rule. Certain as I felt that it applied only to "signing day," I was wrong. A head coach may not attend a signing at any time.

I had to endure an official reprimand by the NCAA for that failure of memory.

Another assistant coach, Jim Caldwell, was more successful in saving me from lawlessness—and from possible excommunication. During the 1987 recruiting season, we visited Leroy Thompson and his mother in Knoxville, Tennessee. Leroy lived just a few blocks from the University of Tennessee, which was also competing for him. The house was surrounded by local television reporters with cameras, newscasters with microphones, sportswriters, everybody waiting for Leroy's announcement of his choice. Inside, Leroy said to me, "Hey, Coach, I'm sorry about all those people. Could we go somewhere and talk? I've got a few questions."

"Sure." I turned to Caldwell. "Jim, let me have the keys to the car. Leroy and I are going for a ride."

Caldwell glared down my stupidity. "You can't do that, Coach. You're not allowed to drive him anywhere."

Of course. I'd forgotten.

Then Jim added, "But if Leroy has a car, *he* can drive *you.*"

So we got into Leroy's car and drove off to his dad's house. There, Leroy and I talked. He soon told me he'd decided for Penn State, but before he signed he wanted me to go back to his mom and explain our school and its standards. She wasn't too excited about his leaving Knoxville, where she could regularly watch him play.

The staging of the letter-signing itself has become a kind of legal bonus payment in the eyes of some recruits and their parents. They ask for and expect TV cameras and a press conference in the home. Sometimes, the kid's school wants to benefit from the letter-signing as a media event. In February 1988, St. Thomas High School in Fort Lauderdale, Florida, was so pleased that eleven of its players won football scholarships that it sponsored a mass signing in the school library and feted its eighteen-year-old athletes like Hollywood stars.

What the recruit usually doesn't know is that when the party's over he is only six months away from the cold-water shower of discovering that he's just another freshman player and that he still has to make the team. Moreover, if he's signed with an honest school, he also has to make it in the classroom.

When I had entered coaching "temporarily" at Penn State, big-time recruiting rules were different and fewer. And I wasn't always up on the last detail of them either. Earl Bruce, our freshman coach, broke me in as we spent weeks together searching for talent through the hills and coal-mining towns of western Pennsylvania, where he knew almost every high school coach because he had once been one of them. Sometimes, Bruce and I drove a kid around for hours tickling his ears with great football stories. We'd do that not to impress the kid, but because we heard a competing coach was in town looking for the recruit and we didn't want any rivals to get their hands on him.

Many of today's NCAA rules on recruiting are uselessly handcuffing, downright stupid, and just about beg some coaches to cheat. Yet, having said that, I think most new rules are better—at least, no worse—than the freewheeling ways of recruiting in the old days.

One example of the old ways: In one of those early years I was hot after two stars of North Catholic High School in Pittsburgh, Matt Szykowny, their quarterback, and Dick Turici, a fullback. At least a dozen other schools were after them, too. One day, North Catholic's coach confided in me, "I think Matt is leaning toward Penn State." He could not have sung me a sweeter song, because Szykowny was a plum. The coach then added with a significant whisper, "Now, the senior prom is coming up, and if you could get somebody to lend him a car, that would really clinch it for you."

I called a Penn State alumnus who owned a Dodge agency nearby and explained the possible advantages to his alma mater if he could lend Szykowny and Turici a car for the prom.

"Sure," the dealer replied enthusiastically. "I've got a fancy convertible for them."

I was sure the glittering car would bag Szykowny, maybe both.

First thing I knew, both kids signed with Iowa.

One night soon after, I bumped into a good friend and rival, Vic Fusia, a smooth talker and tough recruiting adversary on the coaching staff of Pitt who covered the same territory I did. While Vic and I often competed for the same prospects, we had already entered our partnership in searching out the best Italian restaurants in every western Pennsylvania town we covered. Over a bowl of spaghetti, Szykowny's name and his defection to Iowa came up.

"Yeah, I thought we had him," Vic muttered sadly.

"You thought *you* had him? I even got him a car to use for senior prom."

"I was ahead of you," said Vic. "You know where he took that car after the prom? Those two kids took their dates to the nightclub at Holiday House. I'd already fixed it with the manager to send me the bill."

We all know that now, as then, a few coaches look the other way while alumni and boosters provide players with cars and cash support, including payment of rent, or they permit grades to be falsified, or they violate NCAA rules in other ways to give themselves a recruiting advantage. Yet nobody can prove much, and coaches are rarely inclined to accuse others in public. A research team at the University of Cincinnati surveyed coaches in 1987 on the subject of cheating, and they came up with good news and bad news.

About 75 percent of coaches, they found, "believe their colleagues are honest, have high ethical standards and want to run clean programs." Despite their tendency to be clean and sportsmanlike, probably one third of big-time football (Division I) schools, according to the coaches polled, regularly violate NCAA football regulations. Why the contradiction? More than two thirds of coaches said the main cause of cheating is pressure on them to win.

When a school cheats, those surveyed said, it's rarely without the knowledge and endorsement of the coach. He can put a stop to it any time he wants. All he has to do is lay down the law to his assistant coaches, who are usually the bagmen in the recruiting and special-treatment rackets; he has to insulate a wall between his staff and recruits on the one hand and boosters and alumni on the other. Coaches themselves have to stop fawning over green teenagers with promises and lies about their becoming starters while still freshman, about how the kid will become an instant superstar by hoisting the team into a national championship. Coaches of that type talk about college as one big football camp, yet promise—especially to parents— that the kid will somehow come out the other end with a degree and a valuable education. All this would, until recently, be dressed up before signing time by good food and good drink in the best restaurant in town for Mom and Dad as well as the kid. (That kind of restaurant wining and dining is now outlawed.)

A recruit is limited to visiting only five colleges at college expense. Some kids have already decided, of course, which they're going to pick, yet may still make all the visits just for the thrill and ego kick of the travel, entertainment, and the meetings with famous coaches and college players.

The purpose of NCAA rules is to establish a level playing field for all schools. But in my book the obligation to play fair and square is owed not only to other schools. More than to anyone else it's owed to the kid.

A school doesn't have to cheat to be good at football. Honest schools turn out winning teams and conference championships year after year. For every recruit bought off (and miseducated) by a coach's lies, there's at least one other who is repelled by dishonesty and who wants the promise that his school will be serious about his education.

A few years ago, a coach visiting from the Southwest told me that down his way there were established starting prices for talking with recruits, and perhaps with their high school coaches, like minimum bids in an auction. In Texas particularly, he said, you didn't bother approaching a running back unless you knew the starting price and were prepared to outbid other schools.

Sleazy as all that sounds, it does not describe the general condition of college football, although dishonesty exists and often accomplishes its goals. As that Cincinnati survey showed, the majority of coaches are honest with their kids; most kids expect honesty from schools and get it.

In fact, in the very places where scandals have become most visible, we're starting to see strong, convincing acts of leadership to clean up the picture of college sports. In most places when we talk about "legal" and "illegal" recruiting and fair-play practices, we mean that someone is observing or violating NCAA regulations. Those rules usually have no direct connection with actual law. They are a code of behavior adopted and self-policed by member colleges and universities, and are not normally adjudicated by the courts. But recently, after some disgraceful violations that soured many fans and alumni as well as heaping embarrassment on the administrations of leading schools, the state of Texas enacted a *law* prohibiting gifts and payoffs to college athletes by schools, alumni, boosters, or whomever. There's no other law like it elsewhere in the country—although we'll surely see it duplicated in college athletics if we don't clean up our own act. The new Texas law calls for a $5,000 fine and up to a year in prison for violators—and the student is culpable as well as the gift-giver and fixer. Perhaps the most poetic part is that it was signed into law by Governor Bill Clements—the same man who chaired the board of trustees and did not exactly wring his hands in shock and remorse, at least in public, when Southern Methodist University was caught in flagrant violations and was given the NCAA "death penalty."

Our ways at Penn State are plain, maybe boring, compared to some of the exotic recruiting methods used elsewhere, but they work for us, season after season.

During January and February, our assistant coaches and I hit the road, coordinated by John Bove, whose full-time domain is recruiting for football and other sports. It is our hardest-working time of the year outside of the playing season itself. As recruiters, the assistants geographically divide the entire East, down to Florida. I follow later, talk to prime prospects, their high school coaches, and parents.

When we want a kid and think he might want us, we invite him and his parents to visit the Penn State campus for a weekend. That puts Sue almost in the tour guide and restaurant business. Most arrive Saturday morning, the distant ones Friday night. We put up parents as our guests at the Nittany Lion Inn, a famous and cozy hotel owned by the university. The player himself stays in a regular dorm with one of our players so he can get a firsthand look at student life at Penn State. Some schools don't think that's important, a good idea, or flattering enough. They prefer to dazzle the kid with his own importance in a swanky hotel room. That works very well for them—and for us. The two ways help separate our kind of kid from theirs. If we can, we choose as his player-host someone from the recruit's city or region, best of all, from his own high school or a school his plays against. We want the kid to experience what real life at Penn State would be like for him, and we want him to ask questions of someone he might be able to trust, perhaps even already know.

No, we do not arrange dorm parties or dates for the prospect. Some schools do. Maybe we lose a recruit or two for that negligence, but I know it helps us pick up a recruit or two or more. Parents tell us so.

If the parents and kid come Friday night, they and their player-host are taken to dinner by the coach who scouted his region. On Saturday morning, after that same group gathers for breakfast, the family visits Don Ferrell, the team's academic adviser, then goes to see an academic adviser from the college of the university or the department the prospect is most likely to major in. This adviser will explain what's academically required of a student and how he can expect it to fit with his football practice. After lunch, they tour the campus and the academic counselor describes a typical program in more detail. If the family is visiting us as early as December and if we're preparing for a bowl game, the recruit and his father watch our Saturday afternoon practice. In January and February, they'll visit our weight room and get demonstrations of our up-to-date equipment.

Meanwhile, Sue and the wife of one of the assistant coaches—often Jim Williams's wife, Betsy, because they have no young children that require them to arrange baby sitters—take all the mothers to our art museum, the bookstore, and our famous Creamery that sells Penn State homemade ice cream. Some of our experienced old-timers feel it is the best ice cream in the entire world, especially a flavor recently named Peachy Paterno. We're allowed to treat the parents to ice cream, because that's food, but not to a Penn State T-shirt in the bookstore, because that would be influence. Sue used to take the mothers downtown to shop, but no longer. A new NCAA rule says that we can't drive these visitors anywhere except on campus.

On Saturday night, after dinner at the Nittany Lion Inn, the kids go to an athletic event, while the parents gather at my house for informal talk and more food, catered by Sue. Everybody delights in the goodies—except, maybe, the coaches and their wives, who every week pass the same trays of the same surprises: Sue's famous small rolls with hot Italian ham and salami and mozzarella and lettuce and tomato and purple onion and cheeses and chopped vegetables and dips and nuts. Throughout that evening, the kids and parents get to know something about us and, equally important, we get to know something about them. If the kid will not fit in, it usually shows before the evening is over. If we don't like the parents, we get leery about the kid because he is not likely to turn out much different. One unforgettable dad kept trailing me around the veggie trays all evening telling me how super his kid was. The kid went to Maryland, pleasing both us and them, I guess. One family kept jabbing us about wanting flying lessons for their kid—paid for by the university as part of his education—so neat and novel an idea that maybe the NCAA had no rule forbidding it. We didn't go for the idea or the parents or the kid. Another kept telling us they got a speeding ticket on the way to the university and were sure a guy as influential as Joe Paterno could fix it. I told them sympathetically that I got one myself on the way home from visiting *their* high school and that I'd just paid it on Friday. Still another, having promised their kid a car for high school graduation, kept slyly asking where we could get a deal for them. I told them we don't work on deals, we coach football.

People who start off their relationship with us that way usually don't hear from us again. They're giving us a clear message that their kid is likely to be full of "I" and "me," not "we" and "us." Football games are won by what players put into them, not by what they get out of them.

Sometimes my toughest moments are not with those parents but with my wife. I once whispered to Sue, "Really work on that mother, because we really want her kid."

Sue gave me her meltdown look. "In my eyes, every woman here is equal. She's a mother. I don't want to know who the great players are, and I don't want you ever again to tell me to do that."

Actually, when we decide that someone won't fit our style, we usually don't have to do a thing about it. By the time the weekend's over, the kid, who has spent a lot of time with his host player and others, knows that we're not his style either. The communication works both ways, and generally the kid will back off.

18· Throwing the Book

For almost every rule about what we can't do in recruiting, there are another two or three that tell us what we can't do with the squad itself. Most rules address real abuses by unethical coaches and willing schools. But especially in the rule book for dealing with squad members, some rules deserve trophies for causing more problems than they solve.

Over the years, the fat book of NCAA rules has built by patchwork while the world has changed, including the world of athletics. Division I-A football is big business with big box office, big television, big advertising sponsors, and big pro football that has learned to use the American system of higher education as its farm system. The rules are not only patchwork, but a crazy quilt. Carl Lewis, a great track man, became a millionaire while remaining an amateur. All kinds of endorsement money was dumped on him, and all legal as long as the money was paid to a trust fund instead of directly to Lewis. That's legal in track, but not in football. Don't ask me why. A kid can sign a professional baseball contract for a bonus of, say, $150,000. That ends his amateur status—in baseball. Suppose he then decides he prefers a football career. He's still an amateur in football.

A football player is absolutely forbidden from contact with an agent before his college playing days are ended. Why? And why only football players? Why is it so terrible for a kid to talk with or even choose an agent who, within weeks, will negotiate for him with pro teams? I think all parties, including the kid, would be better off if we rethought the timing for freeing the player to talk or sign with an agent during his college career. Also, if he should jump the gun he ought to have a grace period before his signature ends his playing eligibility. That breather would protect him against the plight of Herschel Walker, who, as a Georgia all-American, signed with an agent and accepted a handsome chunk of money. Then he woke up the next morning and said, "I think I did the wrong thing." In most states, even an ordinary consumer buying a vacuum cleaner on time is protected by a grace period.

I'm not minimizing the need to control the access of agents to college players. Money is involved, and these kids are usually naïve about business deals. In competing among themselves to sign players who are likely to be named in early rounds of the NFL draft, it's no surprise that some crooked agents offer money, sometimes dazzling amounts, to players for signing secretly before their eligibility expires. During his senior year, our own all-American wide receiver, Kenny Jackson, had to keep changing his phone number to avoid contact with agents.

An honest and smart coach could have an easy way to protect his kids from the unwanted "advice" of agents—if only the NCAA would let him. All he'd have to do is offer sounder advice—for free. Or the advice could come from somebody more qualified than a coach. A few years ago, Bob Mitinger, a State College attorney who had been a Penn State all-American end in the 1960s, volunteered to give some of our players free advice on launching their pro football careers. A perfect adviser—except I couldn't let him do it. The NCAA rule says we are not allowed to do for an athlete what we don't do for a nonathlete. Fair as that may look on the surface, it isn't. To "equalize" opportunity, was the university to set up a legal assistance agency for tens of thousands of students? Or simply offer every nonathlete advice on how to dicker with the National Football League!

After several years of that silliness, the NCAA finally permitted a panel of three faculty members to advise players about agents. Not a bad compromise. We jumped right in and formed such a panel, although, I'm sorry to say, not many other schools did. Our panel consisted of two lawyers and a psychologist, all in their thirties, so that our kids could identify with them. The sooner we allow honest agents to operate directly and openly within reasonable time limits, the sooner we'll get rid of the hustlers, smooth talkers, and leeches who now have a natural environment in the impractical rules of the NCAA.

If rules governing agents are important, on some other subjects they are downright petty and silly. I mentioned earlier that Sue tutors a small number of players who need an academic boost, usually in their freshman year, until they get steady footing. Some days she wishes she could hold some of these sessions in our own home and get other volunteers to hold them in theirs. But she can't. Why? Because Sue is constitutionally unable (and I think I'd be) to have a visitor at home without offering at least a cup of coffee or a cola. And that would be illegal. So she meets them on campus.

I don't blame the people who voted that rule. We should be grateful, I guess, that NCAA member colleges are that earnest about keeping their skirts clean. But I do heap blame on the minority of win-at-any-cost boards of trustees, athletic directors, and coaches who brought this down on us all—rule flouters like one of the highest paid, reportedly, who quit in a siege of scandal in 1988. There's something out of whack when the guillotine can fall on an honest football school because of a chocolate chip cookie.

Where would I draw the line? Big corporations concerned about gifts that might influence their employees set reasonable limits. If a gift is worth $25 or more, says one rule, refuse it. Another common company rule that might suit us better: If you can't eat it on the spot, it's not acceptable. We can accomplish our goals without being silly.

Rules about giving or lending cars to players, or any disguise

of such a favor, are obviously essential. But I recall one applica-
tion that was more absurd than the time I couldn't drive Leroy
Thompson in my car although he could drive me in his. During
preseason practice in 1968, Dennis Onkotz, our all-American
linebacker, called me one night, panicked:

"My wife's in Northampton having our baby—right *now*.
What do I do? I've *got* to get there."

"Take my car," I said.

In minutes, he sprinted to my door for the keys—and was
off.

Today, under the new rules, I couldn't do that. If his mother
were dying, I couldn't do that. That is a thoughtless, stupid
rule, and I'm telling the NCAA right now: If that kind of
genuine emergency happens again, I'm not going to stand
there and read a frantic kid the rules. I'm going to hand him
my keys.

Far more important than restrictions on cars is the way
NCAA rules systematically insure that broke kids stay broke—
if they're football players. We encourage whole universities to
worship them as stars. Then we embarrass them so mercilessly,
the weaker characters among them go out and break laws. I'm
no softheaded excuse maker for kids who do wrong, but time
and again I've seen good kids break under the money stress we
put on them.

A couple of years ago, one of our kids from an impoverished
inner-city home was taking a taunting from some smart aleck
in town, which players endure a lot. After a while, fist made
contact with mouth, and the taunter had a couple fewer teeth
than when he started. The scrap hit the local papers, it being
almost impossible to keep football players out of the news when
they do something the slightest bit irregular. The injured fellow agreed not to press charges if my player agreed to pay the
dental bill. My player, scared that he might get into trouble
with the team and me, paid the bill promptly—but with a bum
check.

If I had known how broke and stressed he was, I'd have

found a way, preferably legal, to get him a loan. I'd do that with any kid, football player or not. Where was this kid, whose dad was dead, to go for five hundred bucks? So he "postponed" a problem he saw no way to solve. Bad check. Headlines.

Those are my toughest moments with the rules. A kid comes in with a true emergency. Maybe somebody at home died. He says, "I need twenty bucks for a bus ticket." I'm not allowed to give him twenty bucks. I can't even *lend* him twenty bucks. It is absolutely, expressly forbidden by the NCAA rules.

Even if varsity football players could find time to work for their spending money, which they can't, players are *forbidden* by NCAA rules to work while going to school. The reasons are drawn from history, soundly enough. Some well-meaning alumnus (like the benefactor who put me through Brown) will hire a football player at, say, twice or three times a usual student wage, disguising a form of illegal payment for athletes.

Twenty years ago, we were allowed by NCAA rules to pay a student "laundry money." That meant reserving a small piece of a kid's scholarship, usually about $15 a month, to pay him in cash for spending money, making up in small part for the job he's not allowed to hold. I feel strongly—and I urge strongly—that that kind of cash allowance be restored, and I don't care whether we call it "laundry money," or "pizza money," or "walking around money," or, if professors like it better, an "honorarium." All I want to do is see to it that a kid, especially a poor kid, is able to go to McDonald's (where he's not allowed to work) and buy a hamburger when the other kids go. This athlete, sought out socially by others, is proud. He's also young, insecure, and sensitive. Something tears inside him when he has to make excuses for not going, the real, unspeakable reason being he hasn't got the buck and a half. He ought to be able, maybe once in a whole year, to buy a nice hundred-dollar sport coat and ask the salesman, "Can I pay you in four monthly payments?" These kids are not always as strong in mind as they are in body. When we ask so much of them in discipline, in setting an example, in study, in self-improvement, I don't want to help drive a borderline kid over the edge into cashing a bad check or borrowing from a roommate what he can't pay back. Sixty dollars a month could greatly ease that most painful of pressures on our most talented, and sometimes poorest, of kids. I can't think of any way we could buy more fairness and justice at less cost.

Some people say, of course, that if you allow a player $60 a month, some schools and coaches are sure to cheat, finding a way to slip the kid $120, $200, $300 a month. Of course. The cheaters are doing that now, and they'll continue to do it until the threat of getting caught—and the penalties—force everybody to take the rules seriously.

Sure, some athletic directors wince at adding $60–75,000, say, for football and basketball to their tight budgets. They want to go the other way: stretch the kids' season by one game so they can generate a half million *more*, not less. A growing group wants to schedule twelve games a season for Division I teams. Their interest, of course, is simply the revenue. Besides the extra profit at the gate, another game gives them one more shot at television, which can double that profit. That's a sizable attraction for any athletic budget when, as at Penn State, football may support all sports across the board.

Ironically, when someone proposes, as I do, that we choose a national championship team by playoff, these athletic directors and coaches may be the first to holler, "No, a playoff makes the season too long." Actually, some college students already play twelve games. There's now a "preseason" Hall of Fame game, and other promoters may try to imitate its success. If a team is chosen for that as well as for a postseason bowl game, it has to play a 13-game schedule. Thirty teams in Division I-A now play bowl games. So if twelve games were to become a general rule, a team in a preseason and postseason bowl would play fourteen. Compare that against my last playing year at

Brown when we played nine games, everybody's standard season.

The football player doesn't object to subsidizing volleyball, fencing, and repainting the swimming pool. He understands how he's used, even exploited. He may even sympathize with the needs of nonrevenue sports. The main reason he plays football is because he loves playing football, loves the cheers of the crowds, and he doesn't think much about where the money goes. But he does care about—and resents—the humiliations of being broke.

The NCAA, which has 960 member schools, enjoys reminding those members that it is *our* organization, representing *us*. If that's the case, how come 105 Division I-A football schools can't legislate their own division's financial affairs?

While technically governed between conventions by a council of forty-six members, the day-to-day interpretations of imprecise rules are made by jobholders appointed by the executive director who continue in their jobs at his pleasure.

Its first full-time director, Walter Byers, took over in 1951 and stayed until 1987. During that time the NCAA grew into a complex and powerful organization. Byers was a great leader whose ability is best measured by the totality of control the NCAA acquired over college sports. He became so powerful that no member school of the NCAA knew what his salary was at the time Byers retired. In 1983, one report said he was paid $78,450, not an exorbitant sum for such a job, although it was said to be sweetened by $200,000 in annuities, pensions, and deferred compensation, an additional $10,000 a year after his retirement, as well as some noninterest loans he received from NCAA. His influence did not end with retirement. The heads of the four major departments, who had to approve his successor, were all appointed—not elected—under the Byers administration.

A search committee asked if I wanted to be considered a candidate to succeed Byers. I chose to continue as Penn State coach, and I don't mind saying that I preferred a role in the NCAA of an elder statesman, one that seemed to be shaping. The committee later made an excellent choice in Dick Schultz, the University of Virginia athletic director, who took over in October 1987. Now nobody knows what *his* salary is. Unimaginable as it may seem in this day and age, the members, who supposedly own the organization, never see a budget.

While Byers brought growth and prosperity to college football and basketball through multimillion-dollar television and radio contracts, he also presided over the proliferation of rules so that we have rules that explain rules, unenforceable rules, and impractical rules. If someone calls NCAA headquarters in Mission, Kansas, and asks three officials for interpretation of a single rule with a single set of facts, at times he'll get three different answers. If the NCAA can't do better than that with its own rules, how did Walter Byers expect us dumb football coaches to understand them?

This year's NCAA handbook has 311 white pages of rules and another 128 pages of blue pages giving case illustrations because nobody fully understands the first 311 pages. In addition to that, we get a weekly NCAA newspaper with a whole section to update interpretations.

That simply has to be cleaned up. The only way to do it that makes any sense is to have a constitutional convention and start from scratch with the most fundamental questions: What is a student athlete? What is an amateur?

One problem that most schools had with NCAA rules from the beginning was that all member schools could vote on all issues affecting all schools. That sounds democratic, but it was the opposite. What was the sense of letting Pace College of New York City help decide athletic issues affecting big-time football and basketball schools like Penn State, Michigan, and Notre Dame? That finally changed in 1973, when NCAA members divided themselves into three groups. Large schools with major athletic programs became Division I.

This was bound to lead to a forum where those high-stakes

schools could discuss their own problems. In October 1975, a group of twenty-five schools from seven major conferences and most of the major independents got together, among them Ed Czekaj, Penn State's athletic director, the Reverend Edmund P. Joyce of Notre Dame, and Chuck Neinas, commissioner of the Big Eight conference. Out of their meeting grew the College Football Association (CFA). It included all the major independents and conferences—except the Big Ten and the Pacific Ten.

The Big Ten's self-exclusion, I don't doubt, had more to do with personality clashes than anything else. Wayne Duke, commissioner of the Big Ten, and Chuck Neinas, once close friends, were in each other's doghouses. That led to widespread distortion of positions, distrust, and misunderstanding. Big Ten people seemed convinced that the rest of us wanted to bolt the NCAA, take over college football and push for unlimited numbers of scholarships, for lower academic minima for athletes, and larger coaching staffs. No matter how we renounced those goals, they didn't seem to believe us.

What attracted me most was that the CFA formed a coaches committee. Previously we'd had an American Football Coaches Association. I had been a trustee for a while but resigned because I found it a waste of time. We sat around at meetings and shot the bull, but avoided decisions and certainly avoided action. When Charlie McClendon became director of the AFCA, that changed. We now have a dynamic organization, fighting especially to strengthen the security of coaches.

A prime issue we should have addressed—but didn't—was protecting coaches from getting fired capriciously. In the late 1960s, Maryland fired its coach, Bob Ward, on the preposterous ground that his players thought he was too tough on them. I wrote to Paul Dietzel, then president of the AFCA, asking for an investigation, which did not take place. "I don't think it's a good thing," my letter said, "for a college football squad to fire a coach . . . If a university fired an English professor because his class didn't like the way he was doing things, I know darn well that the American Association of University Professors would want to know what happened." Later I testified in court to support Joe Yukica, a Penn State player when I arrived in 1950, who was fired as Dartmouth coach by a new athletic director in 1985. Joe sued to keep his job for the remaining year of his contract—and won.

I was appointed chairman of that new CFA coaches committee. For our opening meeting, thirty-five or forty of us powwowed in a room for a day and a half and changed the whole atmosphere of recruiting. Exactly contrary to Big Ten rumors of what we wanted, we shortened the permissible recruiting period, limited the number of days we could watch a kid play, proposed higher eligibility and academic standards, and required players to meet the same standards for graduating as other students. The big irony is that football coaches came up with those recommendations, not the faculty reps to the NCAA. In fact, the CFA general membership thought our eligibility standards were too tough—because the faculty reps said they were unrealistic.

Why do so many schools abuse the academic welfare of their athletes? It's not just the doings of unethical coaches. Much of it lies at the feet of weak faculties who have been unwilling to stand up to their responsibility as teachers, as protectors of the educational mission of their universities.

When a school recruits students solely because they can help the football team win games, regardless of the students' academic abilities, the college football coach has become, in effect, an admissions officer. Or, put another way, the school has forsaken its education role and entered the sports entertainment business (but, while collecting huge grosses at the gate, exploits its players by not paying them).

Some of the most important decisions about the conduct of athletics are academic decisions. At Penn State, a committee of the faculty senate sets the standards for admission of athletes. A senate committee also sets standards of continuing eligibility and establishes the number of class hours that team members may miss for "away" games. That committee also must approve trips to postseason bowls. The faculty member teaching a course has complete autonomy in grading students—including athletes. (Nobody on our football staff may approach a teacher asking to "go easy" on a player's grade.) A few zealous alumni sometimes squawk at these limitations on the football team's "freedom." They forget that the first mission of a university is the education of its students.

Strong, entrenched organizations are usually not very good at reforming themselves, and the NCAA is not likely to be an exception. But there's an offshoot of NCAA that can do it. The presidents of NCAA schools recently formed a forty-four-member Presidents Commission, which can, if it wants to, become the most powerful instrument for correcting the wrongs in college sports. The Presidents Commission is empowered to review any activity of the NCAA. It can order a study of any matter relating to intercollegiate athletics and propose follow-up action. It can place any issue on the agenda of an NCAA Council meeting or at its annual convention. It can call a special convention of the NCAA, as it did in June 1987, and it can propose legislation.

The presidents have already helped produce dramatic progress by their support of the "death penalty" for habitual rules violators and of Proposition 48, setting minimum academic qualifications for athletic scholarships.

One major reform I would urge the Presidents Commission to support would be to end eligibility of freshmen for varsity football. I know that I'm in a relatively small minority in urging that, but I think it's wrong to allow a seventeen- or eighteen-year-old kid to check into college and immediately get swallowed up by the kind of football played at Division I-A schools.

At some schools, a freshman plays his first game before he attends his first class. He's surrounded so immediately by athletes and gets immersed so fast in a training schedule, he has almost no chance to form friendships with other students, particularly in a school where he is segregated in an athletic dorm. At Penn State, we try to compensate for the freshman's culture shock by putting him through mandatory seminars, hoping they'll teach him in a hurry what he really needs a full year of actual experience to learn right. We try to help him understand his responsibility to the team and to himself to present a healthy image to other students who watch him. We make him aware that a player may get lots of strokes for what he does on a playing field, but that nobody's likely to ask how he's doing in his studies, his adjustment to a strange campus, whether he's homesick, or how he's doing in taking charge of time and personal decisions. We instruct the freshman about the pressures of competition and how to handle the press, about the dangers of drugs, and the techniques of just saying no without embarrassment.

As part of my preferred no-freshmen rule, I'd support having freshman teams that were scheduled against similar teams from other schools for three or four games a year. They'd be limited to practicing only three days a week and would not attend daily squad meetings.

Some coaches argue that if freshmen are crossed off the roster, a school would have to offer more scholarships to keep its team up to snuff. That's baloney. If everybody has a limit of ninety-five scholarships, and everybody has twenty-five for freshmen who are not permitted to play, then everybody plays with seventy scholarship players. Is seventy not enough? Then neither is ninety-five. And if we were allowed two hundred, that wouldn't be enough. Anyhow, if we had to limit scholarships to the very best players, we'd probably have more walk-ons—unrecruited, nonscholarship players—from the general student body.

In the hope of getting a majority of Division I coaches to agree on some kind of plan to eliminate freshman eligibility, I have proposed this as a practical compromise:

1. Expand our present limit of ninety-five scholarships to one hundred.
2. Then, in the first year after that change, only eight freshmen may play; second year, six freshmen; third year, four; fourth year, only two. Finally, in the fifth year and thereafter, no freshmen would play varsity football.

In considering that compromise, or any other proposal on this issue, we should never lose sight of the source of this controversy:

Why were NCAA rules designed to let freshmen play in the first place? So we could "get our money's worth" out of those scholarships by squeezing four years of playing time out of a kid, further exploiting him for the sake of the school, not for the good of the young athlete himself.

19· Sons, Daughters, and Parents

As far back as our first undefeated season, 1968, I found I could no longer relate normally to my own children. Our own fans made it impossible, although they didn't mean to.

When they were small, I took the kids swimming one day at Penn State's huge pool. They'd climb on my shoulders so I could flip them over and dunk them. After my face started becoming a bad habit on the local sports pages, sometimes on page one, other kids began coming over for their turn at being flipped. One day, I realized I couldn't show my face without attracting a crowd. My kids had to push and shove just to get near me. Some days, they felt like they'd lost their father. One day, I took the family to Hershey Park, about a hundred miles from home, and suddenly we were surrounded. Little Jay pouted to his mother, "*We* brought Daddy. *They* didn't." I sent the family off to enjoy the rides and the chocolate treats, while I slipped through the parking lot and hid in my car for the rest of the day, playing with *x*'s and *o*'s on a yellow pad. Our kids felt robbed.

One summer, we all went to the beach for a few days. I'd learned by then to spend afternoons in the motel with my *x*'s and *o*'s. At the beach, Sue made acquaintances, and they asked, "Why doesn't your husband come down?"

She said, "He has some work to finish."

"What's he do?"

"He does things on paper."

They only knew her as Sue, never asking her last name.

Diana became a cheerleader at State College High. The Little Lions, as we call their football team, played Friday nights, so I eagerly grabbed the opportunity once to see her cheerlead. People kept coming over to yell, "Hi, Joe-pa" and stick programs at me for an autograph. I don't mind signing, but it distracted from the cheerleaders and from the game itself. To her combined disappointment and relief, I never tried going again, except one night when Jay was playing. Sue and I sat almost in the end zone, where hardly anyone sits. People kept coming over, so I left and walked home, leaving the car for Sue. I never was able to go see my second daughter, Mary Kay, compete as a gymnast. When Scotty, our youngest, played ice hockey a couple of years ago, I decided that not many people watch pee-wee hockey. But they came anyhow, out of the walls and the ice, wanting autographs. I'd say, "Can you wait till the time-out? I'm watching my son play." They'd say, "Just one, just one." I left, so Scotty and his teammates could feel it was their game.

The first couple of months of the year, those disappointments especially bothered the kids because I'd be away for days at a time, recruiting. When I was away, Sue tied a string on the bed of the youngest of the kids, whoever that was at the time, to hold a number of thick wooden beads. For a five-day trip, five beads. More precisely, as the kids would say it, five beads meant five "sleeps." Each night, they could slide a bead to the other end of the string; only one left, Daddy would be home tomorrow. David tried to shortcut this system. He'd ask Sue at nap time, "Can I put a bead down for the nap?" Sue had to stand firm: "No, only dark sleeps."

One night, after a long recruiting trip, Sue fed the kids early and the two of us went for a quiet dinner at The Tavern (remember, the cozy restaurant I couldn't afford in the early days). Three or four autographs, not too bad, and I settled down to telling Sue about an interesting town on this trip, Walla Walla, Washington. A lady at the next table had a relative there, which gave her a license to join freely into our conversation like a member of the family. I mumbled to Sue, "We might as well eat at home," and the first moment we gracefully could, we left.

One night, at a basketball game where I was waiting to present an award, I stood up and walked in front of the spectators, and an ovation swept through the crowd. But I was only heading for the men's room.

In 1976, toward the end of the season, the office began receiving phone calls threatening harm to Sue and the kids. That was the exact word the caller kept using: "harm." Nothing more specific.

Then the widowed mother of Chuck Fusina, our quarterback, began getting calls. Finally, Chuck himself, a couple of other players, and a couple of the coaches. I saw no reason to upset Sue, so I didn't tell her. Then threatening letters appeared in the mail. The FBI welcomed those because they provided better leads than phone calls, maybe to a disgruntled player or ex-player. They found no clues, however.

Meanwhile, Sue began getting the calls at home and said nothing, because she saw no purpose in upsetting me. Instead, she developed terrible headaches. One of them lasted a month. (She still gets one today when she talks about that time.) Sue started driving Diana and Mary Kay to their piano lessons, something she'd not usually done, which tipped me off that something was going on. Then one night, as we watched the TV news, she couldn't hold it in anymore and told me about the calls. That was four days before the Pitt game, always a tense time. An especially realistic dark hint in the messages both at home and at the office was that we had darn well better not interfere with Pitt winning that game. Even more bothersome, the newscaster kept reminding us that that night was the anniversary of John F. Kennedy's assassination.

Covering over my own tension, I tried to assure Sue that the threats were just a bunch of words, nothing to worry about.

"They *do* kill people, you know," Sue almost screamed. Then she began to cry.

"Tell me all of what's going on."

"I can't." Then, a little piece at a time, she did. And, a piece at a time, I told her what I knew.

Whenever we played at Pitt, Sue took the kids and stayed at her parents' house at Latrobe, not far from Pittsburgh. She said she wanted to break that routine this time, in case the culprit knew what to expect. Sue called her parents to suggest that the kids stay at her aunt's home during the game, which was scheduled at night for television. Her father, nervous about that idea, said he'd hire a private detective, in addition to the usual sitter, to guard the house and five acres.

The detective was introduced to the kids as a cousin they'd never met named "Rex." Four-year-old Scotty climbed into Rex's lap for the game. He felt the guard's shoulder holster and asked, "What's that bump?" Rex, apparently unflustered, said, "I have a broken bone." Exactly the right answer for Scotty. "Oh, my dad has one of those, too," he boasted to Rex. Scotty had always admired my bumpy rib, broken at Brown.

Sue's day was a nerve-racker. She had to attend a luncheon in downtown Pittsburgh, then a gathering in a private club at Three Rivers Stadium, where the game was to be played. There she was to meet Helen Fusina, Chuck's mother, and another group of important alums, all the time shadowed by an FBI man and surrounded by uniformed Pinkerton guards who came close to interfering with her going to the powder room. At the game, two guys in front of Sue kept turning around, scoping her suspiciously. She kept wondering if they were FBI men or murderers.

During the second half, I wished she wouldn't notice, but she did, and it made her more nervous: The FBI, or somebody, insisted when we went out after halftime, that I stay put at the fifty-yard line, which was worse than paralysis. What I didn't know till later was that they ordered the biggest guys on the team to stand close around me. The players were not told why. Early in the game, three calls had come to the stadium office threatening me, one specifying that if I appeared on the field in the second half, I'd be shot. All during that half, says Sue, she prayed, "Dear God, I hope we don't win." (Sue's prayers are notoriously effective; we lost.)

The final hurt was that after the loss, when we needed a morale boost, a gorgeous cake arrived in the locker room— without a card. The FBI stole the cake right from under our noses and brought it to their lab.

The calls and letters stopped as soon as that game did. About two weeks later, my office received a letter apologizing—ha!— for "any inconvenience caused" us by the previous correspondence. Like all the others, unsigned. For the next two or three years, the threats resumed, each year as anticipation built for the Pitt game, then suddenly halted after that game. In 1977, the barrage included an ugly letter to my son Dave, who had just had a serious accident, saying he'd been lucky this time, but wouldn't be the next. In 1978, Sue got two calls at home saying, "Mr. Pohland is dead." That's her father's name, and he's still vigorously alive.

After that, the threats disappeared into the black hole they'd come from.

In midseason of 1977, the day before our sixth game, against Syracuse, my life was jarred into a perspective of what counts and what doesn't.

Usually by midseason, the pressure so envelops the players, coaches, and me that we lose awareness of the rest of the universe. The name of each day of the week only marks where we are in the week's practice, and how many days to the next game.

Sue had left for Syracuse with four or five wives of the

coaching staff. For games a few hours away, they'd often leave a day ahead in a van and make an outing of it with a fun dinner. I took our youngest, Scott, to lunch in a downtown restaurant. When we returned home, the phone was ringing, a call from Our Lady of Victory School in State College, where our two older boys were students. Dave, our eleven-year-old, the voice told me, had had an accident and that I should come to the school right away. Without asking questions, I grabbed Scotty and shot over there, perhaps two miles from home.

Dave was lying, as though lifeless, on the concrete floor of the school's gym-auditorium-lunchroom. They told me he had been asked to remove some audio-visual equipment from the stage. Dave and two classmates couldn't resist fooling around with a trampoline on the stage before returning to their classroom. On one of his high bounces, Dave lost his balance, flew through the split in the stage curtain, and landed on his head on the floor far below. He was now lying about fifteen feet from the stage, unconscious.

An ambulance was already there. I rode it with Dave to Centre Community Hospital, where Dr. Bill Grasley, by coincidence our former team physician, was on duty in the emergency room. He ordered some X rays, took a quick look at them, and said, "Joe, make a choice. We have to get him either to Hershey or Geisinger." Those are two large, up-to-date hospitals—each about a hundred miles from State College.

"Geisinger," I said. That gave me options because it was directly on the way to Syracuse. The state police could locate Sue on the road and get her back to Geisinger. Again, I climbed into the ambulance to ride with Dave, who was still unconscious. It was the longest ride of my life. Every mile, I concentrated on prayers, simply begging God to keep my son alive.

At Geisinger, Dr. Henry Hood, a neurosurgeon, was waiting for us. All night and almost around the clock, Dr. Hood monitored Dave.

Dave was to lie in a coma for the next seven days. The pictures and tests showed he had suffered a fractured skull. One night we almost lost him. I just know he would not have made it without Henry Hood's constant vigilance.

About eight o'clock on Saturday morning, Dr. Hood told me, "Dave seems stable now. If you want to get to the game, I think we'll be okay."

I said I'd hold a chartered plane till the last minute, and would decide later.

Shortly after ten, they told us they were having problems controlling the swelling of Dave's brain. We gave permission to operate if the CAT scan showed a clot. I canceled the plane, and got word to Bob Phillips and Jerry Sandusky, assistant coaches, to handle the game.

That was one game, maybe the only one in my life, when I felt I couldn't care less about who won or lost. Yet one moment in that stadium that day has deeply moved me, and I've never had a chance to acknowledge it. Frank Maloney, Syracuse's coach, needed that game. He'd had a lot of bad luck and was struggling to keep his job. Never having beaten Penn State, if he could outplay us that day he might save himself as well, and he had a fine team that put him within reach of doing it.

A second-half drive brought Syracuse close, at 31–24. In the last minute of play, they gained forty yards on a pass—then lost that gain when the umpire charged them with a holding penalty. With thirteen seconds to go, they dropped a pass that would have given them the opportunity to win.

I know what those players felt. I know what Frank Maloney felt. I've been there. I know how he could have berated his kids in the locker room. I've been there—and I've berated mine for mistakes. But someone told me what did happen in that locker room. Those crestfallen, muddy, bone-sore players gathered around their crushed coach, steeling themselves to get what they expected. Instead, Maloney said, "Before we even say a

word about the game, let's get down on our knees and pray for
Coach Paterno's son."

All my life I've heard some people try to tell me what is bad
and dehumanizing about competition. We hear so seldom
about the respect created by competition and how it may
elevate us to higher ground. That gesture by Frank Maloney,
who I haven't had a chance until now to thank publicly, is right
out of Virgil's vision of honor and courage. He was a warrior
that day who needed a victory and came close to having one,
but he just wasn't destined to win that game.

Frank Maloney that day brought out his best. It lifted his
own kids and, when they learned of it, mine as well.

Since then, Dave has recovered completely. About the only
thing he's been forbidden to do is play football.

My three oldest kids worked all through their college days to
help pay their way. Jay, number four, does so today, and I
expect Scotty to do the same when he finishes high school. If
I were very rich I'd still expect them to work and earn through
their college years. It's an essential part of their education. I'm
sure I'll upset a lot of people by saying this, but any parent who
excuses a college-age kid from earning, on the ground that at
least partial self-support might "interfere" with study, has a
different idea than mine of what education is about.

I have spent almost every working day of my life for the past
forty-three years with college kids on a university campus—
four at Brown as a student, thirty-nine at Penn State as a coach.
I can't think of a single student I've known who got hurt
academically because of a reasonably scheduled part-time job
or a manageable commitment to extracurricular work. But I
have known hundreds of kids who became more self-confident,
more self-reliant, with a better sense of reality and worldliness
as a result of doing well on a paying job, meeting deadlines on
a school newspaper, balancing a budget of a student organization, or meeting the disciplines of a seriously coached athletic
team.

I won't deny our kids may have had some experiences at work that are not quite like those of most kids. Mary Kay, waiting on customers at The Tavern, once was assigned a table for a lady's seventieth birthday party. Table chatter turned to football, and the elderly birthday girl launched into a speech about Joe Paterno: how the Paternos were intimate family friends of hers, but that she really didn't like him. He was overrated as a coach. He also didn't know how to relate to young people. "Joe Paterno didn't make those teams what they are," she concluded with gestures, almost knocking over the birthday candles, "*they* made *him*!" Mary Kay, who regularly helped her mother in home entertaining, knows just about everybody who has ever entered our door, and she'd never seen this lady in her life—nor did the lady recognize her waitress.

Maybe that wasn't her worst moment at The Tavern. Showing up at work one Saturday night after we lost a game, Mary was greeted by a cook: "Fire Joe-pa!"

Mary shot back, "They already did. Why do you think I'm working?"

Not long ago, I pledged a personal gift to start a fund for the Penn State libraries. We timed the gift to help publicize a history-making $200 million capital campaign by the university (later expanded to $300 million). Our gift was peanuts compared to those of people much richer than we are. Many have given a million, two, three—one generous alumnus, ten million.

Sue and I arrived carefully at the amount we gave: Three of our kids have graduated from Penn State, and we assume the other two soon will. The truth is I never wanted any of my kids to go to Penn State. I felt they'd be better off getting out on their own, getting away from the shadow of their old man. But they chose it.

As a faculty member, I get a big discount on their tuition. So we simply calculated how much we saved by not having to put up the normal college expenses for five kids. It came to

$150,000—and that's what we decided to donate to the university that has become our life.

I mention it now to say that if I had a second chance to decide about that gift, I might not give it, or not the same way. The university had convinced us that the football coach giving to his favorite cause, the library, would help publicize the campaign and attract other potential givers. The trouble is, it also got the attention of our two youngest kids, Jay, our present Penn Stater, and Scotty, in high school. If they didn't read the papers the day the gift made the local headlines, their classmates did. They seemed to have picked up the impression that they are rich Paternos and that money doesn't matter anymore. It undermined our long effort to bring up kids with a sense of realism and duty to make their own way in the world.

I have to stay watchful that my kids don't get spoiled by special breaks. In the 1988 season, Jay was on the squad as a reserve quarterback. During the summer, the only time of year when players are allowed to, Jay got a job. Maybe "got" is the wrong verb. Actually, an old family friend who owns a successful business in town mentioned to Frank Rocco, the assistant athletic director, that he had a job for Jay. What I didn't know till later was that the job was for $12 an hour.

When I found out, I said to Frank, "You got a job for So-and-so. What's he making?" So-and-so was a Puerto Rican kid from Philadelphia. I'd been to his home to recruit him and knew how poor and unstable the family was. If he has a father I never met him. The kid, very bright, was farmed out to an orphanage at least once.

A couple of years earlier, under the influence of some wrong friends, So-and-so got involved in a car theft and had to pay some fines. One reason I wanted him to work the summer around State College was to keep him away from that crowd in Philly.

So-and-so's job paid five bucks an hour, Frank told me.

I got mad. Why is my kid earning twelve bucks for an easy,

unskilled job when So-and-so's the one who needs it and makes only five? I told Frank, probably unfairly, I wished he'd convinced my businessman-friend to give the soft touch to So-and-so. Don't worry about Jay, I chewed him out. Let Jay work for five bucks.

You could ask—and Jay surely would—why my kid doesn't have as much right to a lucky break as the next one, and I have no logical answer, except that for the sake of the rest of the team I can't let that happen.

Some days I feel like I've got a hundred sons to worry about. If any squad member gets into a jam, it's like my own kid getting into a jam.

Not long ago, one of our players was driving in midday with his best buddy. He may have had a couple of beers, I don't know. He lost control of his car, it squealed off the road, and his best buddy was killed. Morning after morning, from nervous half-sleep, I'd wake up with anxious questions about how to handle that kid, how to get him through the guilt, how to keep him from going over the edge. Then I'd switch to worrying about my own kids, and what would I do if—. And then, in the confusion of the night, I'd begin to wonder whom I'm really worried about, the whole hundred, or really just my own.

Sometimes, that leads me to another worry: I'm over sixty years old, and I've got two sons still in their teens. It gets tougher and tougher to be patient.

Maybe what saves me is that I'm in close touch with young kids all the time.

One kind of person I've never been able to stand, especially when it's a kid, is a con artist.

Any year I can count on a few phonys slipping into the squad. Usually, I discover they're made that way by their parents, most often by fathers who program their kids to be football heroes. *Hey, kid, what you want to be* [translation:

what *I* want you to be] *is a pro linebacker. Penn State's the place for you to go.* The kid may have absolutely no concept of what we're going to ask him to do. No idea whatsoever of what it's going to mean when we say, You've got to go to class, you're going to have to be honest and trusting with your team-mates, you can't play to get your old man's applause or anyone else's, you're going to have to be a team player, you can't be a hot dog here. That kid may have no idea what I'm talking about when I tell him, you've got to stretch yourself mentally, get more out of college than just going to class. He's coming here because his father has seen Penn State play, or he works with a couple of Penn Staters and he's always dreamed of his kid playing football at Beaver Stadium, and the father may have no more of an idea than the kid why this place may be dead wrong for him. He shouldn't come here, but he comes. And he slips through our recruiting filters.

What that father would never understand is that while his kid doesn't belong here, So-and-so, that Philadelphia Puerto Rican kid, does. In his family, that kid at eighteen *is* the father. He has street smarts spilling out of his ears. His deter-mination is as muscular as his body. And he wants to play football here because he sees a Penn State diploma as a way out of poverty. He may not be an academic genius, but he has a good mind. He tested well enough to get in, but he's much smarter than he tests. Arizona State wanted him, Memphis wanted him, but he came here for the schooling he knew we'd demand of him. He *belongs* here.

But then I think of another kid I'll call Ken. For a year we strung along with him while he cut classes, eked through some courses, didn't even eke through others. I wrote to his parents to warn them of where he was headed. First thing I know, they're sitting across my desk. The kid proceeds to tell them that he's doing great, that my information was all wrong. His mother looks at me with big innocent eyes: "Ken wouldn't lie. Ken never lies."

1973: "Joe-pa," at students' request, delivers commencement speech, asking, "If President Nixon knew so little about Watergate, how could he know so much about football?"

"The Last Interception," Fiesta Bowl, Miami vs. Penn State, 1986. Vinny Testaverde (14) of Miami to Pete Giftapolous (90), Penn State, in front of the goal line, just beyond linebacker Don Graham (53). A fine catch—and a national championship.

Breaking up is not so hard to do, as Penn State's number-one-ranked national championship team presents a Nittany Lion statue and a "number one" jersey to the then number-one man, President Ronald Reagan. A man soon to be voted number one, George Bush, in reserve, holds a white Penn State cap.

(From left) Gregg Garrity (hand in pocket), Todd Blackledge, and Curt Warner (the latter were roommates) celebrating with other students, a number-one ranking, at last.

Bottom: The roommates in action.

This page and overleaf: The changing faces, moods, and ages of a teacher-coach-father: serious or smiling; pensive, uncomfortable; in the heat, the cold; even, once in a while, relaxed.

(PENN STATE)

(PENN STATE)

Here, Paterno with, among others (*clockwise from top*), the cutout "Stand-up Joes," the likenesses of Joe-pa bought by admirers; superb athlete Jesse Arnelle, now a San Francisco lawyer as well as Penn State trustee; All-American, All-Pro Jack Ham as he is inducted into the Hall of Fame and asks Paterno to present him; out-of-uniform but equipped-with-microphone superstar Franco Harris. Franco and Joe did not always see eye to eye, but here they broadcast eye to eye, as friends.

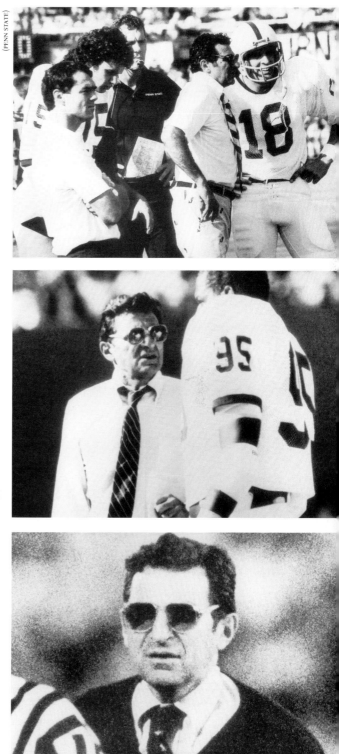

BACK TO BUSI-NESS—and basics. A coach's life is consumed with players, ceremonies, interviews, the retreating backs of officials, even a slightly embarrassing pose with merchandise.

(PENN STATE)

Paterno with Doug Strang (18) and Rogers Alexander (95); and in apparent disbelief at an unidentified official.

Joseph V. Paterno, educator, with friends on campus, the students of Penn State.

Paterno, playing a familiar position, is hoisted aloft in victory by his "designated lifters," Sugar Bowl, 1983.

A photo in the family album bears a caption, in a familiar hand, that suggests *the reason to work*, the reasons why...

The Paternos, Joseph V. and Suzanne P., at home.

The whole team. *(Back row)* Scott, Sue, David, Diana.
(Front row) Mary Kay, Joe, Jay (Joe junior).

What can I say, except that I'll check further. I check and find out he not only cut classes, but to keep from flunking, dropped the courses. He enrolled in summer school to make up, didn't go to class all summer, then told his parents the reason he didn't go was that I said he was in the doghouse and had to practice this and practice that to stay on the team. I told him he needed to leave Penn State, go to some school less demanding where he could succeed—or even stay out of school for a while until he could decide what was worth committing himself to. The parents came running back. The mother glared at me lethally. The kid's "tragedy" was all my fault, because I didn't give him a chance to play. The reason he wasn't studying was because he didn't play. (The truth was that even on the field, the kid didn't work hard and wasn't that good. He lacked commitment in football just as he lacked it in his studies.) Nobody in that family is owning up to anything. The kid's lying to his parents, and the parents can't imagine that the kid's lying, because the parents lie constantly to themselves.

I'm now thinking of another kid, a walk-on, who was here in 1986, wouldn't study, didn't finish his long runs, did poorly in his forty-yard dashes. After the season, I told him he couldn't make it here. He transferred to a small state university nearby. Later, his father wrote begging me to take him back to Penn State, claiming the kid worked hard to get into better shape and pleading that the greatest thing that ever happened to his kid was the year he was on the 1986 National Championship team and that he's so proud of his championship ring.

Is that that father's idea of a pinnacle for his son? I gave the ring to every kid who barely earned the right to wear the uniform. But this kid never once got into a game. I have plenty of kids with less ability, but they work 50 percent to 100 percent harder—and they make it.

What does that unfortunate father think success is?

* * *

When I was growing up, all the tough decisions were made by my family, my church, my school. I knew exactly what I had to do and what I shouldn't do. So growing up was a picnic for me.

At no time in history have the rules of living changed as fast as in the second half of my life. Today a sixteen-year-old has to make value judgments every time something new happens. She or he is the one who is burdened with the self-instruction, the decision to join in, to turn away, to "just say no." The new morality is that there are no clear instructions for morality. Everything seems "flexible" and "relative." Everybody wants to protect our youth, but you're not allowed to tell them what to do and what not to do. A sixteen-year-old player—maybe your own son—goes to parties where you know sex is part of the theme, and you're expected to say, "Okay, you want to lie around with a girl, go ahead—but be careful. Don't get her pregnant. Don't get a disease." The new morality is "Be Careful."

If I have trouble getting the value of rules out of my system, maybe it's because I'm a man of a game. Without strict rules— *strict* rules—games can't be played.

When I talk to my squad about the importance of rules for living, I often use an analogy. Suppose we're playing football on a hundred-yard field, I tell them, but at the end of the field there's a sudden, deep drop, no fence to block falling over the edge. Obviously, we're not going to use that whole field. We're going to play maybe seventy, even sixty yards to have a buffer of protection. You don't go to the edge. Or we put strong fences around the field and we pad them. Now we're free to play the whole field.

The generations that have become parents since World War II seem to have caved in, maybe because the kids outnumbered them, or so it seemed. They made a virtue of saying that kids were smarter and wiser than they really were, kids who might have been smart but were inexperienced. Parents surrendered their traditional belief in the value of roles and rules and called the process "understanding," "modern," and "liberal." For a time, we surrendered manners, duty, even the school curriculum. The problems of the ancient Greeks, we let our kids decide, have little "relevance" to life today. Latin? It's "dead," and anything written in Latin has meaning only for ancients. What bearing can Plato and *The Republic* have on modern civilization today? The Romans and Greeks had no television, no computers, no widespread affluence or social mobility in any modern sense. What's the point of paying serious attention to *them?* So, abandoning the deep roots of our culture, including morality, today's kid has to make daily decisions based on rootlessness, a here-and-now existence.

I'm glad to see that many of the kid brothers and sisters—and the children—of the most liberated baby boomers are rediscovering in some ways that certain rules make life easier and better—and *more* free.

I am a Catholic, but not a conscientious churchgoer. When the Vatican decided the mass no longer had to be said in Latin, I resented it. I'm such a traditionalist that I felt the meaning of the mass had been taken away. Not just because I knew Latin and wanted to be a snob about it, but I resented the notion that the church could suddenly decide to abandon an ancient ceremony. Somehow, that freed me to make decisions of my own—whether I liked a particular priest or whether I felt like listening to his sermon. It's a rare day that I don't think about my obligation to God, but I wish the church hadn't changed the rules on me.

I have trouble accepting that what's right on one day, especially in matters related to eternity, are suddenly not right or not necessary the next day. I believe there are some unchanging rights and unchanging wrongs. I believe there's a God. I don't believe I'm smart enough to design—and keep redesigning—my own God. Making up football plays is as far as my instinct for originality wants to go.

Sue is devout and goes to church faithfully, and so do Diana and Dave. Dave assists in the mass. Sue feels I'm not entirely honest telling the kids not to miss mass while I don't attend regularly—and if I have to confess I honestly think she's right about that. One of my excuses, especially during the football season, is that Sunday morning is an important time for coaches when yesterday's game films arrive.

The existence of the Catholic church is important to me. Maybe I back away because each person has only so much energy and the church faces some critical decisions, and they're not the ones I choose to think through and fight about: whether the church should permit women priests, what its stand should be on birth control. In Norway a cardinal is still saying mass in Latin, and the Pope has told him he cannot consecrate bishops, but the cardinal is consecrating them anyhow. Those issues interest me, which is why I have to stay away, because I'm more interested in thinking through some of our country's problems about low-cost housing, inner-city schools, and civil rights.

I go into a public high school in Brooklyn, one that my older cousins went to long ago, and I see six or seven thousand kids in that one school, and only four or five hundred graduating. There's a cop on every floor, and you say to yourself there's no hope, the problem is too big, and people don't understand the problem, and nobody knows the answer. Then I go to the part of Brooklyn called Bedford-Stuyvesant, where I grew up and what now may be the most impenetrable ghetto in America, and you walk down the street—if you have the courage to walk down that street—and you see young male kids and wrecked older men just sitting, on busted chairs on curbstones. Having nothing else that draws them to something higher, they've committed their lives to the nether world of drugs and booze and hustling and stealing or not going anyplace because there seems to be no other place to go.

You look around and you say, There *has* to be hope because

no hope is not acceptable. It is not acceptable either by humanity or by God.

The older I get the more I feel that no matter what choices of free will I make somebody up there has predetermined my fate. So many times I've gone to bed at night trying to figure out, "Why has life been so good to me? I have a good wife, healthy children, and my own health. What do I have to do to pay You back?" At times I get scared to death that maybe I've used all my chips, and I say to myself, "One of these days, Joe, you're going to get it." Or I wonder whether somebody up there is saying, "You're here to do something, Paterno, and you'd better not screw it up." I'm not sure that's God's specific language, but that's the message I hear.

20· "If a Coach Wants Love, He Also Gets Losing"

WE caught the fever again in 1977, winning ten games, losing our concentration only against Kentucky, 24–20, then on Christmas Day beating Arizona State in the Fiesta Bowl, for a season of 11–1.

That's exactly the record we rolled up in 1978, except that that record was far from the same. Its single loss struck me in the face on New Year's Day 1979 when we faced Alabama in the Sugar Bowl for an undisputed national championship.

Less than two minutes from the end of the game, we were behind, 14–7. At fourth down, we stood less than a yard away from our goal line. This was probably our last opportunity to score. If we made the touchdown, a two-point play would establish us undeniably as the best team in all of college football.

What a perfect moment!

There, steeled against us, the great Red Tide.

And we—*We Are Penn State!*—perennial winners, until now never the acknowledged champs.

There was Bear Bryant.

Here was Joe Paterno. In this play I go hand to hand, my destined chance to outcoach a legend.

I called a time-out and told my coaches I wanted quarterback Chuck Fusina to fake a run and throw a little pop pass to the tight end. I didn't doubt that experienced, poised Chuck would handle it perfectly.

A couple of my soundest coaches insisted I play the percentages—just crash through the couple of feet for the touchdown. "If we can't do this and score a yard," one of them insisted persuasively, "we don't deserve a national championship."

With an eerie clarity, I still remember the sure voice of my instinct: "That's a lot of crap. This is the time to surprise them and throw the football."

But I didn't say it out loud.

Instead, I paused for a most finely split moment to hear another voice in my head: "Hold it, Joe. What if—"

That moment was one of the few in my life when I backed off from a strong instinct and let myself worry about what people might say if a decision was wrong. Especially what the coaching staff would say if they turned out right and I turned out wrong.

I nodded, giving in to caution, choosing the percentage play: handing the ball to our tailback, Mike Guman, an excellent leaper.

Bryant and the Tide lay waiting for him.

To this day down in Alabama, anywhere you go you can find their blown-up photo: an army of Crimson defenders stopping Guman cold.

I have talked about getting angry with myself when I lose. Nothing of the kind ever compared to this loss. I beat up on myself not only immediately but for months afterward, halfway into the next season. Much as I blamed myself, I couldn't tolerate all that self-blame. I let my anger turn against the staff and against the team, even though the decision was purely mine. I had to spill some of it off. Writers and fans said, for all to hear, that Paterno couldn't win the big one at the critical moment. Even former players said openly, for quotation, "He should have won that one."

It got to me. It hammered at my ego. *When I stood toe to toe with Bear Bryant, he outcoached me.*

Sue sensed it. Somewhere in the middle of the next season,

she shook me out of what must have looked like some kind of trance. Leaning into me with a kind of demand in her eye, she asserted:

"Joe, the Alabama game is over! It's just another game you lost."

I still think my distraction and demoralization helped lead to some of the things that went wrong in the terrible season that followed, 1979.

Concentration is the most fragile thing I know. A team that loses concentration can't win. A coach that loses concentration cannot lead a team to win. A coach and team that take winning for granted—or dwell on losses—lose concentration. A winning team and coach have to run scared without letup—but also without actually getting scared. Getting scared destroys concentration.

All those principles of concentration are true, and I could state others, but memorizing principles cannot change how fragile concentration is. A piece of bad luck, or one moment of stupidity by one member of the team, can knock concentration off its perfect center. When it falls to the floor it smashes to a million pieces.

In the summer preceding the 1979 season, the team was shocked by the kind of incident that's not supposed to happen in Penn State athletics. One of our young players was arrested on multiple charges of rape. Then, on opening day of fall practice, I had to bounce three players off the squad for losing their playing eligibility for academic reasons. One of these was all-American Peter Harris, who led the nation in 1978 with ten interceptions. That was not only a loss in itself, but fans felt the pain of it even harder because he was the kid brother of Franco Harris, who had graduated six years earlier. People came down on me as though I had committed disrespect to Franco's memory. When people demanded I explain, I did so bluntly: Pete goofed off. When that's so, I said, I don't care whose brother he is. (Many kids, like Pete, stay unsettled during their student days but find themselves later and mature productively. Today Pete Harris is a successful chef.)

Next, as though we were destined to fall apart piece by piece, our defensive captain, Matt Millen, a tackle, dropped out of an early-fall running drill. If he'd had a cramp or was getting the flu, that would have been one thing. But his reason was intolerable: He simply said he couldn't do it. I had to strip him of his captaincy. What in the world had happened to this team leader was more than I—or he—could explain. Two days later, Matt made the run with no problem, but the morale and concentration of the team were severely shaken. He'd surely be careful for the rest of his life before he'd again say, "I can't," but the surprise taught me that even a demonstrated leader should never be taken for granted. Leadership, like concentration, has to keep renewing and reproving itself. Matt's later atonement was complete, accurately descriptive, yet still didn't explain it: "I was at fault for not pushing myself. I was wrong. Dead wrong. Totally wrong. Personally, I think it set the tone for the team and, psychologically, it hurt the team. It was awful. Every time something would start to go good, something bad would happen. We would start up the ladder and somebody would knock out the bottom rung."

That ladder still had a lot of rungs to go. In the first week of the season, I got a call from the university police. They had come upon two of my tackles guzzling beer on a campus bench. That stupidity destroyed the team's concentration for a week. I suspended them from that week's Texas A&M game, which we lost, 27–14.

Before long, our reserve tailback, Leo McClelland, who had the habit of spreading the unconfirmed news that he was a Heisman candidate, was overcome by some affront or another and quit the team in a huff. Then, in midseason, our tailback, a junior, hours after playing his biggest game ever—scooting 166 yards and scoring three touchdowns against West Vir-

ginia—drove his car over a campus curb and was charged with
drunk driving. So I had to drop him for a week. Again, we lost
concentration—as well as the next game, to Miami, 26–10.

Had enough? That ill-fated team hadn't yet. One of our
reserve fullbacks was told he wasn't welcome at a dormitory
party and chose to get physical about his disappointment.

Also losing to Nebraska and Pitt, we stumbled through a 7–4
regular season. Yet somehow we won an invitation to the
Liberty Bowl in Memphis to face Tulane. One absolute rule
I emphasize is that players must be on time for prebowl team
meetings. Two players showed up late for the first meeting, and
I sent them home. That was tame. Next thing, the Memphis
police were holding one of my reserve tight ends. He'd wan-
dered into a private home—and its owner pointed a gun at
him. The player told police he was looking for a place to sleep.
What was wrong with his room at the Hyatt Regency? Police
charged him with first-degree burglary and told me he was
lucky that the self-defense bullet didn't kill him. Later, the
player got the charge bargained down to malicious mischief
and was given six months probation.

As Richie Lucas, our All-American quarterback twenty years
earlier, said one day, "There's such a thing as a good eight and
four and a poor eight and four. We had a poor eight and four."

The grapevine started buzzing that at last the truth was
coming out about Penn State—that we always looked like an
Eagle Scout troop because we're hidden in the mountains and
hide our troubles from view. I can understand the suspicion,
but it wasn't true. It had been twelve years since I last had to
bounce a player for the crime of poor grades. All those other
troubles truly were unheard-of around here.

I think one reason was that *I* had relaxed. Because I had
softened my intensity I think the kids lost that fear of Joe
Paterno. In fact, I said that to a writer and was gratified that
he went for confirmation to Charlie Pittman, our star of a
decade earlier, who said, "Deep down, all athletes yearn for
discipline."

The more I thought about it and the more I called players in to sound them out on what happened, the more I concluded that my loss of concentration—or even theirs—was not the whole story. These kids were different from those I'd coached earlier and those I'd gone to school with. Values of young people had changed. This crop had shifted, subtly but importantly, toward every man for himself. Some change in the air of America had left them less ready to understand that giving themselves to the interests of a group means getting more for themselves in return. I also found them less willing to get involved empathically in someone else's life. I didn't want to quarrel with where they put their personal values, but I knew—and know—that we couldn't win with everybody just going his own way.

Whenever I recruit, I always state my feeling that a player's first duty is to his team. My assistant coaches do the same. Kids listen, they like the romantic music of it, and they nod. But it's hard to know if they really get what we're saying. It was clear that before the dark season of 1979 we had mistakenly recruited some athletes who didn't understand in their gut what I was saying and that I meant it. I knew we had to examine more closely a recruit's ability to pass up a good time to stay tiptop as a football player. We had to examine a recruit more carefully to see how much the new permissiveness of the seventies had softened him. Sure, it softened a whole generation, yet many kids slipped through with the tough values of self-demand from an earlier day.

I also hardened my hostility toward the rule that permits freshmen to play. At the same time, I lacked the toughness and resolve to rule flatly that freshmen would not play for Penn State. That's where I was the phony and the hypocrite. I avoided laying down that rule because I knew it would hurt our recruiting—when other coaches were actually promising some hot prospects that they'd play as freshmen—and would shave our chances of winning championships.

That season told me I had to reexamine my role as surrogate

father to many of these kids, the hardest of my tasks. Team members, new ones as well as old, were preached at constantly, "Don't do anything that will embarrass yourself, the team, or the university." After the sudden outburst of so many kids embarrassing all three and suffering for it, they needed support.

In December, after the Pitt game and before the Liberty Bowl, I talked to player after player trying to find out what went wrong and what we needed to do. I learned that if they came for counsel or support, they felt I wasn't there for them. Kid after kid told me, one way or another, that I always seemed too busy. True. I often am. That year even more so perhaps because I had accepted the additional job of becoming athletic director. Many people complained I had too much power at Penn State, and now kids were saying I'd lost my influence with them. What they didn't say, but what they must have sensed, is that I had grown not to like them as a group the way I'd liked other teams. I had to admit to myself that I began thinking of them as a bunch of jackasses.

Was I demanding too much? Was it out of date to ask that much? Was strong discipline a thing of the past?

How was I to measure these things?

Some hints came from a *Sports Illustrated* writer, Douglas S. Looney, who evaluated my predicament. (His title quoted me: "There Are a Lot of People Who Think I'm a Phony and Now They Think They Have the Proof.") His article reached out to some of my best players of the recent past for hindsight evaluations of me. I thought they spoke truthfully—and realistically.

Lydell Mitchell, now a San Diego Charger, said, "I enjoyed playing for him much more after I was through playing for him."

Charlie Pittman: "There is not any like or love for Joe by the players. But he gets you on top of your game. If a coach wants love, he also gets losing. What Joe wants is your best effort, that's all."

Denny Onkotz: "Like any coach, Joe has to make decisions for the good of the team, and that means bad things for the individual."

The writer rightly concluded: "If a guy wants friends, he can go bowling; if he wants to win in big-time competition, sacrifices must be made."

Friends? Love? One of my 1978 players recently broke me up with a lesson in how deeply a coach may burn himself into a player's memory. Ten years after his graduation, Joe Lally revisited State College for a charity golf tournament. The tournament used a brand of golf ball that has my picture on it (which they advertise with a slogan, "Guaranteed to go up the middle three out of four times").

After his game, Lally told Jim Tarman, "I could hardly wait to tee up so I could hit Joe. But you know, it was just like when he was on the practice field. I just looked at the ball—and it started to yell at me."

21· The Prize

ONE day Indiana basketball coach Bobby Knight passed through State College and we spent an hour in my office shoptalking about college championships, more specifically, why college champions seldom repeat for a second consecutive year. One obvious reason is that a championship grows out of experience—and experience usually belongs to seniors—and seniors graduate. But Bobby and I found ourselves agreeing on a subtler, more pervasive reason: At schools that expect athletes to be successful students, too—like Indiana and Penn State—a team simply can't sustain two years of the concentration and intensity required for winning a national championship. Taking that a step further, I was starting to believe that great college football programs peak about every four years, with luck, maybe three.

After our hairline miss of a recognized championship in 1978, I could have done without, thank you, the debacle of 1979 to support my theory. But I was not surprised that we started an upswing in the seasons of 1980 and '81—each with nine wins and two losses plus a victory at the Fiesta Bowl in both seasons.

Could the fourth year, 1982, be our year? And if it were, would the press polls be ready to acknowledge a first-rank eastern team? To the first question, the answers started falling our way. A pair of Penn State roommates had matured into leaders and stars: Todd Blackledge, a superb quarterback, and our fine running back Curt Warner.

Our first four games were scheduled at home, helping us to a fast start. We beat Temple (31–14), Maryland (39–31), and Rutgers (49–14), then conquered a big test against Nebraska (27–24).

Maybe "conquered" is the wrong word. The hand of fate was on our side that day to help us win. With seconds to go before the final gun, we were losing, 24–20. We gambled all on a pass to Mike McCloskey, who snatched the ball at the outer edge of the ten-yard line. We went on to score—and win. At the postgame press conference, reporters raised questions about whether Mike caught the ball out of bounds. How was I to know from about the fifty? All I knew was that the officials called it a catch, and the game was over. Next day I looked at the film. Sure enough, without question, Mike's foot had come down outside the boundary. I freely admitted it to the media. But that didn't change anything. The decisions of officials, wrong or right, are among the breaks of the game. A few days later, so I heard, the state of Nebraska was flooded with T-shirts emblazoned PENN STATE FIELD. Beneath the words was an illustration of a gridiron—with a bump sticking out of its side.

That victory, by whatever means, made us feel ready and anxious for our trip to Birmingham—for Alabama and Bear Bryant, who had beaten us the previous year, 31–16.

Maybe too anxious. This time they beat us by three touchdowns, 42–21. Any coach can imagine our locker-room mood after that trouncing. But not every coach has had the luck to see what I saw then: the seizing of leadership by somebody on the team who had the genuine feeling and the simple nerve to seize it, and the way a leader can change the world. Our fullback, Joel Coles, not a headline maker, not a hall of famer, just let his inner voice take possession of him, and he got up on a bench and let it out in a yell:

"Listen, you guys, we've still got six games to prove that we're a good football team!"

You could just see a dark cloud of discouragement explode and disintegrate. The kids began to cheer for themselves.

In the next four games we did begin proving the team we were, each victory stronger than the last:

Syracuse. 28–7.

West Virginia. 24–0.

Boston College. 52–17.

North Carolina State. 54–0.

On Friday night, November 12, 1982, climbing off a plane at the South Bend, Indiana, airport, we stepped into a blast of frozen air and began boarding our buses when two TV reporters aimed cameras and mikes at me. One of them, with a twinkly television grin, asked, "How will it feel tomorrow, Coach, to be taking your team for the first time into the great tradition of that Notre Dame stadium?"

"Well," I stammered, trying to be polite, "I guess, I think— we've played a lot of big games and it's great to be playing Notre Dame."

Then the other guy, almost word for word, asked the same dumb thing.

I wondered to myself: "Who the hell do Notre Dame fans think they are?"

At the hotel that night before bedtime I got my team together. Still irritated, I said, "You're going to hear all about Notre Dame tradition, and you know what? It doesn't mean a thing unless Knute Rockne leaps out of the ground and tackles you. Their field has got a hundred yards and two goal posts just like every other football field. When you put those black shoes on tomorrow, and you put on that jersey without your name on the back, and you put that plain helmet on, *that's* tradition, Penn State's tradition."

Next day we won, 24–14.

And finally, we closed a successful season against Pitt, 19–10.

Some fans of short memory enjoy knocking my caution in calling for passes. They might be jolted to be reminded that some sportswriters called the 1982 team "Air Paterno." Blackledge threw 292 passes, completing 161 of them, for 2,218 yards. The twenty-two touchdowns he threw still stand as a school record. As a team, we gained 2,369 yards passing, making it one of those rare times when any team has gained more yardage by passing than running. We also ran for 496 plays and 2,283 yards, depending chiefly on Todd's equally outstanding costar, Curt Warner, who gained 1,041 yards.

Warner was a sure bet to become a Heisman candidate as one of the great backs of the country. That puts terrific pressure on a young kid. The media focused all eyes on Warner in the opening game, but we beat Temple mainly on four passes thrown by Blackledge. Warner caught one of them, but he didn't get to carry or gain as much as the writers (or the opposing coach) expected.

I could see Warner was distraught afterward. I'm sure he felt good about his catch and was excited about Blackledge's great day. One white and one black, those two had been roommates for four years and are still as close as can be today. But the reporters wanted Warner to start his potential Heisman year by breaking new records on the ground. Even though our passing game had surprised the opposition, he probably felt let down about himself. Amid the celebration by the other players, the media guys circled around Curt, who sat glumly by his locker. They badgered and badgered him for "comments" on whether he thought Blackledge or the coach should have called more running plays, on his "feelings" about not making much ground yardage, on not helping himself toward the Heisman. Suddenly Curt turned his back on them, threw down a shoe or something, and he was crying—trying to keep those reporters from seeing.

The main story the next day was not about Todd Blackledge and his great achievement. It was about Curt Warner, his "failure" to meet the crowd's expectation, and his loss of control in the locker room.

Chief Justice Earl Warren used to say that he turned to the sports pages first because he wanted to start the day reading positive accounts of people doing their best. That's changed. Because of their superficial view of the meaning of success, too many sportswriters miseducate their readers, corrupt the meaning of athletics, and inflict unjustified pain on players.

Today, the sports-page headlines shout about basketball stars shooting up drugs, ex-sluggers going to jail, Billy Martin getting mugged in a barroom, George Steinbrenner refiring Martin, and Dave Winfield suing Steinbrenner. They quote a wonderful star, Isiah Thomas, saying about another wonderful star, Larry Bird, that if Bird were black he'd be just another player, hardly noticed. I don't know if Thomas said it just that way or just what he meant by it, but I do know that some unfortunate reporter, or his editor, thought that that was one of the great athletic events of the day. There's no way that I know to reconcile that kind of judgment with the message I constantly preach to my squad—and would like to preach to the fans: Respect the other guy, do your best, and if you lose, give the other guy credit.

Some media people are preoccupied with taunting, badmouthing, and emphasizing mistakes and slip-ups instead of achievements. I wish they'd pay—and educate fans to pay— more respectful attention to the strains these young kids endure in a hard-fought game. I wish sports reporters wouldn't try to make themselves look good by putting words into the mouths of stressed and inexperienced nineteen-year-olds, leading them to say something about their teammates, or their opponents, or their coach, so that the reporter can get a headline and by-line by making a kid look bad.

Stories like the one on Curt Warner appear often, and that's how far we've come from Earl Warren's idea of "positive accounts of people doing their best." Sportswriters should be striving for fresh and compelling ways to report results and the quality of play, especially when it's outstanding, inspiring play. That's what we pay our way into the stadium to see.

Maybe this is the result of television. More of us see games than in the old days. Maybe reporters feel that because we see the games, their duty is to go "behind the scenes" where the gossip is—and the playing isn't. Maybe the sportswriter's job is harder today. He always has to look for something beyond the play itself that can be made to sound important. That takes imagination, experience, skill, sometimes artistry. And the trouble is, a lot of sportswriters are young, inexperienced, artless, and not very good. The good ones—guys like Bill Lyons, Robert Lipsyte, Roger Angell—are wonderful. But the less wonderful ones, especially a lot of young people on smaller city papers, sometimes labor to produce an angle that's inaccurate, negative, and hurtful:

QUARTERBACK SACKED THREE TIMES; BLOWS GAME

SLUGGER HITLESS FOUR DAYS IN ROW

HEISMAN CANDIDATE FUMBLES FOR LOSS

PATERNO PROVES HE CAN SCREW UP

That kind of reporting was later to typify the simple-headed explanations of our 1985 Orange Bowl loss to Oklahoma: Quarterback John Shaffer lost it! If Penn State doesn't win, somebody's got to be blamed.

Before the next season, a Harrisburg paper polled its readers on who should become the 1986 starting quarterback, Shaffer or Matt Knizner. Knizner won their fan poll in a runaway. Knizner was very good, and my decision between Shaffer and him was very close. But I hope those fans—and sportswriters—didn't think I was going to abandon someone who gave this team as much loyalty and hard work as Shaffer because of one football game.

Are these carping, hurtful reporters devoted just to giving the fans what they want? Are the fans really the villains? True, a lot of fans just want their team to win—win big. They want to be able to shoot their mouths off, riding the backs of somebody else's achievements. Yet I still have to love them. When

I get up before more than a thousand Nittany Lion boosters, they're not enemies of mine. Some are very knowledgeable—and some are like children. I try to make them understand. I want them to enjoy. They live and they'd die for Penn State football. I don't want them to get screwed up by the press. I want them to rise above feeling bitter after we've lost a game. Maybe some won't forgive me for saying this, but I want them to understand that I love the Notre Dame and Pitt alumni too. There's plenty of glory for both sides if we all play as well as we can play.

I can't help but hold the media partly responsible for the increasing tendency of fans to boo, catcall, wave handkerchiefs—and gamble—rather than admire the spectacle. Too many fans would rather cheer when their team rolls over the other side, 39–0, in a lousy one-sided game than see a great football struggle in which one team—either team—goes down by a point. Either way, the players come out of a close game like that feeling fully alive, one team feeling better simply because of a feather stroke of luck. I feel my very best coming away with the thought, It's a shame the other team had to lose. They were as courageous and good as we were.

People who come to games with a genuine desire for excitement often have an undeveloped sense of what's going on out there—they are more interested in the scoreboard than in the fine points of play and players.

I won't forget one story about how much—or how little—the most devoted and excited fans see. In 1953, when Syracuse played at State College, one of our kids—Dan DeFalco—blocked a punt during the last minutes. We won. After the game I went to a cocktail party where a guy I ran into, a football worshiper and major in the university ROTC, began hailing the wonders of Penn State football for building character, courage, and all those nice things.

"I just wish I could have had my whole ROTC outfit there," he sang, like an aria, "watching that Danny DeFalco just plunge in there without fear, and how he blocked that punt. He just made up his mind to block it, and nothing was going to stop him. He played off two big blockers and threw himself at that football, stopping it on sheer guts alone. God, if I could only get that across to my men."

Of course, I had seen it, too, but I didn't know what the hell DeFalco had done. It happened too fast. Danny, a good friend of mine to this day, was a good solid player, but not so reckless that he won the Congressional Medal of Honor every quarter. Later, checking out the films, I got to that climactic ending and remembered what the major said. What the film showed, so help me God, was that nobody blocked Danny. Absolutely nobody interfered with him. When he suddenly found himself in front of the kicker, he was so surprised he didn't know what to do and he ducked. The kicked ball hit him and almost knocked him on his tail.

Oh, the character-building wonders of football!

After games, at those quickie press conferences in our media room, one of those newspaper experts, showing off to his fellow experts, will ask, "What do you think made their running back decide in the third quarter to cut around on the outside when—" Maybe I flabbergast them, but I have to say, "Geez, I don't know." What am I supposed to tell them? There are a thousand things going on out there in the same split second. Your mind's going on what your plan was, what happened to your plan, all the things that went wrong, you're trying to figure out what you're going to do next. Who knows why their man ran on the outside? A coach probably sees a hundred percent more than the most experienced fan, but even then, when you look at the film, you don't see a lot of what you think you saw.

The best of it, of course, is that if you confuse your opponent enough, he doesn't know what's going on either.

The prebowl polls at the end of 1982 were just right for us. Georgia, undefeated, untied, ranked first. That couldn't be better because we were listed second and had already signed to play Georgia in the Sugar Bowl on New Year's Day. If they won, we'd have no beef about their championship. If we won, nobody could question our claim. In third place stood Nebraska, whom we had already beaten. And fourth was Southern Methodist University, for whom I had sympathy because they were unbeaten, but had one tie. I knew how they felt about the poll. I'd been there.

Against Georgia on New Year's Day, we scored the first touchdown and ended the opening quarter with a lead of 7–3. By half time we had shut down their running machine, named Herschel Walker, and led more comfortably, 20–10. But they came back in their first possession of the third quarter to score, making a game of it again, 20–17. Early in the fourth quarter, on a first-down play from the Georgia forty-seven-yard line, we pulled our "Play 643," a routine fake in which Blackledge motions to hand off to Warner who's plunging for the middle of the line—while four receivers zigzag downfield. With only two or three defensive backs to go after them, one is bound to be open—if Blackledge can find him. One was, and Todd did. He heaved a perfect arc into the arms of Gregg Garrity, who, racing down the left sideline, plunged into the end zone to score.

Now, at a more comfortable 27–17, our job was not to make mistakes—and we made a big one. Our punt returner, Kevin Baugh, who had played heroically with a sixty-six-yard run and another for twenty-four, dropped a punt that gave Georgia the ball on our own forty-three. The fault was as much mine as Kevin's. I should have told him to let the punt drop, untouched. Accepting the gift, Georgia soon scored. Coach Vince Dooley decided to go for a two-point conversion. If they made it, a field goal would give them a clean win of 28–27. We stopped them. Score: 27–23.

With 1:37 to play, we were in third down, three yards to go for a first. The timing was the worst possible for us. A fourth-down punt would give Georgia the ball with time to score and leave us no time to get the ball back and retaliate.

We had to keep the ball. We simply had to get the first down. But how?

Time out for conference.

The irony of the moment clutched at me. How could fate make this so resemble four years ago? Same stadium, same event, the Sugar Bowl, another southeastern conference team, and forced to gamble the whole year's marbles, a national championship, on a single short-yardage play.

"Let's run it," the coaches urged, correctly, according to the percentages. "We can't risk an interception." My basic approach, exactly.

I looked at Blackledge.

Blackledge said, "I think we can throw it for a first down."

My gut believed him. Maybe analytical judgment would lead me differently, but the moment pleaded for strong instinct. This quarterback was just an eager kid, bucking the probabilities and all the combined seasoning of his coaches. But my gut believed in him because he was afire with belief in himself.

I said, "Throw it."

He threw it. The Georgians were stunned as the ball went up, and Gregg Garrity seized the dinky pass a measly six yards downfield. The first down and the ball were ours. Control of the remaining time was ours. The game was ours—and so was our first recognized national championship ever, after all those years of winning and waiting.

That moment's crucial decision had come easier for me than on New Year's Day, 1979, because I was not the same person I was then. Facing Bear Bryant four years earlier on this very spot, I wasn't big enough, strong enough, grown enough to face the ridicule if we had thrown the ball and the pass had been intercepted. The scare of it faced me down, and I lost. This time I didn't care about the ridicule. I cared about the first down, the pass, and the thrill of the risk.

I knew this time that I was not afraid to lose. And I knew

this time that listening to your heart and going with it is a winning principle.

When the players swarmed all around and carried me on their shoulders all the way to the locker room, I loved sharing their celebration of themselves. But that isn't what I'll tell my grandchildren about that victory. Before the trip was over I learned as never before how much this team and its successes are an expression of so many people.

Central Pennsylvania is a broad, diverse, hard-to-get-to region of farms and small industries so evenly and thinly spread that it doesn't have a city of as many as 60,000 people. When we landed at Harrisburg, thousands of those people stood waiting in the cold to cheer us. And that wasn't what I'll tell my grandchildren either. The total and moving surprise came after our buses groaned out of the airport for the three-hour journey to our remote mountain home of State College. Through county after county, for country mile after country mile, U.S. Highway 322 was lined with people, people, people, cars, cars, cars, honking horns, horns, horns, no end of them, waiting through that winter night just to wave, to shout a greeting, to clap their hands for an all-too-brief moment as their champions passed by. Towns along the way sent out their fire engines to greet us. With emergency lights circling, each town's engines escorted us up the highway to deliver us to the care of the next town's engines in a hundred-mile relay of joy and pride. I never saw such love between people who didn't know each other. And never in one place at one time have I sensed so many football players in their private darkness sneaking so many silent, exultant tears.

22· A Bigger Number One Than Football

A couple of weeks after the Sugar Bowl, the Penn State board of trustees invited me to address them. I seized the opportunity to cough up some things long stuck in my craw.

For years I had been upset—in fact, astonished—at Penn State's unwillingness to go out and raise money, except in the most obvious ways: big institutional grants and reminding rich widows to remember us in their wills. Now and then, our development office asked me to go out and stroke a corporation president who was a football fan, and I always went when I could. After visiting our millionaires, we usually dropped in on a gathering of alumni. These gatherings always struck me as strange. I shook a lot hands, the alumni did their share of fawning over the visiting coach, my development escort smiled a lot, and that was it. Nobody lowered themselves to utter a single word about money. About the only money raised from alumni in those days was by the athletic department—and only for athletic scholarships, which we steadily increased in number.

My feelings came to a head in about 1978 on one of those trips with Charlie Lupton, our director of development at that time. During one speech to an alumni group I decided to open up.

I told them about my days at Brown, about playing football in the Ivy League, about the nice publisher who put me

through school, and so on. Then I slid over to one reason why
Ivy League schools accomplish so much academically that we
can't—because they have the money to hire the best minds and
finance the most advanced research. And they can do that
because they raise that money from their own alumni who are
expected to give every year as part of their life's obligation, like
tithing for their church. I said, as best I recall:

"If we're going to move our university ahead—as a university as well as in football—we've got to stop crying like a bunch
of babies that the state is not giving us more money. The state's
got their own problems. If we only do what the state gives us
money to do, we'll be just another mediocre state university.
We should be better than that. We need to raise money from
our alumni. You people have a responsibility, and you're not
being asked to face up to it. You're all doing well because you
got a big-league education—and you got it cheap."

I could hear my friend Charlie gulp. When we left, he said,
half chuckling, half in a sweat, "Joe, you broke the unwritten
law. That's the first time I've seen anybody ask for money in
an alumni meeting."

Then what were those meetings for? I guess their purpose
was to say nice things about ourselves and our school and to
keep everybody happy so when the time comes for the alumni
to elect their representatives to the board of trustees, the right
kind of people will keep getting elected. Sure, every university
administration has a right to worry about that.

Something needs to be explained here. Despite its name,
which may mislead, Penn State is not a state university in the
sense that, say, the State University of New York (SUNY) or
the University of California are. We call ourselves a state-
related university because we get only a minor part of our
income, about 25 percent, from the government in Harrisburg.
The rest comes from tuitions (which pay only a small part of
a student's education); from the overhead component of large
research grants from private industry, foundations, and government; and from endowment income.

Pennsylvania, an otherwise wonderful place, should be embarrassed to have it known that out of fifty states it ranks forty-seventh in its support of higher education. I can't explain why its good citizens, who themselves rank high in their average level of education, tolerate that scandal. For the state money we do get, we have to lobby in competition with Pitt, which is located in the heart of the city of Pittsburgh, and Temple, located right in downtown Philadelphia, which share our status as state-related. In that competition, Penn State consistently falls short. When you count the state legislators from the combined Philadelphia and Pittsburgh areas, they just about dominate the legislature, especially when they decide to join hands for their mutual benefit. Our charming rural location leaves us relatively cloutless in the state capital during budget time, even though Penn State sprouts alumni throughout the state like our famous Pennsylvania mushrooms.

For the trustees I didn't write out a formal speech but scribbled some notes. From them, here is a reconstructed summary of what I said:

"This is the first board meeting I've been to in thirty-three years, so if I look a little shocked and scared, bear with me.

"We've been able to get to where we are by playing *our* way. We've not cheated. At least not deliberately, despite a rule book that thick. We've done it with players who legitimately belong in college.

"This is a magic time for Penn State—for our whole university. We have never been more united, more proud, and maybe it's unfortunate that it takes a number one football team to do that. But I don't think we can afford to lose the opportunity this moment presents—and I don't mean an opportunity for athletics.

"It bothers me to see Penn State football number one and then, a few weeks later, to pick up a newspaper and find a report that many of our academic departments and disciplines are not rated up there with the leading institutions of the country.

"I have been all over the country in the last few weeks. I've been in Florida, California, Chicago, Atlanta, other places. I've been there recruiting and, during this time when we can capitalize on our position of success, trying to correct some abuses in intercollegiate athletics. Everywhere I go I hear nothing but 'Boy, Penn State, what a great bunch of people. What a great institution.' So we do have a magic moment and a great opportunity.

"We have to start right now to put our energies together to make this a number one institution by 1990. I don't think that is an unfounded or way-out objective.

"I want to talk to you not as a football coach but as a faculty member, as someone who has spent thirty-three years at Penn State. Also as someone who has two daughters at Penn State and will probably have three sons go through Penn State, whose wife graduated from Penn State, and who has two brothers-in-law who graduated from Penn State. Also as someone who has recruited against Michigan, Stanford, UCLA, Notre Dame, Princeton, Yale, and Harvard, great academic institutions, and who has had to identify some things they have that are more attractive for some students than what we have and has had to identify some of our problems.

"People out there know we have some excellent departments that could be outstanding in a short time. We also have some departments that are lousy. We have some lazy profs who are concerned only with tenure, or only with getting tenure for some of their mediocre colleagues. Some of those mediocrities could turn Happy Valley into Sleepy Hollow. They are certainly not invigorating . . .

"Big public universities today are like Pirandello's play *Six Characters in Search of an Author.* They are in search of their modern purpose, their soul. I think what we're looking for is the soul of this institution. We've got to come to some decisions about where we want to go—how far we're *willing* to go.

"We need brilliant, aggressive, vibrant teachers and scholars. We have some. We don't have enough of them.

"We need to raise money so we can endow chairs for star professors. Stars attract ambitious young faculty, and both of them attract the best and brightest of students. We've got to offer scholarships to get the star students that star professors get excited about. We've got to compete for stars by offering them the best and latest facilities—laboratories and equipment—for their research. We need the best in libraries. All this is within our reach. But we've got to go out and raise the money that will get all that for us. We have alumni out there who can do it, who are eager to do it.

"Doing all that is not so different from doing the essentials in building a great football team. First, it takes a vision and determination. It takes belief in ourselves. It takes a plan. It takes concentration. And it takes the daily *doing* of it.

"There are some people among us who flinch at aspiring to the status of Brown, or Yale, or Harvard, or Stanford. Some people say that wouldn't be true to our mandate. We're not intended, they say, to be an elitist school. But I think we can be more than we are and make students better than they think they can be. Maybe it will take us fifty years, but that's what we should be aspiring to.

"Dr. Eddy [Ted Eddy, then our provost, who is now president of the University of Rhode Island] said it the other night better than I can. He said—and he almost sounded like a football coach, but that's not bad: 'We have a great chance and challenge to make our university number one in many areas, and in coming together to do it we may find out we will have as much fun doing it as we had fun doing it in New Orleans [at the Sugar Bowl].'

"It would be nice to say we can take three years putting together a major fund-raising campaign. But we can't. We can only hold up our finger as number one for six more months. Then we have to play the game again. And we may not be number one. Six short months to capture this magic moment. We have to raise seven to ten million bucks in the next six months to get up the impetus we need, or we are going to lose an opportunity.

"I'm a football coach. I sit down with my staff and we look at our schedule and our squad and we say, 'This is what we want to do, and this is what we can do.' Then we set priorities and make decisions as to how we can achieve our objectives. We put a plan together. We stick to it. We don't jump from one plan to another. We bust our butts to get it done and that is what has to be done with Penn State in the eighties.

"When we stick that finger up as number one, today it's only for football. I'm ready to help where I can to make number one mean more."

That vision wasn't invented out of my own pipe smoke. I knew that others were thinking about it, talking about it, wishing for it. But nobody was taking leadership—saying it out loud, ready to start laying out a plan, to execute a plan. That's what I hoped my speech might do: set a fire under the feelings of others that I knew were already there.

People applauded. But what I wanted to know was what they really were applauding for. Was it for the entertainment of a locker-room pep talk? Was it for the victorious team and the championship? If that's what they were cheering for, they had missed my purpose.

Lots of letters said that what they read in the papers was just what people needed to hear, and they were glad the challenge came from me. Frankly, I wish the challenge had come from our president. But President John Oswald had recently come through a heart attack, and it had not left him the energetic leader he had once been. He was on his way to retiring within the year.

Before my speech, I had learned that a search committee had quietly, in fact secretly, come up with a new president, a fellow named Jordan who ran the Dallas campus of the University of Texas. The job had been offered and the deal made. The way I learned it was that Sue heard it from an employee at the Nittany Lion Inn who knew of Jordan's secret visit to campus and saw the superduper treatment he got. Some way to find out. I was miffed and made no secret about that.

Certainly the choice of a new president didn't require my approval, but I felt that someone might have made a courtesy call to say, "Joe, we're letting you know just so you're not surprised, and we think you're going to like this guy." I felt that after all my years of total devotion to this place, and now having put the university under a spotlight that could bring us benefits in every way, including academically, I should not be treated like an outsider. I have to admit that the wound hurt for a good while.

The appointment of Dr. Bryce Jordan as our new president turned out to be one gem of a choice. He arrived with a vision and a plan—and a commitment to raise large-scale money to back his plan. Within months, he laid out a drive to raise not the seed money of "seven to ten million bucks" I had mentioned in my speech, but a five-year capital campaign to raise $200,000,000, enough to expand the character, resources, and goals of Penn State University.

The purpose of that ambitious campaign, chaired by alumnus Bill Schreyer, head of Merrill Lynch, was to push forward on Penn State's remarkable history—and remarkable contradictions:

As a land-grant university, we are rooted in agriculture, yet we pioneered and lead in aerospace technology.

We are known everywhere for our sports, yet we are the birthplace of the field ion microscope, which allowed scientists to "see" the atom for the first time.

We are the research center that first synthesized progesterone, giving the world the birth-control pill.

We computerized weather forecasting and have graduated one out of every four meteorologists in the United States.

We invented the first long-term pacemaker as well as the

artificial Penn State heart, the work of fifteen years of partnership between our Colleges of Medicine and Engineering.

We have devised almost two hundred improvements on nature by altering the genetic strains of plants.

We have shown the world how to create diamonds in the laboratory as film coatings on crystal silicon surfaces, and that may revolutionize some manufacturing processes.

Through pooling the findings of biology, psychology, and sociology, we have led the way to understanding what happens in the body and mind as human beings grow old.

Our creative writing programs have turned out students who wrote the screenplay to *Casablanca* (Julius Epstein) and the stage play *Agnes of God* (John Pielmeier).

The National Research Council ranked Penn State sixth in the nation in producing undergraduates who later earn a Ph.D. We are tenth in turning out graduates who receive National Science Foundation fellowships. Our faculty is fifth in winning Guggenheim Fellowships (1985–1986) and fourth in Fulbright Fellowships.

Penn State has contributed more alumni who work at IBM, General Electric, and Armstrong than any other university. A group of Fortune 500 executives ranked Penn State's business executive education programs the best in the country.

One of our professors of pharmacology, Arthur Hayes, was chosen chairman of the Food and Drug Administration; a dean of engineering, Nunzio Palladino, became chairman of the Nuclear Regulatory Commission; and our vice president for research, Charles Hosler, is a member of the National Science Board.

After our five-year capital campaign was only three years old, alumni generosity brought us so close to the goal that Jordan and Schreyer announced an expanded goal of $300,000,000, and it looks like we'll top that.

Already we have established and recruited more than two dozen scholars of international reputation for newly endowed chairs in the sciences, liberal arts, medicine, and engineering, as well as in agriculture, business administration, education, and telecommunications, and there are more to come. We have created a Biotechnology Institute dedicated to "putting biology to work for a better world" and, purely on a foundation of alumni gifts, built a five-story state-of-the-art laboratory building for the institute.

All that is a beginning of Penn State's bigger, broader drive to go for another kind of number one: a more important game in a tougher league.

23· The Happiest Hundredth

SURE enough, the Knight-Paterno Law of Letdown after a championship whacked us across the head in 1983. In our first three games, we lost, lost, lost—all in front of the dropped jaws and disbelief of mostly our own crowd.

The first of those losses, a preseason exhibition at Giants Stadium, knocked us off balance, not because of the opponent, always-powerful Nebraska, but the score: 44–6. In the shameful second, at Beaver Stadium, we failed to reach the end zone, and lost, 14–3—to Cincinnati???!!! Finally, again at home, our offense found itself, but the defense stayed lost: Iowa beat us, 42–34.

After recovering our pride with Temple (23–18) and Rutgers (36–25)—before *their* home crowds—we moved into three big games and took them all, Alabama (34–28), Syracuse (17–6), and West Virginia (41–23), only to get licked at Boston College, 27–17. That year, for the first time in history, Penn State played my old alma mater, Brown, and I was grateful that my kids preserved my good name, winning, 38–21. Next week, Notre Dame returned the courtesy of our visit, venturing into the mystical tradition of Beaver Stadium, although I don't think any TV reporters asked their coach any nincompoop questions. We beat them again, 34–30, but ended the regular season with only a tie playing Pitt, 24–24.

Our mediocrity brought one special reward. The big bowls—Sugar, Cotton, Orange, Fiesta—probably wouldn't have returned our phone calls. But the Aloha Bowl invited us to play Washington—in Hawaii! Besides enjoying our 13–10 victory there, the kids (including those in my own family) had the time of their lives on the beach.

Next year, 1984, was worse. Please, don't press me to name names or give details. Just be satisfied that we had a "winning" season, 6–5, and that was mainly because William and Mary, a kindly and gentle little college whom we had not played before (or since), accommodated us, 56–18. We disbanded for a not-too-merry Christmas, without a bowl for the first time in fourteen years.

1985. Third year after our glory. If we were impatient to wait for the natural cycle of the fourth year, this could be *it,* right? Right, except you wouldn't know it by the way we began: swamping each of our first two opponents, Maryland and Temple, by all of two points (20–18, 27–25); the next two by a single touchdown (East Carolina, 17–10; Rutgers, 17–10); then another two-point devastation of Alabama (19–17). The big consolation was that Alabama had been undefeated until we nicked them. The season kept going like that until we finally shut out Pitt, 31–0—and even surprised ourselves to be rated number two in the nation, undefeated and untied! Even more surprising, our match against Oklahoma in the Orange Bowl would again produce a clear national champion.

Todd Blackledge, a hard quarterback to replace, had not been replaced. In 1983 I played the best we had, a senior named Doug Strang, spelling him off in spots with a steady but not spectacular freshman, John Shaffer. By 1985 I was starting Shaffer. But this "best we had" came up with strikingly better results than anybody would guess from his arm, his legs, or his individual stats—because many people didn't take into account his brains and temperament. Throughout his high school career and at Penn State, Shaffer had started in forty-three games—and *never once failed to come up the winner.* Now, in 1985, leading a team that did not appear any more spectacular than he did, he had started every game, won every game, and run his streak up to fifty-four, a perfect lifetime of winning as we now headed for the Orange Bowl to play for the gold.

Well, we weren't ready yet. On New Year's night of 1986, Oklahoma did us in, 25–10, despite our strong defensive effort. The fans and the press box, always in search of single, simple explanations, put the blame on Shaffer.

In 1986, Penn State's hundredth year of football, we were ready. We knew it. We could feel it in spring practice, in fall practice, from the opening of the first game against Temple, which we took, 45–15. No matter that we had come so close in 1985, the expert pollsters started us near the bottom of the Top 20 in 1986, a place I found comfortable. I'd rather inch up than slip down. And inch up we did as, week after week after week, somebody above us tumbled—and we knocked off our opponent: Boston College (and Doug Flutie), East Carolina, Rutgers, Cincinnati, Syracuse, Alabama, West Virginia, Maryland, Notre Dame, and Pitt.

Jimmy Johnson's Miami Hurricanes, with Vinny Testaverde, the sure Heisman winner, at quarterback, owned the polls the way Republicans own New Hampshire. By season's end, we had climbed to second. Perfect. And the Fiesta Bowl's success in matching Miami to play Penn State on the night of January 2 set up the perfect national championship game.

For me it was also a perfect matchup for testing the crucial elements of my way of playing football: *The strongest team is the strongest defensive team. The surest strategy is to minimize the risk of losing the football. Kick the ball deep into the opponent's territory and scrap like hell to keep it there.*

Miami and Jimmy Johnson represented just the opposite. His team, his style of play, his recruiting, his tricks of intimidation of opposing teams are all built to support his refined taste for spectacular quarterbacks. And this year he had a miraculously talented daredevil in Testaverde. Loose and slippery as a goldfish. Spry as a grasshopper. Quick as a jaguar. Accurate as a hawk. Almost invulnerable.

Except for one thing. A dazzling, great passing quarterback lives in an environment that is the essence of vulnerability. His job description requires that *he part with the ball.* The better the thrower he is, the more his coach organizes his team, his practice sessions, his strategies, his play selection, around him. They *depend* on him to throw—and then *somebody else has got to be there to catch it.* That's where the advantage shifts to the superior defensive team.

In preparing, we played and replayed and again replayed film of the Hurricanes until we knew every one of them better than their mothers did. We set as our main target not Testaverde but his receivers. Instead of concentrating on sacking and shutting down the quarterback, we said, we'd let him throw— but change our coverages so frequently we'd confound his receivers.

While we were watching film, the Hurricanes were giving interviews. Dan Sileo, their defensive tackle, told one writer, "We played for the national championship on September 27 [when they beat Oklahoma, the previous year's champs]. As far as I'm concerned, Friday's game [the Fiesta Bowl] is just the end of the season."

Testaverde threw and threw, and completed more passes than I cared to count. But we kept their receivers off balance, which forced Testaverde to throw into crowds of football players. When he did, our secondary walloped their receivers as pure punishment for going after the ball, caught or not. As Shane Conlan said later, "They kept talking about how little our defensive backs were [Ray Isom, five-foot-nine; Duffy Cobbs, five-foot-eleven], but they'd never been hit by them."

The clear message of our hard knocks reached those receivers. They dropped seven of Testaverde's passes. I don't mean missed them. I mean dropped them. Far more damaging, we intercepted five of them—a stunning experience for a great quarterback who had heaved 116 consecutive passes in 1985 without an interception and had another streak of 114 in 1986.

The best of the interceptions, of course, as any Penn State fan will not soon forget, was the one that came eighteen seconds before the end of the game. We held the lead, 14–10, their ball. Fourth down, eight yards to a first. They stood only thirteen yards from a goal that would snatch the game and the championship from us. We didn't need a management consultant to know, first, that Johnson had to go for a first down, and, second, that he would probably go for it in the air. (Later, Jimmy told the press he wanted to run the ball, a gutsy impulse. But he didn't call a time-out to discuss it or order it. I don't know if Testaverde signaled him, or if Johnson signaled Testaverde, or if the quarterback decided on his own. Testaverde did say later that he just knew he'd score on a pass. Not just go for the first down, but score.)

Our defenders were trained for this moment.

"We knew in key situations," little Ray Isom explained later, "that he [Testaverde] would stare at the receiver he was going to throw to. On first-and-ten he may be the best quarterback in the country. But on third-and-eight, or fourth-and-thirteen, he maybe needs to work on it."

Testaverde dispatched three receivers. But his eyes had never loosened their grip on his split end Brett Perrimen. As the ball took flight toward Perrimen, Nittany Lions mobbed him, and our Pete Giftopoulos, in loving embrace, gathered that ball into his belly. Then he fell with it to his knees. For a split second I thought he was praying, until suddenly he raised the ball like a holy grail.

We beat Miami not because Testaverde didn't pass well, but because Miami had come to believe he would pass well no matter what. Jimmy Johnson's dependence on his greatest strength, the year's best quarterback and one of the best of all time, probably did him in.

* * *

Jimmy Johnson remained a puzzle to me. He ran across the field to shake hands just as my "designated lifters" swarmed to take me over. I didn't know what to say to him. He had wanted that game, and I'd been on both sides of that feeling. Minutes later, he came to our locker room to congratulate the Lions, which he didn't have to do and which was hard to do. Yet on the field he hadn't flicked an eye when, after John Shaffer threw a pass and the officials were watching the ball downfield, one of Jimmy's players slammed Shaffer across the back of the head dangerously and illegally, knocking him down with no purpose but to injure him. It was one of the dirtiest things I've ever seen in football, and I wondered whether Jimmy was troubled by that style of play.

I don't know whether Jimmy helped his kids plan their disgraceful walkout of a dinner in advance of the Fiesta Bowl that was to honor both teams. But I know he was there. Nor did he raise a finger of caution when we were climbing out of our bus for the locker room as his team, representing the University of Miami and supposedly higher education, just about blocked our path, waving and taunting and yelling, "We'll get you, you mothers." (I'm only using half their word.) The Penn Staters were so shocked I placed myself between the two teams and ordered my guys, "Just keep going."

What puzzled me most was that, year by year, Jimmy had grown into an outstanding coach. The main reason he didn't get the kind of credit—and professional respect—that would naturally have come to him was that the sideshow of bully tactics, thuggery, and goonery stole the attention from his true skills.

He remained not only a puzzle but a stranger to me. Some years Jimmy and his wife showed up at Nike's annual resort party for its endorsing coaches. I like the Nike deal best for this one annual opportunity to socialize with other coaches while eating and drinking a little more than we should. Each time, Jimmy struck me as standoffish, a bit filled with himself, not comfortable in a social group. The Fiesta Bowl championship game that we won added to a reputation he was getting—with which I sympathized from experience—of being good enough to get to a championship game, but not good enough to win it.

Then a change came over him. Soon after he repeated his Fiesta Bowl trip in 1987, but this time beating Oklahoma for the national title, the Nike group gathered again. As we faced the hardships of St. John's in the Virgin Islands, I ran into him in a hotel elevator.

I said, "Congratulations, Jim."

He surprised me with a big hand grasp and said, "It's like somebody took a monkey off my back."

That was the first trusting, unguarded thing I'd ever seen him do. During that trip, he became one of the boys, as though he no longer chafed to prove something, as though he'd suddenly grown up.

I was glad to see him get hired in 1989 by the Dallas Cowboys. Pro football may be good for him, and I know he will be good for it.

In certain life-style ways, Johnson reminds me of Barry Switzer (who resigned from Oklahoma under fire as I was writing this), another member of our Nike endorsing group. They're both drawn to a fast track. Barry, a more appealing guy than one might guess from the behavior he tolerates from his team, has no hypocrisy in him. He never hands out any baloney publicly about what his kids' grades are or how many graduate.

I always regretted my intended off-the-record wisecrack to some newsguys who asked about my leaving college coaching. I tossed back that I didn't want to "turn over the game to the Switzers and the Sherrills." Barry is a great kidder, practical jokester, and fun guy to be around, but my crack bothered me and I apologized to him as soon as I could. I didn't give a damn about what Sherrill felt.

Jackie Sherrill is a different art form. As far back as 1978, when he was coaching Pitt, he stopped existing for me. We had been competing to recruit a good linebacker in Paulsboro, New Jersey. I went with an assistant coach to Paulsboro and phoned the kid's home from a motel. His mother said, somewhat harried, that she didn't know where her son was. Sherrill's style of sportsmanship already being well known, I assumed Pitt had stashed the kid away somewhere.

At 1:45 A.M. my motel room phone rang. It wasn't the kid or his mother. It was Sue. She was crying. Sherrill had called her at our home in State College in the middle of the night, demanded to know where I was, and then yelled:

"I know that son of a bitch has that kid, and I'm going to find him and beat the crap out of him."

When Sue refused to tell him where to reach me, Sherrill pinned a few vile names on her, too. Brave, heroic man.

Neither of us got the linebacker. The kid chose Minnesota.

There's one bit of gratitude I guess I ought to express to Sherrill. When he later signed a fat-money contract with Texas A&M, which got a big press, Steve Garban, our senior vice president, called me in and asked, "Joe, are we paying you enough?"

I said, "I don't know. Why don't you call Don Canham [the athletic director] at Michigan and find out what they pay Bo Schembechler. I ought to get about the same as Bo."

So, thanks to Sherrill, I got an instant $25,000 raise that I probably never would have thought to ask for.

Johnny Majors (who had preceded Sherrill at Pitt, where he was good for both Pitt and eastern football) and I would share those split-second handshakes running off the field, but I never got to know him until our Nike get-togethers began a few years ago. A lot of other coaches cross paths working together on other staffs, but Penn State's is the only staff I've ever been on. Some guys live on the phone with each other. They gab about job openings, exchanging opportunities for their assistant coaches, or saying, "So-and-so beat you last week. Is there some new tactic going on in your conference?" Some guys are phone people. When I can avoid it, I don't even like to return calls. Maybe I isolate myself because I'm considerably older than all of them except Michigan's Bo Schembechler.

So I didn't know Johnny Majors until we got embroiled in a drama the year Nike brought us to St. Thomas. Our airline lost Sue's and my luggage. In St. Thomas, we were assigned a condominium room that connected to the Majors' through a common living room and kitchen. By this time, he was coaching at Tennessee. I was left without a stitch of clothes except what was on my back. Johnny said, "No problem, I've got plenty." The amazing thing was that he handed me a sport coat exactly like one I'd lost, down to the tiniest herringbone, and exactly the same size. He wore the same pants size, same shoe size. I'm the kind who packs three days of clothes for a five-day trip. John packs eight days for five, including twelve pairs of pants. For the next few days, I was better dressed than ever in my life—and found out what delightful people the Majors are.

And I feel the same about Vince and Barbara Dooley. What people! In 1982, right after we beat Georgia for our first national championship, I came out of the locker room to board our bus. Who's waiting for me but Barbara Dooley! We'd already grown to like the Dooleys on the Nike trips, and the four of us had spent time together during the week preceding the game. But here we'd beaten them for all the marbles. People often don't understand the high stakes and emotions that ride on a game like that. Winning is heaven—and losing crushes the soul. Anyhow, Barbara grabbed me at the door of the bus and gave me a great big kiss. I stammered, "Geez, Barbara, I don't know how to feel."

"Bull," she replied, in part. "Just enjoy it."

24· The Hellfires of '88

As any two-bit fortuneteller might have predicted, 1987 was a letdown year. In fact, that year, following our second championship (8–4), was close to a carbon copy of the year that followed our first championship (8–4–1). Both times we got postseason bowl invitations that probably resulted more from our power at the box office than the power of that year's team. In 1987 we went to the Citrus Bowl, where the orange of Clemson squeezed us like lemons, 35–10.

By far the most important play of that game happened three weeks before the kickoff. On December 11, in a routine workout at our indoor practice field, Blair Thomas, our tailback, caught a cleat in the artificial turf and went down in pain. We soon learned the worst: He had torn the anterior cruciate ligament of his right knee. On January 11, our doctors operated. Playing in his forthcoming senior year would be out of the question.

The loss to us—not for the Clemson game, but for 1988— was incalculable. I've said this out loud and I'll say it here again: There is absolutely no doubt in my mind that Blair Thomas was to become the leading candidate for the Heisman Trophy in 1988. Not just one of them, but *the* leading candidate, regardless of whoever else managed to get nominated. People know I don't often talk like that. Blair Thomas is the best all-around back I have ever coached in thirty-eight years. Lydell Mitchell might compare, but Blair is quicker.

Am I exaggerating? Ask Notre Dame coach Lou Holtz, who

explained one reason he lost to us in 1987: "I said before the game that Blair is the best back we've played against all year."

Or West Virginia coach Don Nehlen: "That Blair Thomas . . . We must have missed five million tackles on him alone."

The evaluation I like best is by Blair himself: "I really don't have that many moves. I just run."

As a junior in 1987, Thomas caught twenty-three passes for 300 yards, rushed for 1,414 yards, the combination giving him a Penn State yardage record, and he scored thirteen touchdowns.

We had to go into 1988 without a tested quarterback. Matt Knizner, Shaffer's backup, who took over for 1987, had graduated. In fact, the hallmark of this whole team was inexperience. More players faced their first year of college football—either as redshirts or "true" freshmen—than on any team in my coaching career. Our defense team was to have seven new starters.

In two years, three years, there might be no stopping this band of raw and potential football talent. We had recruited well. The players drilled well and with high spirit. I felt good working with this happy new bunch. But the attitudes of winning mature slowly. The even more delicate factor of leadership also seasons slowly before it leaps out from unexpected sources. On this year's depth chart, the potential leaders, those who lift the others to a vision of winning, had not yet stepped out to stake their claim. I couldn't remember opening a season with fewer hints of what to expect.

In our annual preseason media conference, reporters, who routinely ask for the secrets of the future, pressed me for championship predictions. I think reporters think that for every possible reporter's question a coach has an answer. (The coach may not tell it, but he secretly *has* it.) I said, "We talk about a national championship every year, but this is not a national championship team. If the pieces fall into place, hopefully it will be in a couple of years. But it's going to take a while."

The only thing I knew for sure was that if I tried to make this unusually young squad as good by the middle of 1988 as they could be by the middle of 1989, I might lose them. I could rush them so badly they could lose their emotion and self-confidence. All I could do was say, for example, to Tom Bill, our new starting quarterback, "Tom, here are legitimate goals for you. Here's how good I expect you to be after five or six games, or—" And I might not even tell that to Tom. We had two great freshmen receivers. Terry Smith and Dave Daniels, unless I'm dead wrong, are going to be great football players—but that's not written in the sky. If I give them too big a load too soon that they can't handle, they might never be. I'd rather be a week too late playing a kid than a week too early. A coach has to have a feel for that, and he better feel it right. But when reporters ask *how* I make those decisions, sometimes I want to answer, "I wish to hell I knew." After forty years in this business, all I know is that you better know.

In my weekly summer newsletter to our players, I sized up what they'd have to face in our opening game:

> *Virginia*—This is the biggest game Virginia has ever played . . . They changed the date of their William and Mary game to September 3 (the week before we play them) so as to give their new QB a chance to get some game experience. This will be the best football team in Virginia's history, and they have great momentum after their [All-American] bowl win over BYU [Brigham Young University]. They have superb speed on defense and I mean superb speed. One of their wide-outs will be a #1 draft pick, a marvelous athlete. Although their QB is inexperienced, he is an outstanding prospect. He has a big-league arm, is big, and can really run. Coach Welsh was on our staff for nine years, and several members of his

staff either played at Penn State or were graduate assistants for us. They have been waiting to get at us and they will be ready. *So will we.*

On Saturday, September 10, as the players were having their knees and ankles taped at our hotel in Charlottesville, I found a letter from one of the kids in my box. The writer of it, who chose not to sign his name, clearly had been concentrating harder on practice than on fine points in his English class, but the letter gave me a lift:

9/9/88

Dear Coach,

Good morning. I'm writing you in regards to tonights game. I've been around a long time, and I have learned alot since my tenure here. I know what it takes to win, and I know this team can with our current attitude. As you know, this team is youg, lacking maturity. But I am encourage because its a hardworking team.

These are things you already know, so why am I writing. I want you to remember back to the 1986 season when we were at Alabama. It was an afternoon game and we were eating our pregame meal. As usual, after every pregame meal, you give a talk on what it's going to take to win.

This talk was of itself, different, special, and unique. You gave the up date of Alabama's season and their opponents. While the press was making them (Bama) to be something, you told the true story. After sharing your thoughts with us, you then came on strong with a tenacious voice crying, *"They're nothing."* It was an emotional transition that turned the whole atmosphere completely around. Young men who were nervous inside, with pregame butterflies, were transformed into conscious, stoned face, hard nosed football players. You were a big reason why we won that game. It takes a particular kind of person to get 78 players, as a unit, to forget about their fears and to know that they have what it takes to win.

It is unbelievable what the power of speech can do, especially when you pour out your heart. Because, as you know, what comes from the heart people can feel and be moved from one direction to the other. I'm encouraged about tonights game and I'm praying that the Lord will use you in the way that He sees as being beneficial to us as a team.

God bless you Coach
Go for it!!

In traveling to the stadium, we observe a custom that Rip Engle followed during my playing days at Brown and through all the years I assisted him at Penn State. I have no idea what other teams do, because I've never gone to the stadium with another team. We make that solemn trip (from the hotel when we're away; from our athletic building when we're home) in three buses, the first for the offensive team, the second for defense and special teams, the third for reserve players and nonplaying personnel. I ride that first bus, in the right front double seat at the door; directly behind me on the right is Fran Ganter, the offensive coordinator; next, on both sides of the aisle toward the front, are the offensive coaches. And behind them, the offensive players. Except for one. As we ride to the coliseum for the joust, across the aisle from me, directly behind the driver, the double seat is occupied by the first gladiator among equals: the starting quarterback.

Every couple of years or so, I look across at a new profile of some silent, brave, tense young warrior in that seat of honor and challenge. Right arm wrapped around his huge plain helmet, he gazes straight ahead, ignoring the stream of fans, the startled faces of those who recognize their uniformed heroes, the traffic, the hoop-la; he just looks ahead, fine-tuning his concentration, opening the faucets of his will and absolute resolve, dousing the sneaky flame-licks of his fears, getting secure in the deepest privacy of his soul. I do something of the same in my seat. But sometimes, without turning my head, I might pick up in the corner of my eye a hint of how the new kid is doing.

On this evening in Virginia, the fellow in the front seat, Tom Bill, looked just fine. Good sculptured warrior's face, head erect, world shut out. Like he had been waiting for this night all his life. And he had. Two years back, in 1986, I got a first good look at the cool steel in his freshman bones when we were drilling, drilling, before meeting Miami in the Fiesta Bowl. No, we didn't expect to call on him for the game. But in his practice role on the "foreign" team, Tom Bill played—*was*—Vinny Testaverde. He was tough on us, and we were tough on him, and I knew we had a good one. Tonight he'd be okay.

On our first possession, Sam Gash, a sophomore, climaxed a strong march with a one-yard touchdown run.

Then we kicked off to them, and they fumbled the kick. Darren Perry snatched the ball for us, and Gary Brown, another sophomore, scored from the five. We intercepted a pass, and Tom Bill threw to Michael Timpson, our track-star wideout, for a five-yard touchdown. All in less than eleven minutes!—and we were leading, 21–0.

Tom Bill completed fifteen passes out of twenty-two that night for 179 yards and two touchdown hits. During the second half, feeling pretty secure, I relieved him for a few plays to give Tony Sacca, fresh out of high school, his first taste of college play. I felt I had to. Bill's backup, Lance Lonergan, had stubbed his thumb against a helmet. Doug Sieg, a sophomore with an extraordinary throwing arm, was out with a bad back. We needed the protection of some game experience for Sacca.

Every break that game fell our way. Final score: a surprising and heady 42–14. Had I made a big mistake? Did we have some kind of miracle team here? If they were this good on opening night, how good might they get by the end of October?

Only a truly tough opponent could give us a reading on who we were. Boston College rode into Beaver Stadium the following week for that purpose, although they left no clear answers. Deep into the fourth quarter, we were tied, 20–20, after a game of trading turnovers and goofs, competing to find out not how good we were, but how green, jumpy, and sloppy each team could be. Our side lost ninety-eight yards and ninety-nine months off my life to eight penalties. One of them had kept alive the BC drive for their tying touchdown—a pure gift from the treasury of our inexperience. Another nullified a gorgeous touchdown pass lofted by Bill and snatched perfectly by Dave Daniels, the promising freshman. The worst of it was that both fouls were committed by older players who should have been setting examples of poise for the younger ones. Despite ourselves, we failed to throw the game away. With fifty-eight seconds remaining, Ray Tarasi, our walk-on field-goal kicker, centered one perfectly from thirty-seven yards out. We survived, 23–20.

So our test now became Rutgers, who had already upset Michigan State. At half time we led 10–7, but they rapidly ran two more touchdowns to go ahead, 21–10. Then, late in the third quarter, the terrible happened. Two teams of players untangled themselves after a blitz, leaving one guy in blue lying on the field, unable to rouse himself: No. 12, Tom Bill, our quarterback. The worst kind of injury: his knee. In all my years of this game, I had never lost a quarterback to a serious injury. I was soon to learn that that moment was the last of Tom Bill's season.

With Lance Lonergan's thumb wound persisting stubbornly, I had no choice but to send in lanky, leggy, too young Sacca to take over. This time, not for game experience but for real. Two touchdowns behind, we had to go for broke. Fifteen times we signaled Sacca to pass. Five times he completed, for ninety-five yards, not bad at all for a rookie who shouldn't have been out there at all. He led a ninety-yard march to the two-yard line. But too much was being asked too soon of a kid who, under real pressure, had never played before a bigger crowd than they collect at Delran (New Jersey) High School. At third down, his pass flew inches above the fingertips of Dave Jakob, who was in the clear for it. On fourth down, he just missed Timpson. Either pass, as it turned out, would have won the game. Sacca's legs were not only long and fast, but almost too good. He depended on them too much, whirling and scrambling out of the pocket, reaching for the magic tricks of escape that had been so easy for him as a high school star. Overuse of his natural agility exposed him not only to sacking but to injury. We needed to teach him to throw the ball away or go down before taking a serious loss. We'd have to drill him more in that, and in time he'd learn it. Finally, Gary Brown ran the ball across once more to reduce our margin of loss to 21–16.

Next week, Lonergan's thumb still wouldn't come around. This time, the bus ride to meet Temple—on their turf—was all different. Tony Sacca, this kid I scarcely knew, whom the players he was to lead didn't know, who hardly knew himself or knew who he was supposed to be in this sudden central role, rode the front seat. The strangeness of it. In all my years, I had never started a freshman at quarterback, never imagined I would. His fingers dug into the helmet in his lap. Was he struggling to control a telltale habit of nail biting? Those strained, glossy, fixed eyes—was that a look of being confident or stricken? Someday I'd know every flick of his lashes, but now I didn't know how to begin reading him.

It turned out to be a good night. Sacca threw for two touchdowns. Leroy Thompson ran for two more, and Andre Collins blocked a punt that Willie Thomas grabbed and ran across for a fifth. We beat Temple, 45–9, and did it again the following week to Cincinnati, 35–9, when Tony threw two more for scores.

On national television from Beaver, the reality of our plight hit home when we simply didn't have the strength to handle Syracuse. They took us, 24–10. Next week, Alabama's defense tied us in knots, and ours tied them in knots, but they did it better, and we lost, 8–3. Again, we could have won.

But we saved our worst for West Virginia. Leaving aside the domineering performance of their quarterback, Major Harris, we took a penalty for, of all things, twelve men on the field and another for a personal foul that canceled a sack of Harris and led to a West Virginia score. We blew a sure interception on our own five-yard line, then had a field goal blocked. Despite all that, we did score thirty points. But our greenness and absence of concentration helped them to an overpowering fifty-one.

Lonergan's thumb finally healed in time for Maryland, and I was able to relieve Sacca with respect and a few prayers that we hadn't damaged his natural growth. Immediately, the whole team played better—not because Lance is a more talented athlete than Sacca, which he's not, but because he was a four-year veteran at scrimmaging, a sharp-eyed and experienced reader of defenses, master of the playbook, and strong in the huddle. The kids knew him and trusted his steadiness. We won, 17–10, making us a winning team again, although barely, at 5–4.

The Pitt game, on our ground, crystalized more clearly than ever what was lacking in this team. For example, running backs were aggressive as hell if they had the ball, but were not adequate blockers. These kids did not yet know that winning takes that small, critical, unreasonable extra commitment. They didn't know it because winning in Division I college football was not programmed in their memory. They had virtually no teammates who *did* know from having done it. These kids had not been here in '86. Winning was not something they had stretched for, wept for, accepted pain for. Despite my best speeches, they didn't know how you have to believe in yourself to get it. Victory, they still felt, was something that came automatically with their high school stats, the Penn State colors, and the famous winning coach.

If this team couldn't learn the price of winning by the experience of winning and by playing beside winners, how were they to learn it? Maybe from the shame and pain of losing.

At half time, on his side of the locker room, calm, gentle Jerry Sandusky, the defensive coordinator, tore into a rage with the defense. Literally, he roared through clenched teeth: "This is a *football* game! You go after your guy and you get him and you don't let him go until you *know* he's down! No matter what, you get that guy down and you *keep* him down. That's where the game *is*. This is a *football* game. You want to play? That's how you play it!"

As the whole team, offense and defense, crowded at the locker-room door for my signal to cram through the tunnel, I hit them, too, bringing out that bulging vein in my temple:

"You *want* this game? You go out there and *take* it. Don't give it away. It *belongs* to you. The game belongs to whoever decides to *take* it!"

Doubt sows doubt. Lack of confidence spreads and undermines confidence. Feelings spread not only from coach to player, but from players to coach as well. I take responsibility for losing that Pitt game. There was a moment that maybe we could have won it. The score was 14–7 against us halfway through the fourth quarter. We were sitting on Pitt's twenty-two-yard line. Fourth down. Two yards to go for a first.

Those are the glorious, yet the most terrible, moments of coaching football. Do we go out there and *take* that game that *belongs* to us? Of *course* we do.

But which way do we take it?

Only one way made any sense. Only a fool would not take the field goal. Look, the wind was headed straight-on between those goal posts. That pretty wind was giving me a message, singing me a tune. The clock was on its knee pleading. If the kick was right and we made it 14–10, there'd be time for a shot at the touchdown—and a clean win. If I did the foolhardy thing and went for the first down, we'd have to get the touchdown, then still need a two-point conversion to win. In this hard-luck year, how much luck do you have a right to expect? You can't be frivolous with the fate of these kids. Percentages are percentages. You're a coach. You've got to go with the coach's play.

Damn, that's what I did. With a pat, I sent little Henry Adkins out to make the kick. Henry's instep hit the ball too squarely. He kicked a low line drive that never had a chance.

I hear now, this very second, the cry of eternal melancholy that wailed through my chest. Why didn't I listen to my heart? Why didn't I go for the first down? Why didn't I give my kids their chance to win? Damn those good common-sense reasons, the wind, the timing, the percentages! Why didn't I give my kids the kind of call that would have let them *take* their football game?

I gathered the team around me in the locker room after the loss. After a silence, I said: "You played hard tonight. You played well. But mostly you played hard. You weren't coached well. I didn't give you the chance to win the game, and I want to tell you I'm very sorry. I didn't make the decisions that would have let you win the game, and I want to tell you how sorry I am."

I don't know if the kids knew for sure what play I was talking about. Later, people told me that players, in postgame radio interviews, puzzled at being asked, said their coach was right to make the field-goal call. But my gut still pounded at me for not having gone the other way. All the way home on a short ride that took forever, a friend tried to cheer me with reminders that we might not have made the first down either. But I heard myself muttering to him my most cursed words: "I *hate* to lose. Been that way all my life. I can't *stand* losing."

Yes, I know, I needn't be reminded. I'm the guy who preaches that winning isn't everything. I'm the first to say you've got to be willing to lose, that you mustn't be afraid to lose. But something deep in my belly fights weeping and gets angry when I have to suffer losing. I didn't promise, when I started this story, to be consistent, or to resolve contradictions, or even to try to avoid them. Like suffering, contradictions are life and have to be endured.

So we headed for our final game, nationally televised, with undefeated Notre Dame, who might become national champions. What was on the line for me was a tough football game and a chance to show we had improved by winning it. But what was on the line for every reporter who covered it was that the game would either bring us another winning season (barely, at 6–5) or Penn State's first losing season (5–6) in fifty years and the first in my coaching career. I kept saying to writers, to callers on my weekly radio show, to TV interviewers, that the losing-season prospect was an overblown issue. What's the big-deal difference between 6–5 and 5–6? I threw back that question so often, I hope I got the clear force of my answer across, and only Sue knows that late at night in the privacy of my own kitchen the prospect of a losing season irritated the hell out of me.

The Irish came out playing hard and clean and ready for a stronger opponent than we were. Spare me telling the details. Final score, 21–3.

On the sideline in the closing seconds of that game, when the clear intent of the *fata* could no longer be frustrated—we were going to lose—my mind raced back to a moment like this at the end of 1966, my first year as a head coach. We were closing our season at five wins, five losses. Everybody I knew was saying that Paterno had been a good assistant coach, but didn't have it to be a head coach. So now I said to myself, "Okay, I'm taking the same attitude now that I did then."

In the five games we lost in 1966, two teams who beat us were UCLA and Michigan State, who went on to face each other for the national championship in the Rose Bowl. Another we lost to Syracuse in the year of Larry Csonka and Floyd Little, two of the greatest college football players ever. One of the remaining two, Georgia Tech, remained undefeated and went to the Orange Bowl.

We were not a great Penn State football team in 1988, but our losses were to a lot of great football teams. We played possibly the toughest schedule we'd ever had.

Rutgers was the only loss we could not excuse ourselves for. They played well, but were not as good a football team as we were. Aside from all the bad luck and injuries, some officials' decisions that went against us and that shouldn't have, the erratic kicking, we lost four games to four teams that lost only six games combined all season.

Still, I couldn't just explain the season away like that. I had to make sure there wasn't something else. Because we've always been able to come back and put together a championship football team out of the ashes doesn't mean it's going to happen simply because we want it to happen. I had to make sure there wasn't some hidden factor we were concealing from ourselves. What was there in the coaching? Was there something in the morale of the squad?

I had to talk with *everybody*. And before I talked with my coaches, I wanted to talk with the players.

And then, with nobody to talk to, I had to make a tough decision of my own.

25· Phoenix

A discovery startled me not long ago when I was thinking about those four-year up-and-down cycles of college football teams, including my own. Yes, we've had great teams as well as our share of postchampionship letdown teams. What surprised me was that since I took charge of this team in 1966, *every* Penn Stater who has played out his football eligibility has fulfilled one or more of the college player's highest dreams. He has

played an undefeated, untied season, or
played in a bowl game for the national championship, or
played on a team that won the national championship.

I have not hesitated to state that to any high school recruit we go after. It is not a campaign promise, but a fact.

And I do not plan that any member of the team of 1988 will become an exception to that unbroken twenty-three-year experience.

The design of life is cycles, the back-and-forth interplay of opposites. Dawn is the beginning of a journey to nightfall, and nightfall leads to dawn. Food satisfies hunger, and eating starts us toward hunger again. The eye absorbs light, light makes us blink, and the blink restores the eye for light again. We score, the opponent gets the ball; they score, the ball is ours.

Careers go in cycles, too. In 1967 and '68, I closed myself in a room, alone. Because nobody could help me, alone I rethought the game of football to fit my team. I taught a new game to my coaches and my players, then watched and tested every move, trusting no one and not letting a detail slip my notice. When a guy stakes his life on something new, there's no other way.

So I learned how to win football games, and there were some years it looked as if I'd learned it better than anybody else.

A cycle was in motion. The coaches learned the new ways well. The better they learned, the more I relied on them, not just to follow my plan, but to bring their intelligence, their own inventiveness, their love of the game, to making the plan work better and better, to make Penn State football better and better. Over a span of years, the more these staff coaches grew, the more I released my grip, gave them room to develop kids according to their instincts, to analyze our opponents for themselves, to call their own plays on the field. We kept winning, and the more we won, the more self-assured they became.

Until the hellfires of '88.

Then I knew, leaving the sidelines of that final game at Notre Dame, that I had to restart a cycle. I had to go back to 1967 and get my hands into *everything* again. As our coaches had grown better and better, I let them watch and analyze game films by themselves and I went home and watched mine. Maybe we began to see different things. Worse, maybe we had begun to think different ways and didn't know it. Meanwhile, some old-timers had become head coaches elsewhere or retired, and I had new assistants with whom I had never worked as closely as the earlier ones.

In the cycle of leadership style, there is a time for letting go, for giving people room to move, to make their own mistakes, and grow—and there is a time for tightening the reins and getting a team into a single, unified rhythm.

This year, one part of our problem was that our offense had

become fancy. The press and the fans cheer a fancy offense, whether it makes good football sense or not. Contrary to the basic strategies that have steadily kept us a winning team, I think we threw the ball too much. Too often we were at second down, five or six to go, and we threw the ball. The less jazzy but sounder game was to just run that football tough until we got our score. Especially after we were forced to send in Tony Sacca, we should have immediately said, "Okay, there's only one way we can go. We've got a young kid in here and we can't be a sophisticated, daredevil football team. We've got to be a physical football team." We didn't say that. If we had, people might have missed a few thrills watching our impressive freshman quarterback, but we also might have won a couple of football games that we didn't win. I had to face that I have a very young offensive staff that needs more from me. First-rate guys, but young. In the past few years, I have not been giving them enough direct leadership.

On the other side of the ball, on defense, a superb staff of great teachers has grown in its own directions, too. Over the years we've developed some differences of opinion as to whether it's better to give a kid, especially a young one, fewer assignments to master or a greater variety to confuse the opponent with, whether to emphasize more repetition in practice or less. We differ about that—and on both sides of the difference, we're guessing. That staff has a great defense package. But each kid's got to be able to master that package. He's got to be able to execute it and make his adjustments under a lot of pressure. Too often our young kids have made mistakes that I don't think we had to make. I had to face the fact that strategic questions like that one need my direct, hands-on leadership.

I took a lot of heat from the media about one decision in 1988—and I would make the same decision again, although with one important change. After the loss of Blair Thomas, and with no compelling choice for a replacement, I decided to rotate running backs among three talented young players—Gary Brown and Leroy Thompson, both sophomores, and Sean Redman, a junior—until one of them clearly won the job. Naturally, none of the three kids was crazy about that arrangement.

What I would do differently is that I'd be tougher with them. We babied several of the best younger kids, particularly the young backs, and I think we paid heavily for it. So did they. We babied Gary and Leroy. They both wanted to start and both wanted to carry the ball, but they weren't much interested in blocking for the other guy, and that's what loses football games. We couldn't miss the rumors that Brown was thinking about transferring and that Leroy might want to go back to Tennessee. Letting that kind of talk affect the way we pushed those kids was the worst thing we could do. We should have simply said, "I don't give a damn if you're going to transfer or not. You're going out there to block that guy, and I won't put up with any crap. If you don't like it, go." That's always been my way. But letting up this year for this unusually young bunch affected the way they played. Despite what some fans and writers thought, the rotation had nothing to do with it. I've rotated kids before, and they got better because the uncertainty made them practice better. These kids didn't get better because we were worried about losing them and didn't press them hard enough. I was thinking long-range, when I needed to take care of first things first, and failed to.

One after another after another I called the players in. I sat down with each on my big office couch and probed for what he had on his mind. What surprised me most was that not a single kid even hinted at some hidden problem. None reported any cliques developing in the squad. No enmities or damaging rivalries or even kids who didn't like each other.

What came out most was the naïveté and immaturity of the younger players. They griped about not playing more. They didn't yet know that you pay your dues before you play. Some

of the older guys regretted that they hadn't sat down some of
the younger kids and said, "Look, your time is going to come."
But that was correctable. And with time would come the
leadership that lay waiting in them.

A lot of nights I lay awake replaying the year's games in my
head.

I saw ever more clearly what needed to happen, but that
didn't answer the looming question: how to make it happen.

There were three ways I could go.

I could keep doing what we had always been doing and hope
it all would get better.

I could back out. Thirty-nine years was long enough for
anybody. In twenty-three years as head coach, with more than
two hundred victories, nineteen bowl games, more than four
dozen all-Americans and over one hundred players in the National Football League—wasn't that enough for anybody?

Or I could start over. I could put myself back to where I was
in '65, '66. I could go through some new equivalent of that
summer of '67 in the upstairs room—except this ordeal would
have to be on the field, with coaches, with kids, with drills and
repetitions, repetitions and drills, until we got it right. Start all
over for one more cycle of freshmen recruits to proud seniors—

Yes, start all over one more time *and end this thing in four
or five years in a blaze of glory.*

The memory of '66 brought tingles. How I loved to coach.
How I loved to be on the field.

How I love *now* to coach, to be on the field.

When, how, why did I let all this other stuff happen? When
how, why, did all this time-consuming, distracting celebrity
sneak up on me and my real work, trying hard to change me
into a man for all seasons: fund raiser, philanthropist, endorser
of causes, banquet speaker, symbol? Yes, I've used my pulpit
of football victories to try to get some good done in the world

and I feel good about that. But none of it has brought me as much fun as coaching football.

In those first dark days of December, something was missing. No bowl game to start practicing for. A bowl during Christmas break had become part of my routine, the coaches' routine, the older players' routine.

The younger kids felt disappointment, but not in the same way. A bowl was in their dream, but not their routine. They had other experiences that needed absorbing, and the new job to which I had just appointed myself was to bring these kids and those experiences together.

To start, I gathered the whole hundred-plus of them, rookies and graduating seniors alike, in the squad room, a theater with rising tiers of seats, for a most direct kind of indoctrination in Penn State football. Only two years earlier, we were champions of the nation—yet to most of these kids that was only legend. A story. A story from history. They hadn't thrown their bodies into our vanquished opponents. They hadn't even *seen* the games that still pounded in the blood of the rest of us.

We showed them an hour-long film of the highlights of 1986, play for play, stretch for stretch, every game without fail coming through with the big play when we needed it, down to The Last Interception. I could feel something stirring in the room, though I don't want to read too much into it. This was not just exciting football film. This was their team. Their uniform. Their numbers. This was the tradition thrust on them. This *was* them.

The games weren't won just because the players were talented. Those players won because they used their talent—to known limits and beyond. They didn't have luck. They made luck, and they *used* luck. The games were not played. They were seized.

I thought I felt something begin to happen in the room. No way to be sure.

A few days later, just before they left for Christmas at home, I gathered the players again in the same room. In my hand I held some notes from my files of more than two decades earlier. I also held some notes of reports that had come to me that week. The fresh notes disturbed me and, at the same time, gave me an opportunity that I would now make the most of.

I talked to my future champions and said approximately this:

—Since we met last Sunday, I've been asking a lot of questions and I've talked to a lot of people. I've found out some things I probably should have known but didn't take enough trouble to know. We have people here who cut classes and are late for classes. We have two or three guys that have out-and-out just bad grades, and I'm not sure they're going to survive. We've already lost one.

—Another thing that got back to me is that we've got a few arrogant young jackasses in the study hall who have alienated a lot of other athletes from other teams because they go in there and kind of shove people around and take over the computer and do anything they want to do, including playing games on them when other people want to use them for study. Because they're football players, they're big shots. I'm mostly talking about some of the freshmen.

—You guys have had your fun. Some of you are going to come down to earth in a hurry.

—If there's anything I can't stand—if there's *anything* I can't *stand*—it's an arrogant football player who thinks he's better than somebody else. I can't stand it, and I'm not going to put up with it. I don't care how good a football player you are or how good you think you are, I'll make your life miserable for you. And don't think you're going to transfer out of here, because I'll kick your rear end out of here with your tail dragging and you'll never go anyplace else.

—Some of you are getting C's and D's in courses where you should be getting B's and think you're doing okay. You think you're doing okay because right now you're being milk-fed, whether you know it or not. Last week, after the 1986 film, we talked about a commitment by everybody. Maybe I didn't stress a couple of things. I wasn't talking only about a physical commitment. I was talking about a commitment to getting an education. If you don't get the grades you're capable of getting, don't come to me and say, "How come I'm not playing more, Coach?" Every time I look at you, I'll know your grade-point average. I'm going to know every single time you cut a class. If you don't do what you know you have to do, don't expect to play. Don't kid yourselves about that. Don't come and ask me what's wrong.

—Last week, I went back to notes that I made in 1968, 1967. At that time, I was selling an idea called the Grand Experiment. Some of you guys have never heard about it. I came to Penn State from an Ivy League school. When I came here I was determined we were going to have good football teams with people who belonged in college. People who could go out on a football field, knock somebody on their rear end, pick them up, not taunt them, and when they walked off that field, people who could be gentlemen, in some cases scholars, and be the kind of people everybody would look up to. I didn't want what I saw going on in colleges around the country: jock houses and animal houses and all that kind of junk. I wanted a bunch of guys that could walk onto a football field and be tough and mean and ornery, but play the game the way it's supposed to be played, and be somebody everybody liked to be around. Not arrogant, not bullies.

—I want you to understand that you are a Penn State football player. Ten years from now, you'll walk into an office and put your card down, and somebody will say, "Oh, you're the guy who played at Penn State." The players who have gone through here have respect. I can bring guys back here—Jack Ham, Franco Harris, Curt Warner—or I can bring guys that nobody in this room ever heard of. People respect them because people know what a Penn State player is all about.

—If you don't want to go along with me, I think we can start talking about getting you out of here in January, if that's what you want. If you want to stay and not be part of this football team, we'll work something out. But I'm not going to horse around anymore.

—I said in those days that to have a great team you've got to have *we* and *us* people. We won't have a great team unless you as an individual work at making this squad a team. At making so deep a total commitment to every guy who wants to win that he puts aside any thoughts of personal glory. Everything for the team. Don't look for what you're going to get, but for what you're going to contribute. Praise each other. Help each other. Be interested in each other. Learn what makes the other guy tick. Don't grandstand, because grandstanding only causes resentment. Don't sulk and pout and shoot your mouth off. All that does is alienate your teammates. Don't boast. Have confidence that you're the best—but don't talk about it.

—A lot of people wonder why I'm so insistent about how you dress, how you look. It's got nothing to do with you as a person, but it does have something to do with the team. The only reason I ask you to be better groomed and to take care of your personal appearance is out of respect for your teammates. I think each one of you has an obligation to your teammates to do your best and be your best and look your best. Again, your reputation is as good as the poorest person on the team. If I allow some bum on this team, he affects the reputation of every single one of you. Ten years from now, when you say you were a Penn State football player, people will sit up and respect you. You can't get that with excessive styles or by being exhibitionists, because exhibitionists turn the public off. Other people may look like bums, but you can't. I have to get that across to you young guys particularly. You cannot go downtown and make a jerk out of yourself without people knowing it. You've got to start to assume the responsibility that comes with some-body in the limelight.

—I want you to get more out of life, maybe more than you ever thought you could get out of life. Life is nothing but striving to be the very best you can be. Life is competing. As sure as there's going to be a sunrise tomorrow and as sure as the seasons go one after another, life is no fun if you just want to go through it nice and easy. If you're just satisfied to be mediocre, it's no fun. Believe me. I'm sixty-two years old and I'm telling you: I'm going to enjoy the next few years as much as any years of my life. Because living is competing. Compet-ing, striving, stretching, trying to do something that's hard to do—that's the only time you're going to be happy.

—I want you to understand the exultation of victory. We haven't had much of that lately. Winning is a matter of *know-ing how* to win. This team did not know how to win last year. Part of being a Penn State player is knowing how to win. I'm not just talking football. Anything. *If this is what I want to do, I can and I will.*

—I want you to be able to look at each other in a locker room and say, "Hey, we're national champions." And to understand that you've lost yourself in something that's bigger than you are. Most of you have not shared that. I can't describe to you the feeling of losing yourself in something bigger than you are.

—People quote me as saying, "We want Penn State football to be fun." Because of that some people think we joke and have a lot of fun on the field. The fun is not that. The fun is knowing you're prepared. Knowing that you're ready to play. The fun is not what some of you had this year when you went out on the field scared to death you were going to make a mistake, that you weren't ready. That's not fun. All you had was work last fall. The fun is when you're ready to go. The great defensive end for the Green Bay Packers, Willie Davis, said, "We prac-ticed so hard that the games were fun." And that's exactly what we're talking about. Fun is knowing you're good enough to take a chance. That you can gamble. That you're at your best, and that you're not afraid to lose. And that you won't play for a tie.

—I want you to remember this as the years go by: You will forgive me for the hard work. You'll forgive me for the driving, the yelling. You'll call me every name in the next nine months, ten months, because I'm going to be tough on you. And I don't expect you to like me. And I don't give a darn if you like me. I want you to make sure you understand that. We're going to get a job done. I'm going to drive you. I'm going to push you. I'm going to shove you. I'm going to yell at you. And I'm going to make you do it my way or I'm going to get rid of you. And you'll put up with every one of those things.

—The only thing you won't put up with is if I sell you short—if I *don't* work you hard enough. You're not going to come back here and be able to say, "Paterno let us down. He didn't work us hard enough. He didn't know how good we wanted to be. He deprived us of the chance to be as good as we could be." I'm not going to do that to you. I've done enough of that. You're going to come back and I'm going to make you stretch and I'm not going to underestimate how hard you're willing to work. You came here wanting the best of both worlds. You wanted to get a good education where you could also play on a great football team. I'm not going to sell you short.

—I have not slept a night that I have not replayed in my head four or five of our football games. I wake up every single morning figuring out how we could have won a couple of those games.

—We want to be number one. I want it, too. But I don't want to be number one with bums and losers. I want to be number one with people we can all be proud of, people we all went to war together with. Proud to be Penn State football players.

—Life is such that you can't have everything. You cannot get your name in the paper, you cannot have the thrill of playing out there before 85,000 people, you can't have all the adulation that comes with playing a football game and not expect to have some responsibility to act accordingly.

—You're here to represent a great university as well as to develop intellectually, socially, and emotionally. We want you to add to the life of all the students on this campus. There are a lot of kids out there who aren't sure of themselves. They don't have the kind of self-esteem most of you guys have. Haven't had the success you guys have had. You can add a great deal to this academic community, to the experience of a lot of other kids out there.

—I'm asking you a lot. But you guys aren't ordinary people.

—Let me end with this one statement. Get on your books. Run scared. We can't lose anybody else. If you're willing to pay the price, we'll be celebrating a lot. We now know how to play against the best. Now we have to learn to beat the best. We've already got fingers up for number one in the locker room. We are going to be national champs.

—If you can't see yourselves doing what I ask you to do—being considerate of other people, being the best you can be academically, not cutting class—don't waste our time, and we won't waste yours. We'll find something that's better for you. The guys that are going to stay, the ones that want to do it, our day is coming.

—I'm going back to coaching on the field. I told you last Sunday that I'm starting over, going back to coaching the way I did when I was young and felt like taking on the world. That's exactly how I feel right now. I want to take on the world with guys who feel the same way I do.

—Have a good holiday. Get on those exams. Do the best you can. Don't be too proud to ask for help. We'll see you January ninth at five o'clock.

And so they wished each other a Merry Christmas and went their separate ways—for a while. The way they looked—the way I felt—I knew they would grow into a team of winners. If not next year, the one after that. They had time.

This group of Penn State kids, like all the others before them, would have their undefeated season. Or a bowl game for the national championship. And maybe, like two teams before them, they'd bring that championship home.

Index